This Was Not Our War

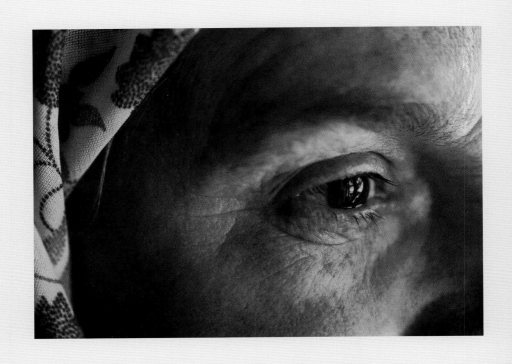

Swanee Hunt

This Was Not Our War

Bosnian Women Reclaiming the Peace

foreword by William Jefferson Clinton

Duke University Press   Durham & London

2004

© 2004 Duke University Press

All rights reserved

Printed in China

Designed by C. H. Westmoreland

Typeset in Dante with

Helvetica Neue display by

Tseng Information Systems, Inc.

Library of Congress Cataloging-in-

Publication Data appear on the

last printed page of this book.

Second printing, 2005

This book is dedicated

to my daughter,

Lillian,

also a survivor determined

to reclaim the peace.

Contents

PHOTO CREDITS

Photos by Swanee Hunt: xiii, xiv, xxx, 8, 14, 21, 31, 60, 96, 116, 136, 146, 168, 191, 192, 296

Photos by Tarik Samarah: ii, xxv, 7, 115, 198, 200, 202, 204, 206, 208, 210, 212, 214, 216, 218, 220, 222, 224, 226, 228, 230, 232, 234, 236, 238, 240, 242, 244, 246, 248

Photo by Charles Ansbacher: 250

Illustrations

Foreword

Bosnia was one of the toughest challenges I faced as President. In 1995, I addressed the nation, describing the situation: *For nearly four years a terrible war has torn Bosnia apart. Horrors we prayed had been banished from Europe forever have been seared into our minds again. Skeletal prisoners caged behind barbed-wire fences, women and girls raped as a tool of war, defenseless men and boys shot down into mass graves, evoking visions of World War II concentration camps and endless lines of refugees marching toward a future of despair.* Bosnia was a small spot on the map of the world where humanitarian and geopolitical considerations collided, forcing the conscience of a superpower to come to grips with its role in the world.

As the war raged in Bosnia, Swanee Hunt, serving as our ambassador to Austria, brought to my attention news not making headlines: that the women of Bosnia had been organizing to try to prevent the war, and they were still doing everything they could, even in the face of ruthless "ethnic cleansing," to hold together their culturally diverse communities. She came to me again in early 1996, right after the Dayton Peace Agreement was signed, to discuss the bridge-building work of those women. I immediately recognized a good idea and was proud to announce a few months later a $5 million start-up contribution by the U.S. government to a new Bosnian Women's Initiative. Through training and microcredit loans, that program has enabled many war-weary women to improve their families' situations, and, at the same time, help regenerate a ravaged economy.

The United States supported numerous other endeavors, public and private, to promote lasting peace and prosperity in Bosnia. Whether in economic activity, democracy building, or cultural exchange, our assistance has aided those who believe in bringing people together rather than dividing them. We Americans enjoy a great many privileges, but we also have a responsibility to be true to the values behind those privileges whenever and wherever we can. It's in our best interest.

Women must be included in this work. Coming out of a vicious war in which so many men were killed in the fighting, Bosnia's future may depend more than ever on its women. A democracy functions best when *all* its citizens are engaged. Replacing tyranny with justice, healing deep scars, exchanging hatred for hope . . . the women in *This Was Not Our War* teach us how. Peace isn't an event, it's a process—and as the Middle East and Northern Ireland have shown us, it doesn't always move forward. These women inspire us with their courage to hope. In return, we owe it to them to help them lock in their gains and keep their momentum.

I keep near me in my office the following lines of verse by Seamus Heaney, which I have repeated often around the world:

> *History says, Don't hope*
> *On this side of the grave.*
> *But then, once in a lifetime*
> *The longed-for tidal wave*
> *Of justice can rise up,*
> *And hope and history rhyme.*
>
> *So hope for a great sea-change*
> *On the far side of revenge.*
> *Believe that a further shore*
> *Is reachable from here.*
> *Believe in miracles*
> *And cures and healing wells.*

With those words in mind, I think of Slobodan Milosevic and others indicted for crimes against humanity in The Hague. And while, yes, that looks as if it's a miraculous achievement, much work still remains to be done in Bosnia at the grassroots. Peace is built every day through ordinary exchanges and events. The women of *This Was Not Our War* know that, as they know unity and strength can come from diversity, that it's possible to honor their distinctive traditions and still relish life with their neighbors, and that the source of lasting peace is the human heart. I salute their foresight and their courage, their action and resolve. In their stories, we read the history of humankind. In their vision, we glimpse possibilities for our future.

WILLIAM JEFFERSON CLINTON

Civilian targets. Bus outside the Sarajevo maternity clinic, in the line of fire of Serbs shelling from the surrounding hills. December 1995.

Preface

September 11, 2001, I was sitting at my desk, writing captions for my photographs of shelled buildings in Sarajevo, for the Bosnian edition of this book. With shock written across her face, a colleague summoned me to the TV. I watched as a plane hit the second World Trade Center tower. Then I returned to my desk, not daring to say aloud what I was thinking: "Now maybe we'll understand what the people in Bosnia felt."

How naïve. Wasting no time on reflection, America's leaders launched into bellicose breast-pounding. Human rights were flagrantly disregarded. The world map was painted in black and white: "You're either for us or against us," President Bush declared. The terrorist act was transformed into an excuse for attacking Iraq, whose leader, our erstwhile friend Saddam Hussein, was suddenly worth spending hundreds of billions of dollars to bring down.

The "opportunity costs" of that decision were staggering. With the same resources, America could have solved most of the humanitarian crises in the world and become the friend of billions. Instead, legions of Muslims feel humiliated by the arrogance implicit in our go-it-alone foreign policy and have vowed revenge.

What went wrong?

The swagger in our current foreign policy leadership is not only unseemly but also dangerous. To quote a wise bumper sticker, "We're making enemies faster than we can kill them." In contrast, this book proposes a decidedly unswaggering view of foreign policy. It looks to long-term relationships rather than short-fused rhetoric. It grapples with issues in the gray middle—issues like accountability in the midst of mass hysteria, the preservation of privilege cloaked in victimhood, and the psychological demand for justice. It elevates the voices of those who can distinguish between religion as a path for life and religion as a pretext for killing. It empowers leaders invested in a safe place for their children more than territory for themselves. It listens to the cries of women in war, understanding that their experience is instructive and their perceptions insightful.

Such common sense is often ignored nowadays by the foreign policy establishment. I certainly wasn't taught it in my ambassadorial training. In fact, just
how I became aware of the importance of listening to women's stories is a story
in and of itself, beginning a decade ago.

On July 4, 1994, during a lull in the fighting, I flew down to Bosnia in the belly
of a cargo plane, strapped in between 50,000 pounds of flour—supplies urgently
needed to feed the 200,000 Sarajevans under siege since April 5, 1992. I was bringing greetings from President Clinton to a few hundred Bosnians gathered in the
American embassy yard to celebrate our "national day." On the patio next to the
bare building (our flag flew over an embassy not yet furnished or inhabited), I met
with seven women who, in bizarre juxtaposition with the grittiness of war, wore
pearls, high heels, and carefully applied makeup as they relayed accounts of practicing medicine in hospitals without anesthetics and teaching architecture classes
without pencils. A cardiac specialist described how she had not seen her octoge-
narian parents for two years, even though they lived only a fifteen-minute walk
away—but across a war line she couldn't penetrate. This was the jagged disconnect of their lives: sophisticated, educated women coping with blunt barbarity.[1]

I was not in Bosnia and Herzegovina out of duty. My job as ambassador to
Austria should have confined me to American-Austrian relations. Truth be told,
during my posting the relationship between Washington and Vienna was solid
and didn't need extensive tending. Meanwhile, a few hundred miles south of the
erstwhile imperial capital, the Balkans were ablaze. I couldn't ignore the weary
pain written on the faces of the 70,000 refugees who had spilled over the border into Austria, whose testimony of atrocities our embassy personnel gathered.[2]
My host government might have resented my looking south, to the Balkans. But
trouble in Bosnia, in the center of the former Yugoslavia, affected the entire region. My involvement was more than tolerated by the Austrian government. It
was anointed.

Soon after my single-day introduction to Sarajevo under siege, the war heated
up again, and the U.S. State Department barred my returning. Washington was
loath to risk a nonessential visiting ambassador serving as a sniper target. But I
couldn't forget the images and stories of that first visit. Now the word was out
among Bosnians: an American official had come to listen to the women. Not
only that, I was nearby, in their former capital. Bosnia had been an outpost of
the Austro-Hungarian Empire, and Vienna was psychologically familiar. Women
like the ones I had met in Sarajevo began to come to me. They sometimes risked

their lives crossing war lines, finding their way to my office in Vienna to plead for U.S. intervention to stop the carnage, which they insisted was politically—not culturally—driven.

I sent their accounts back to Washington and raised questions about U.S. intelligence descriptions of this conflict as a religious or ethnic war we could only let play out. Those intelligence reports, sent to the White House replete with tales of "Muslim extremists," might as well have been crafted by President Slobodan Milosevic's public relations team. Meanwhile, the women's pleas were being drowned out by the shouting match inside the Beltway. President Clinton was receiving strong advice from Chair of the Joint Chiefs of Staff Colin Powell and others not to get involved. My voice blended with those of U.S. Ambassador to the United Nations Madeleine Albright, Assistant Secretary of State for Europe Richard Holbrooke, and U.S. Ambassador to NATO Robert Hunter, insisting that our intervention should have been early and forceful, and that we still needed to lean forward into the fray.

With the death of Tito and demise of communism, Yugoslavia was in chaos. So was the State Department, which, I was told, had not been so split since Vietnam. The lack of U.S. intervention had been a theme in the 1992 presidential debates, with Governor Clinton castigating President Bush for inaction. But Bush realized that the American public knew, and cared, almost nothing about this country outside Western Europe, with towns whose names suffered a chronic shortage of vowels. There Serbs lived in Croatia, and Croats lived in Serbia, and a smattering of them all ended up in Bosnia. Few could, or wanted to, decipher the internal politics resulting in the flood of media accounts that led with tales of stomach-turning depravity.

Ignorance was not an option for our embassy. I learned, however, that within the foreign policy establishment my close interaction with women in the conflict was an anomaly. In thousands of hours around tables where the fate of Bosnia was shaped, Bosnian women were systematically and consistently absent. The same was true in meetings organized by Bosnian officials or by leaders of "the international community," that unwieldy amalgam of military, political, and humanitarian organizations that rush into fragile countries, trying to do as little harm as possible while doing good. Although women were highly organized—over forty associations, linked in an overarching union—they were almost never present in policy-making settings.

One exception was Tatjana (TANJA) Ljujic-Mijatovic, the only woman in the seven-member Bosnian presidency, and one of the women profiled in this book.

We became friends in early 1994, with frequent contact through the diplomatic corps (she was the Bosnian ambassador to the UN in Vienna), in addition to collaborating on half a dozen projects for Bosnia. Another woman at the policy table was Biljana Plavsic, a key Bosnian Serb leader and first president of the postwar Republika Srpska, who later turned herself in to the war crimes tribunal at The Hague.[3] Plavsic confided to me that she was put in the top position by Radovan Karadzic (sociopathic Bosnian Serb president, barred from political life after being indicted as a war criminal) precisely because he thought he could control her since she was a woman.[4] And finally, there was Mirjana Markovic, head of a small communist party in Serbia, wife of Milosevic, and reputedly a more ideological Marxist than her husband, known better for his political cunning. Markovic never figured in the scores of policy conversations to which I was privy, even though her influence over Milosevic was said to be significant.

The wartime roles — positive and negative — of these women raise the age-old question of whether or not the world would suffer less war if women were sharing power, a query that usually provokes a chorus of "What about . . . ?" followed by a litany of women known to be tough as nails: Indira Gandhi, Margaret Thatcher, Golda Meir. . . . In fact, Plavsic and Markovic stand out as exceptions among the large majority of Yugoslav women, who held moderate political views. Aggressive and bellicose women may force their way to the policy table; for the moderate majority, there is no easy entry. So it was in Bosnia. Although women comprised well over half the adult population after the war, their opinions were not sought, nor were their ideas welcome. That omission marred international peace efforts before, during, and after the war.

Though my involvement with Bosnian women was considered a breach of boundaries and a nuisance by several midlevel officials in the U.S. State Department, the naysayers were trumped by President Clinton, who encouraged me privately and publicly. Likewise, our ambassadors to Bosnia — first, Victor Jackovich,[5] later, John Menzies[6] — urged me to come down to Sarajevo whenever and however I could. Even when I couldn't go into Bosnia, I was closely involved from Vienna. In addition to organizing several international conferences, I hosted the 1994 negotiations, led by Ambassador Chuck Redmond, that created the Federation of Bosnia and Herzegovina, a key turning point in the war, bringing the Bosniaks and Croats together to literally join forces against the Serbs.

In those weeks of meetings, I met dozens of Balkan political leaders deciding matters of war and peace, as well as lawyers debating and crafting a new constitution. All were men. One was Ejup Ganic, whose wife, FAHRIJA and children were living incognito in Vienna (an option not available to most Bosnians) while he continued as a political leader in besieged Sarajevo. The signing of the Federation agreement at the White House was presided over by President Clinton. Among the policy players I counted ninety-nine men and only five women, all Americans (including Madeleine Albright and me).[7] Although Bosnian women held more graduate degrees than men, there were no women among the lawyers, diplomats, and political leaders. U.S. hosts did not think to invite them, and Bosnian leaders did not think to send them.

The "men only" pattern continued in every meeting I witnessed as the conflict continued to rage. In mid-1995, U.S.-led bombing of Serb positions reinforced the negotiating process that brought an end to the war.[8] At the subsequent Dayton peace talks, which allowed nationalists to carve up the country and governance system, the strong view of the women that the country couldn't be divided along ethnic lines would have been an important corrective. But there were no Bosnian women at Dayton, which was, in effect, a conference of warriors, each deciding how he could leave with the greatest advantage possible.[9]

Women's exclusion from that policy table may have been intentional on the part of the war makers, who may rightly have believed women would have pursued peace above nationalist aims. After the war, for example, Plavsic turned away from Serb nationalism and moved toward the democratic West. But for the United States and others attempting to end the conflict, ignoring women was patently counterproductive. Perhaps because of their familial and social roles, most Bosnian women were ardently committed to ending the violence. Likewise, in the postwar search for talent to fit the daunting tasks of reconstruction, the exclusion of the majority of the population was a serious and systemic policy flaw. In the end, those who waged the war were selected to plan and implement the peace — a ludicrous tradition rarely questioned by otherwise enlightened leaders within the international foreign policy establishment.

Within two weeks of the peace signing in December, my husband, symphony conductor Charles Ansbacher, and I spent a week in Sarajevo at the invitation of Ambassador Menzies. At the ambassador's request, we brought space heaters in our suitcases, and we unrolled sleeping bags on army cots in an embassy office, down the hall from the office of the plenipotentiary U.S. official who slept next to his desk for seventeen months, rather than dodging snipers to travel to a separate residence. While Charles worked with the remnants of the Sarajevo Philharmonic, which he would conduct on New Year's Eve, I met with women from all over the war-torn city.[10] I was haunted by their pain, inspired by their courage—and concerned at how their voices weakened when they were in the presence of men.

On the evening of December 31, 1995, I watched my husband cajole the soul out of the strings of the Sarajevo Philharmonic (seven of seventy had been killed). At my side was a new friend, MEDIHA Filipovic, the only woman out of forty-two members of the national parliament, with her handsome son, Bojan. This was the first public gathering since the end of the siege. Mediha and I looked out on the hopeful faces of international journalists, including Roy Gutman and Christiane Amanpour, who had covered—and uncovered—war stories such as the Omarska concentration camp and the massacre in Srebrenica.[11] In the front row were a dozen other women activists with whom I'd spent the previous evening strategizing—by candlelight after the electricity suddenly went off. Looking at familiar faces sprinkled throughout the audience of the elegant National Theater, I realized that we were not merely subjects and observer, or citizens and American official; our thoughts and emotions were as blended as the Beethoven.

That week in Sarajevo was a turning point: I decided to invest my political capital in the women of Bosnia. In the spring of 1996, I invited a group of Bosnian women leaders to spend several days in our embassy residence in Vienna. There, journalist NURDZIHANA Dzozic proposed a conference in Sarajevo with women of diverse backgrounds determined to transform their devastated communities. I offered to help and was pulled even deeper into the work of Bosnian women to rebuild their country and secure the peace.

Postconflict Bosnia brought tremendous challenges. Bitterness, anger, and anguish lay under every pile of political rubble. As the international community moved into positions of authority, I received encouragement from Michael Steiner,[12] a German diplomat who served as the "number two" in the Office of the High Representative, set up in Sarajevo immediately after the peace agreement was signed. Steiner had been approached by women who had joined forces across conflict lines to find their missing sons, fathers, and husbands. He was convinced they were a symbol of new possibilities for the country—not as victims, but as a potential force for stabilization. He repeatedly urged me to meet with them, help find outside funding, and find ways to elevate their voices. They were transforming personal tragedy into energy to restore their homeland. Perhaps their example could cut through the thick pessimism that clouded many reports among influential international media.[13]

Convinced that Washington was ignoring an important untapped resource, I approached President Clinton. He immediately made a mental connection between these Bosnian women and the vital role of women in stabilizing Northern Ireland. On his instructions, the State Department appropriated five million dollars to launch the Bosnian Women's Initiative (BWI), which was designed late one night around my dining table. The BWI funded hundreds of cottage industries, such as one-room sugar cube production, as well as modest animal husbandry and medium-sized businesses. The Initiative also encouraged the growth of local nongovernmental organizations (NGOS) to manage the funds. (ANA and VALENTINA Pranic, as well as ALENKA Savic, were involved in that program.)[14] The president's public announcement of the Bosnian Women's Initiative at the G-7 meeting in Lyons, France, in July 1996 signaled the place of Bosnian women in restoring a peacetime economy and establishing a democratic political system.

One day in early 1996, TANJA came to my office to urge, *If there's one more thing you can do for my country, help the survivors of Srebrenica.* After a year of scant aid, feeling forgotten, and their pleas for help unheeded, the women had organized public protests, taking to the streets of Tuzla, a city swollen with refugees. They'd thrown a rock at the window of the Red Cross office. The surviving widows told me privately that their frustration was not only over the lack of information but also the indifference of Red Cross employees. That organization, on the other hand, was stymied by the Bosnian Serb authorities, who continually refused to provide information about the missing or access to the mass graves, despite guarantees in the Dayton accords.[15]

The desperation of Srebrenica survivors like KADA Hotic was backfiring. A midlevel State Department official insisted I should not get involved because the women were "dangerous." "I didn't realize they were armed! And what are their weapons? Rocks?" I asked, facetiously. Ambassador Menzies intervened, saying my help was not only welcome but needed. In mid 1996, I helped the widows (a term they rejected, hoping it wasn't true) stage the one-year commemoration of the massacre. The afternoon was not only a ceremony of grief but also a protest of their having received no word of their missing boys and men, who had, in fact, been executed and thrown into mass graves.[16]

And so it was, working with the women of Bosnia: A few official voices of encouragement prevailed over warnings for me to stay away. A seminal grant from the U.S. Agency for International Development supported technical assistance to Balkan women's NGOS.[17] Similarly, the Organization for Security and Cooperation in Europe devoted part of a staff member's time to encouraging women across Bosnia to organize politically.[18] In both cases, the women could have used ten times the help, but at least the gesture was there.

Support for Bosnian women was clear and unambiguous from General Wesley Clark, who became NATO's Supreme Allied Commander in Europe shortly before I left Vienna.[19] In August 1997, my husband and I were dining in Brussels with Wes.[20] General Clark was about to escort U.S. Senator Kay Bailey Hutchison (R-Texas) to Bosnia. The senator had repeatedly called for the pullout of U.S. troops. General Clark asked if I might gather some women, to try to impress on her the importance of the troops in maintaining stability. The next week, I brought together a multiethnic group of thirteen activists from all over the country. That group included journalist RADA Sesar, who had interviewed me two years earlier, and JELKA Kebo. When the senator arrived for her one-hour meeting with the women, perhaps poorly briefed on the political nuances of the situation, she urged them to "just put the past behind you and invite your enemies over to your kitchens for a cup of coffee." The former principal of the Srebrenica high school told the senator she'd had a house, two cars, and a mountain home. Now she had no kitchen to which to invite her enemy for coffee. Instead, the women presented to Senator Hutchison the plan for a new League of Women Voters of Bosnia and Herzegovina they had just worked on creating, complete with governance structure and first-year action steps. The senator didn't seem convinced by the women. I thought they were magnificent.

On my departure from the State Department in late 1997, I opened a Sarajevo office of my private foundation, from which I continued my work with Bosnian women for several more years. Among a number of initiatives, we brought together several women, including NADA Rakovic, to Washington, to collaborate across political parties. The next step was convening a large conference, which helped inspire a quota for women in the parliament. Vacillating between hope and depression, my Balkan friends were putting back together their lives and their country, piece by piece, their creativity and skills frequently outstripping the sluggish and uneven pace of postwar politics. Their vision jumped into bold relief against the backdrop of Milosevic's campaign against ethnic Albanians in Kosovo.[21] As the Serbian leader tightened his noose there, Bosnians writhed. The parallels between the new war and their recent nightmare were too deep for dispassion, given only four years between the conflicts. For people from the former Yugoslavia, the terror was the same, whether inflicted in Croatia, Bosnia, or Kosovo. The carnage stemmed from one political source, and the security of Bosnia rested in part on the success or failure of Milosevic in Kosovo. Several Bosnian women I knew were housing Kosovars who had fled the region. FAHRIJA told me that listening to their accounts of the growing crisis reopened Bosnians' wounds, which had not had time to heal.

That political and psychological connection between Bosnia and Kosovo (and further, Macedonia) is clear in the words of EMSUDA Mujagic, ball-of-fire organizer from the town of Prijedor, who witnessed the barbarity of the Bosnian war. She is a talented entrepreneur, which made her a target for elimination in the concentration camp, a fate she escaped through wits and luck. But Emsuda is extraordinarily generous as she describes the Serb army that held her captive. She gives the soldiers the benefit of the doubt. *They were fed myths by Milosevic's regime. They still don't know they committed crimes against everybody, including themselves.*

A vignette of Emsuda's words and work shows the juncture where postwar healing encounters hard-core Realpolitik. In the new democracy, Emsuda agreed to teach Bosnian Serbs how to organize NGOs.[22] She relayed to me an exchange during a training session in Bosnia, as NATO was bombing to keep Serb forces from overrunning Kosovo. *Even before "Hello," the workshop participants said, "We can't believe they're bombing Serbia! They've targeted the tobacco factory! And they bombed the bridge in Novi Sad![23] Do you understand? Sick people can't get to the hospital!" I thought to myself, "I sure do understand. In Sarajevo people couldn't go fifteen meters to the hospital because of snipers." I wanted to ask why they didn't think of other people who'd suffered just because they had a different religion. But they didn't want to talk to me. They said, "Radovan Karadzic was our president, and even though he's been accused of war crimes by The Hague tribunal, we won't renounce him."[24]*

Here is Emsuda, rising above personal trauma to train those who may be making life easier for her former torturers. But she's no Pollyanna. And she's no saint. In words sometimes profound, sometimes petty, she lays bare essential truth as she sees it. Emsuda, champion of peace, is no pacifist. She knows the danger of non-action, and she will not simply declare herself withdrawn from the fray. Still, she lets loose her frustration: *What am I supposed to say? When people we think are moderate and rational swear allegiance to Karadzic, can you imagine what the rest of that community is like—the ones we say are more radical? That's why we have to respond radically. I'm sorry there had to be a NATO action against Serbia, but if NATO had acted seven years earlier when the Serbs attacked Bosnia, there wouldn't have been a crisis in Kosovo.*

Bosnian women have earned the right to make such bold statements. They've suffered the effects of the mixed messages, hesitation, and foreign policy meandering of the "international community," led by Americans, whenever we chose to get involved.[25] In their words and deeds are lessons citizens and policymakers alike can ponder. This book was written to bring the extraordinary message of ordinary women into earshot of those who shape the world order. With that goal, I was warned by several Bosnians that I should change the title, which was tainted on two counts. First, it was reminiscent of President Izetbegovic's disavowal of war as the Serbia/Croatia conflict heated up, a stance some say led to the Bosnian government's lack of preparedness and subsequent vulnerability when Bosnia became the target of violence.[26] Second, "This is not my war," delivered with a tone of disgust or apology, was associated with people finding ways to escape Sarajevo—a distancing, denying at the same time their identification with the violence and their responsibility for the survival of their country. My Bosnian publisher, on the other hand, was intrigued by the ambiguous twist. The women in this volume disavowed the violence, yes, but they leaned forward, rather than pulling back, to confront the challenges of postwar Bosnia.

Indeed, it is precisely because this was *not* their war that they should shape the peace.

Context

The Balkans

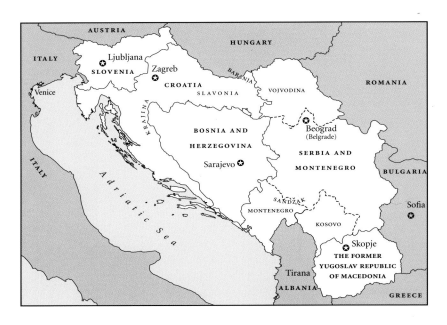

Former Yugoslavia. *Source: United Nations.*

Bosnia and Herzegovina. *Source: United Nations.*

Key Terms and Places

Banja Luka: in northwest Bosnia, capital of Republika Srpska, second largest city

Belgrade: capital city of Yugoslavia, and of Serbia

Bosnia and Herzegovina: full name of "Bosnia"

Bosniak: preferred term by many Bosnian Muslims

Chetnik: Serb guerillas during World War II; pejorative for Serb nationalists

Croatia: Yugoslav republic, majority Catholic, declared independence June 1991

Contact Group: representatives of Britain, France, Germany, Russia, and the United States, who charged themselves with finding an end to the war

Displaced persons: in-country, as opposed to out-of-country, refugees

Dobrinja: Olympic Village, suburban neighborhood of Sarajevo; front line of siege

Federation of Bosnia and Herzegovina: 51 percent of Bosnia, delineated by the Dayton Agreement, controlled by Bosniaks and Bosnian Croats

FRY: Federal Republic of Yugoslavia, post-breakup

Gorazde: town in eastern Bosnia, like Srebrenica a "safe haven" under siege

HDZ: Croat Democratic Union, nationalist party with strong connections to Zagreb

International Criminal Tribunal for the Former Yugoslavia: established in 1993; referred to as "The Hague" in this text

JNA: Yugoslav National Army, controlled from Belgrade

Kosovo: in south Yugoslavia, 90 percent ethnic Albanian, disputed Serb heartland

Ljubljana: the capital of Slovenia, population about 350,000

Mostar: city in central Bosnia and Herzegovina, claimed by Croat nationalists

Mount Igman: accessed by tunnel under Sarajevo airport as an escape route

NGO: nongovernmental organization, international term for "nonprofits"

OHR: Office of the High Representative, established by Dayton Agreement

Pale: ski village outside Sarajevo, used by Bosnian Serbs as political headquarters

Partisans: anti-Nazi communist resistance forces, led by Marshal Tito

Prijedor: city of 120,000 in northwest Bosnia, concentration camp run by Serbs

Republika Srpska: 49 percent of Bosnia per Dayton, controlled by Bosnian Serbs

Sarajevo: Bosnian capital, under siege 3 years, population approximately 500,000

SDA: Party for Democratic Action, Bosniak-dominated, headed by Izetbegovic

SDP: Social Democratic Party, espousing multiethnicity and united Bosnia

SDS: Serb Democratic Party, nationalist party, headed by Radovan Karadzic

Serbia and Montenegro: name for successor to FRY, February 2003

SFOR: multinational Stabilization Force, replaced IFOR (Implementation Force)

Slovenia: northernmost Yugoslav republic, declared independence June 1991

SNS: Serb National Alliance, headed by Biljana Plavsic

Srebrenica: safe haven in eastern Bosnia, site of July 1995 massacre

Tuzla: city in northeast Bosnia, to which Srebrenica refugees were transported

Ustasha: Croatian Nazi collaborators, slur for modern Croatian nationalists

Zagreb: capital of Croatia

Shattered dreams in Dobrinja. December 1995.

Key Players

ALENKA SAVIC: engineer, Tuzla, widow, Slovene/Serb parents, two kids

ALMA KECO: engineer, Mostar, Bosniak paramedic, founded veterans' organization

AMNA POPOVAC: Mostar, Bosniak university student, resettles refugees

ANA PRANIC: Bosnian Croat, sixties, small town, livestock from microcredit loan

BILJANA CHENGICH FEINSTEIN: Muslim convert to Judaism, cosmetician

DANICA PETRIC: grandmother, florist, refugee in Croatia, Catholic

EMSUDA MUJAGIC: Prijedor Bosniak, designer, Trepoljna camp, runs two NGOS

FAHRIJA GANIC: Albanian royalty, dermatologist, political leader husband

GALINA MARJANOVIC: Serb from Banja Luka, worked twenty-five years with deaf

GRETA FERUSIC-WEINFELD: Sarajevo, Auschwitz, professor, government minister

IRMA SAJE: Catholic/Muslim parents, adolescent during siege, tunnel escape

JELKA KEBO: Mostar, Croat, organized youth center, son died in accident

KADA HOTIC: textile factory worker, Muslim (Bosniak), survivor of Srebrenica

KAROLINA ATAGIC: Catholic in Muslim part of Sarajevo, son in army, husband died

KRISTINA KOVAC: Sipovo in Republika Srpska, two daughters, Serb teacher

MAJA JERKOVIC: manager Mostar regional hospital, Croat, Communist Party

MEDIHA FILIPOVIC: orthodontist, Bosniak, only woman in first national parliament

MIRHUNISA ZUCIC (KOMARICA): accounting professor, Bosniak, aided refugees

NADA RAKOVIC: pediatrician, refugee, Republika Srpska Parliament

NURDZIHANA DZOZIC: Dobrinja journalist, Bosniak, published *Zena 21*

RADA SESAR: Bosnian Serb, broadcast testimonies of victims, two children

SABIHA HADZIMORATOVIC: Gorazde, Bosniak journalist abroad, organized aid

SUZANA ANDJELIC: Bosnian Serb, young journalist for *Free Bosnia*

TANJA LJUJIC-MIJATOVIC: Sarajevo Serb, member of parliament and presidency

VALENTINA PRANIC: daughter of Ana, married Bosnian Serb at end of war, BWI loan

VESNA KISIC: Bosnian Serb, League of Women Voters, "Antonia" organizer

"Arkan": notorious paramilitary leader, elected to Serbian parliament, assassinated

James Baker III: secretary of state, chief of staff for Bush reelection campaign

George Bush: U.S. president, 1988–92, adopted nonintervention policy

Bill Clinton: U.S. president, 1992–2000, supported Dayton talks, women's initiative

Richard Holbrooke: under Clinton U.S. assistant secretary of state for Europe

Alija Izetbegovic: Islamic apologist, head of SDA, lawyer, president of Bosnia

Vic Jackovich: first U.S. ambassador to Bosnia, later U.S. ambassador to Slovenia

Radovan Karadzic: psychiatrist, Bosnian Serb president, indicted war criminal

John Menzies: second U.S. ambassador to Bosnia, oversaw Kosovo peace agreement

Slobodan Milosevic: president of Yugoslavia, now at The Hague

Ratko Mladic: head of Bosnian Serb army, indicted war criminal

Biljana Plavsic: Karadzic deputy, president Republika Srpska, confessed war criminal

Colin Powell: noninterventionist Chair of Joint Chiefs of Staff for Bush, Clinton

Haris Silajdzic: wartime prime minister, poet, playwright, non-nationalist party

Franjo Tudjman: general in former Yugoslavia, nationalist president of Croatia

Warren Zimmermann: last U.S. ambassador to Yugoslavia

Timeline

1918   Kingdom of Serbs, Croats, and Slovenes formed as outcome of World War I.

1929   The monarchy's name is changed to Yugoslavia, "Land of the South Slavs."

1941   *April*: Nazi Germany attacks Yugoslavia.

1945   Yugoslavia becomes a socialist state under Marshal Tito, with six republics (Serbia, Croatia, Bosnia and Herzegovina, Macedonia, Slovenia, Montenegro), and two autonomous provinces (Kosovo and Vojvodina) within Serbia.

1980   Tito dies. Rotating presidency instated.

1983   Izetbegovic sentenced to fourteen years in prison for Islamic writings.

1987   Milosevic stirs the crowd with rabble-rousing speech to Serbs in Kosovo.

1989   *June*: Milosevic warns of conflict on 600th Battle of Kosovo anniversary.

1991   *June–July*: Slovenia and Croatia declare independence from Yugoslavia. Slovenia breaks away after ten days of fighting. Fierce fighting in Croatia ensues.

      September: Macedonia declares independence from Yugoslavia.

1992   *January*: UN brokers truce in Croatia, leaving Serbs in control of the Krajina.

      March: Bosnia and Herzegovina declares independence.

      April: Serbia and Montenegro form Federal Republic of Yugoslavia, with Milosevic as de facto leader. Bosnia erupts into war. Serbs begin shelling Sarajevo.

      May: Milosevic and Tudjman meet and discuss plans to divide Bosnia.

1995   *July*: Srebrenica massacre, worst European atrocity since World War II.

      August: Croatian army launches Operation Storm against Serbs occupying one-third of that country; massive exodus of Croat Serbs into Bosnia and Serbia. United States leads NATO bombing against Serb targets to lift Sarajevo siege.

      November: Izetbegovic, Tudjman, and Milosevic initial the Dayton Peace Agreement.

1997 Conflict escalates between Kosovo Liberation Army and Milosevic's forces.

1998 *Summer*: Guerrilla war breaks out in Kosovo.

1999 *March*: Rambouillet peace talks between Serbia and Kosovo fail. NATO launches air strikes against Serbs.

2000 *September*: Opposition candidate Vojislav Kostunica wins FRY presidential elections. Milosevic refuses to step down.

 October: Popular uprising in Belgrade. Milosevic steps down. Kostunica takes office. United States, European Union begin to lift economic sanctions and offer aid.

2001 *June*: Milosevic transferred to The Hague tribunal.

2002 *September*: Milosevic trial begins. President Clinton opens memorial in Srebrenica, with an exhibit by Tarik Samarah, the portrait photographer for this book.

 October: In Bosnian election, nationalist parties regain power.

2003 *February*: Biljana Plavsic sentenced to eleven years for persecutions.

 March: Serbian prime minister Zoran Djindjic—key in October 2000 popular uprising and in turning over Milosevic—assassinated.

 November: Agreement to unite two former warring Bosnian armies into national force.

 December: World Bank reports that four-fifths of war refugees and internally displaced persons are back home.

Introduction

This book isn't ultimately about Bosnia. It's about the way we think of the impre-
cise art of war making. As U.S. exploits in Iraq remind us, we repeatedly enter war
without adequate intelligence, in every sense of the word. What can we learn,
looking through the eyes of a diverse group of women who experienced the carnage of Bosnia? Hindsight is invaluable when trying to avert the next conflict;
but more important is insight, probing the social core and moving beyond con-
vention. Whether the crisis is Croatia, Congo, or Korea, we must bring women
who have their fingers on the pulse of their communities to join the war makers
around the decision-making table. This book lays out the case for their inclusion.

Raising Their Voices

Most accounts told and listened to by Westerners convey little grasp of Balkan
culture. Prewar Bosnia was a poor region, behind the Western European standard, with hard-line communist political officials. On the other hand, Sarajevo
was more thoroughly multicultural than most American cities. Socially, traditional rural values blended with avant-garde urban thinking. People in villages
worked their fields and tended livestock. Intellectuals traveled frequently outside
the country.

This cultural complexity was obscured as the barbarity of the Bosnian war
was thrust on the world by international media. Many journalists oversimplified
the story. The result has been many easy, but wrong, assumptions that have been
salt in the wounds of women like FAHRIJA, who tells a pithy story from her time
in upstate New York, as a refugee: *Since skin is my medical specialty, I decided to
work as a cosmetics consultant, handling brands such as Dior, Clinique, Clarins. I would
dress nicely every day for work, regardless of how I felt. That was my way of fighting
back, showing I was alive and not broken. My clients, rich ladies, would ask, "Where*

are you from? Paris?" I'd answer, "No, I'm from Bosnia." They'd say, "But there's a civil war going on there!" I would explain that it was not a civil war but a war of aggression. The women would say, "But aren't you fighting Muslims over there?" Then I'd say, "I'm Muslim." They were always surprised. Most people I spoke to in America thought all Muslim women were uneducated, repressed, and covered in black cloth. I'm obviously the last person to fit that ridiculous notion.

Indeed, debunking "ridiculous notions" is one of the goals of this book. Bosnian women themselves are the most logical ones to address these errors. My role was to record their voices. In our sessions over the course of seven years, my training in psychological counseling was more useful than a degree in international relations as I taped multiple interviews with each of the twenty-six women in this book. They are advocates, politicians, farmers, journalists, students, doctors, businesswomen, engineers, mothers, and daughters. They're from all parts of Bosnia and represent the full range of ethnic traditions and mixed heritages. Their ages spread across sixty years, and their wealth ranges from jewels to a few chickens. But for all their differences, they have this in common: Each survived the war with enough emotional strength to work toward rebuilding her country, whether in modest or grand ways. Together, their perspectives provide a complex portrait of the war, as well as possibilities for peace.

For an anthropological review of the life of Bosnian women before or after the war, historical analysis of the Balkans, or comprehensive accounts of the war, the reader can find many excellent sources listed in the bibliography. I've tried to include just enough information to provide a context for the stories the women tell in these pages. Generalizations are inevitably flawed, especially when encompassing twenty-six persons with such different backgrounds, experiences, concerns, and hopes. Nonetheless, I've found several broad themes consonant with their values and convictions.

I've resisted the temptation to launch into a polemic on gender differences, even though some of the women I interviewed have strong—some might say strident—views about the differences between men and women in war and peacetime. Elsewhere we can argue about whether women are more or less bellicose than men. I've included a few comments of the women, with virtually no discussion. Likewise, this book is not an in-depth exploration of the terrible effect of war on women. True, Bosnian women have suffered far out of proportion to any complicity in causing the conflict. It's important that their suffering be documented and addressed; but that's not my emphasis. These women may have been victimized, but they approach the reader grounded in strength.

In fact, I expect the women portrayed in these pages will become new friends to the reader—even as they have become important influences in my life. Here, traditionally muted members of Bosnian society speak out, for the betterment of their own lives and communities.[1] Their understanding of the causes of the war and their wisdom regarding the path toward peace are not only instructional but also inspirational for anyone dealing with conflict (which is, after all, everyone). My original intention was only to illuminate the most outstanding examples of women-led activity that has gone into rebuilding Bosnia since the recent war, embodied by women like EMSUDA, who sighed to me once, *I wish I could sit down by myself and tell my story—from beginning to end. I just haven't had time.* But over the hours as we talked, the women brought up personal material so important—and so intriguingly consistent—that I added the first section, to give context to their descriptions about their work. The result is two major parts: lessons learned from the personal experiences of the women during the war, and the basic principles by which they are working to heal their country—and themselves, in the process.

At its most leveraged use, this book may serve as a wake-up call for policy shapers about the basis of our assumptions. In these women's words are insights that could, or should, change the fundamental scope of foreign affairs. But shifts in the public policy paradigm are insidiously difficult. In the pages that follow, I'm critical of the shortcomings I perceive in many who've steered international Balkan policy through treacherous waters these past ten years. At the same time, I recognize that they made agonizingly difficult choices, often with limited information.

Many of the women in this book I met while in my diplomatic or humanitarian roles in the mid 1990s. I had no intention of writing about them. But over time I've read one account after another attempting to describe the war. Most chroniclers have focused on historical prelude and horrifying statistics: 150,000 dead; 2,300,000—more than half the prewar population—expelled from their homes.[2] They've described the exploits of political leaders and warriors (overwhelmingly male). Conspicuously missing is the ground-level story lived by well over half the adult population:[3] women who tried to hold family and community together against overwhelming odds. This book addresses that gap in the current understanding of the war, reorienting what became a dramatically gender-skewed account of Bosnia in the last decade of the twentieth century.

We've much to learn about how to foster change in alliance with women who wield influence not only in their families but also throughout their communities.

Top-down policies should be critiqued by ground-level actors—men or women. In this account of Bosnian women's actions to heal their country are examples of work policymakers ought to be funding in every conflict area of the world. When I selected the key characters for this volume, my primary criterion was that they be actively working on rebuilding their society. I wasn't even aware of their hardship stories or their views about the reasons for the war, expressed in part 1. Quite apart from what they have suffered, these are strong, capable women. Supporting their work, launched in the most discouraging conditions, should be a goal in foreign policy work around the world.

In an age of instant communication, where our *guerre du jour* is served up with breakfast bagels, the conviction that change is possible can preserve the public's capacity to care. To borrow from Justice Richard Goldstone, former chief prosecutor at the International Criminal Tribunal in The Hague, I hope my readers will be "rescued from the numbness of our over-intellectualization and transported into a realm where human emotion—sorrow, empathy, and finally hope—are alive."[4]

Listener's Guide

A few thoughts, as my reader enters Bosnia during and immediately after the war. First, the question of fairness. When advised that this book has an anti-Serb bias, I asked two State Department officials who had spent more time than any others in Bosnia during the war if they would help me with revisions. One warned, "Don't let your critics mitigate the Balkans. The international community has always tried to do that, because they don't believe in right and wrong." The second shot back, "So you're supposed to say why you weren't on the side of the people in the hills, firing shells onto the city? Is it a virtue to be neutral in that situation? No! Don't let them neutralize you." Given that advice, I've decided not to artificially adjust my portrayal of what I heard and saw.

What I bring, then, is the most accurate portrayal I can manage of the world of twenty-six Bosnian women. The words are theirs, the framework mine. Gathering, analyzing, and editing their accounts has been a task with public purpose and personal meaning. In the public realm, their work is prototypical for policymakers on the cutting edge of war and peace. On a private basis, we were friends. I use their first names, not out of lack of respect, but because of the trust between us. In my text, they arrive in a passage in capital letters, which seems only fitting.

I've also edited the often-stiff language of the translator into casual speech truer to the tone of our interviews.

My task was complicated by the labels used by outsiders to describe the parties to the conflict, specifically ethnic-based classifications that became prominent during the war.[5] The use in this book of "Serb," "Croat," "Bosniak," "Muslim," "Bosnian Serb," etc. is as misleading as it is clarifying. It was the strategy of nationalist war makers to accentuate divisive group identities to justify the land grab known as "ethnic cleansing."[6] But ethnic categories belie the large number of people with mixed parentage. Using those labels also implies that people thought of themselves and others in those terms. I have been told scores of stories that indicate an obliviousness to ethnicity before the war. Thus on the one hand, using ethnic labels is consistent with the "divide and conquer" methods of the nationalists. On the other hand, the reality of the Bosnian war is that those labels did become commonplace and were written into the political structure of the Dayton Peace Agreement, which ended the war. So I'm left with an uncomfortable inconsistency. In choosing the subjects of this book, I noted and balanced ethnic background. But using those categories to describe the women, I do them a disservice.[7]

In particular, finding the right term for Bosnians with a Muslim heritage is problematic. It's certainly logical to speak of those Bosnians as "Muslim" when referring to others as "Catholic" or "Orthodox." But using a religious term for one group, while speaking of others in nonreligious terms ("Croat" or "Serb"), reinforces the idea that the conflict was the remnant of a religious war waged by or against the Ottomans. Therefore, several women in this volume identify themselves as "Bosniak," rather than "Muslim."[8]

Others maintain an emotional distance from the question of labels. KADA, for example, from a small rural community, insists that she's always called herself "Muslim," and that's the term she'll continue to use. "Bosniak," to her, sounds artificial. But MEDIHA, a medical professor and parliamentarian, and JELKA, who runs a cultural center, wanted to be sure I use the word "Bosniak." Since my goal is to convey the voices of the women themselves, I'll use "Bosniak" when speaking of a people who, although they may have not thought of themselves in terms of such a distinction for decades, now must. When I use "Muslim," it's because I am focusing on religious faith, or because the speaker herself used the term.

In spite of the difficulties of language and categories, the women and I have been shaped by our relationship, and we're relatively comfortable with each other. The reader, however, has the not-so-easy task of moving through the following collective discussions, hearing one voice, then another, then another—no doubt daunted by not remembering who is who. Better for my readers to suppress the hankering for an easy story line. Brief profiles of the speakers, alphabetized by first name, appear after the main text as a reference, along with photographs; and there are occasional cues throughout the text. Still, it's probably a mistake to try to connect the dots in every woman's story. If the plots swirl together, that's more true to life anyway.

The endnotes provide a few more details of the complicated context underlying the women's words. But I'm uncomfortably aware of how much is missing, given the limitations of a book spreading across twenty-six lives. The reader may find inconsistencies, and those are not mistakes. For whether we live in war or peace, whether we're producing or consuming policy, whether we call home the Balkans, the States, or the world, our actions, our thoughts, our lives spill messily across the lines of simple narrative. Like the women here, and like the policymakers who have shaped their destiny, we consistently hold inconsistent views, disregard well-founded expectations, and confound those who know us best as we adapt to and evolve with experiences that come our way. The women in this book remind us that life is not a jigsaw puzzle. The pieces don't fit.

I

Madness

From the stairwell to the *Zena 21* office. December 1995.

I

Madness

ALMA: *War is madness, where everything abnormal becomes normal.*

RADA: *In the center of Sarajevo, normal life was continuing. It could just as well have been sunny California. Nobody knew that on the edge of town, this craziness was happening.*

ALMA: *It was a crazy, crazy time. God forbid that this happens ever again. I'd rather die than live it over.*

DANICA: *Then the nationalists came in, and people just went crazy.*

MAJA: *They say only insane people are not afraid.*

Alma, Rada, Danica, and Maja are not insane. Fear was in their voices as they described to me UN soldiers protecting food supplies, but not the people who should eat; neighbors raped, by long-time neighbors; dazed refugees sleeping on the floor, the banker, high school principal, mayor. In short, madness.

These women grew up in an ordered society, with clear rules and norms. Their lives were set on a course. They had lovers, found jobs in factories, tilled farms, completed university, raised families. In a socialist society without entrepreneurial surprises, with low divorce and child mortality rates, as well as relatively low unemployment, they had confidence in their futures.

Suddenly, war came flooding into their lives. Swept up in a political tidal wave, they grasped for whatever might keep them afloat. They hoped the United Nations could save them. Apart from limited delivery of humanitarian aid, the UN failed. Hampered by weak internal leadership, a cumbersome bureaucratic process, reluctance among pivotal member states (particularly Russia), insufficient resources, and the arrogance of some key officials assigned to the field, the response of the UN to the crisis in Bosnia was woefully inadequate. Europe was disunited, and American leadership wasn't forthcoming: Governor Clinton, in the 1992 presidential campaign, had criticized President Bush's inaction, a result of discord within the upper echelons of that administration. But once in office, President Clinton faced the same split between the State Department, which advocated intervention, and the Pentagon, which didn't want to get involved. Clinton waffled. U.S. and European pundits argued about the line between a state's sovereignty in determining affairs within its borders, versus the justification of military intervention to halt genocide. Meanwhile, the death toll was climbing toward 200,000. Eventually, in mid-1995, Clinton abandoned the "dual key" arrangement that required UN sign-off for NATO action, saying that NATO's role as a stabilizing force in Europe was called into question by the paralysis, and the humanitarian cost of inaction was unconscionable.

The international community's paralysis was due in part to discrepant interpretations of Balkan history. Local nationalists revised the past to fit their desired future, with tales steeped in stale victimhood that reached back centuries. The region was painted as one giant battlefield stretching across hundreds of years. Outsiders could throw up their hands. "They made their bed, let them lie in it," commented a British diplomat to me in late 1993. It was a particularly odd remark, disregarding the fact that the Balkans had been invaded, divided, and ruled by one outside imperial regime after another over the centuries, leaving behind a hodgepodge of cultural identities.

The country once known as Yugoslavia resulted from the post–World War I dissolution of the Habsburg and Ottoman empires. Bosnia and Herzegovina had been part of both of these opposing empires, and its population — Orthodox Serbs, Catholic Croats, Muslims converted under Ottoman rule, and Sephardic Jews — was integrated. Yugoslavia was first known as "The Kingdom of Serbs, Croats, and Slovenes." This monarchy fell apart at the onset of World War II. A Nazi puppet regime ruled in Croatia and fascist collaborators in Belgrade nominally controlled much of the rest of Yugoslavia, although they were fiercely resisted. Contrary to outside perceptions, that was the first time Bosnians witnessed ethnic conflict on their soil. Throughout Yugoslavia, one million people died in fighting among Ustashas (supporters of the fascist Croatian regime), Chetniks (royalist Serb supporters), and Partisans (communist resisters). The Croats were infamously ruthless in their slaughter of Serbs, but Serb paramilitaries also committed massacres of Muslims and Croats. In addition, 60,000 Yugoslav Jews were murdered by Nazis.[1] Josip Broz (better known by his nom de guerre Tito) led the Partisans to victory. Soviet forces entered Belgrade in 1944.

Yugoslavia under Tito enjoyed a unique position in the world. After break-ing with Stalin's Soviet communism in 1948, Tito developed policies of economic decentralization and independence from the two superpower security blocs. He understood how high the geopolitical stakes were: Truman and Eisenhower wanted to convince Eastern European countries that they could survive outside the Iron Curtain. Yugoslavia's independence was a thorn in the side of the Soviet Union. Western powers showered Tito with favors.[2] He, in turn, skillfully played the game of balancing East and West, developing socialism on his own terms with the benefit of loans from the International Monetary Fund. Tito also established a delicate balance in Yugoslavia's internal politics. He proclaimed an ideology of "brotherhood and unity," and Yugoslavia's constitution created a complicated system of six republics (Serbia, Croatia, Bosnia and Herzegovina, Slovenia, Mace-donia, and Montenegro) and two autonomous regions within Serbia (Vojvodina and Kosovo), tied together by one man at the top: Tito himself.

Although it was the most affluent country in communist Europe, after Tito's death in 1980, Yugoslavia's economy drifted. Its republics entered a rotating power-sharing arrangement that quickly fell prey to nationalist politicians. In 1987, Slobodan Milosevic, a second-rung Belgrade politician, began to accrue power, leaving a wake of embittered colleagues.[3] Using the official Serb media, he stirred up World War II memories of division and encouraged those calling for "Greater Serbia," particularly turning up the acrimonious volume against the ethnic Albanian majority in Kosovo. These tactics of social division raised alarm among many of Serbia's progressive citizens and throughout the other repub-lics. Croatia responded with its own nationalist politics, led by former general of the Yugoslav National Army, Franjo Tudjman. Known as the "Father of all Croats," Tudjman was openly anti-Serb and anti-Muslim.[4] He was hugely influen-tial, not only in Croatia, but also the western part of Bosnia, where many ethnic Croats lived.

Milosevic was artful and experienced. A party apparatchik and sometime banker, he had visited the United States; and his English was excellent. At home, his rhetoric was consistent with the tide of Serb nationalism, but he carefully con-solidated his power through purges within his political party, key media outlets, and ultimately the Yugoslav National Army.[5] When he had reached the limits of power he could achieve peacefully and shifted to military means, he held the high trumps.

History is still sifting and sorting the views of those who participated in or ob-served the disintegration of Yugoslavia over the next years. The first fighting was in the republic of Slovenia. Conflict there between the Yugoslav National Army and resident Slovenes lasted about a week. Hundred of civilians were killed and wounded as the JNA bombed private homes and farms, or shot citizens sitting in cafes or tilling their fields.[6] Slovenia had virtually no Serbs, so the war cry of "Greater Serbia" inspired no one, including the mothers of Serb soldiers who confronted military commanders and urged their sons to come back home where they belonged. These women-led public demonstrations spread. On July 2, 1991, the mothers demonstrated at the Serbian Assembly in Belgrade, shouting: "We haven't borne sons to die for Milosevic!" The next day, hundreds of women went to Ljubljana, the capital of Slovenia, to find their sons and bring them home.[7]

Croatia's fate was not so tempered. One-third of its territory was overtaken by the Serb army in a ruthless onslaught.[8] Tens of thousands of non-Serbs fled the barbarity. Many who tried to stay in their homes were killed or forcibly expelled. The tactics were sadistic and grotesque, replete with summary executions and throat slitting.

Bosnia, with a population of about four million, was the third largest of the republics by land mass and population. The 1991 census recorded that Bosnian citizens were approximately 44 percent Muslim, 32 percent Serb, 17 percent Croat, and 8 percent "other." In two-thirds of the districts, none of the three ethnic groups constituted more than 70 percent of the population. The other one-third was evenly divided: 11 percent were mostly Muslims, 11 percent were mostly Serbs, and 10 percent were mostly Croats. Division along ethnic lines was, thus, out of the question, without great disruption of the population.[9] Thus in 1991 Bosnians watched fearfully as Serb forces destroyed whole towns and villages in neighboring Croatia, torturing and executing non-Serbs who did not flee. Their apprehension was well-founded. When, unstopped by international onlookers, the Serb-controlled Yugoslav army and paramilitaries had overpowered large chunks of Croatia, the military turned its attention to Bosnia with the same bloody campaign, cruelly understated by the euphemistic term "ethnic cleansing," driving Bosnian Croats and Bosniaks from their homes.

Listening to details of the women telling me about their lives, I thought of Europe sixty years earlier. Their stories, like those of refugees being interviewed by my embassy staff, harkened back to the Nazi regime: ritualized torture, gang rape, and killings. Those of us who only studied World War II in history books had the luxury of attributing the Holocaust to the failure of other people, in another era. But Bosnia was happening on our watch. We, not our parents, were sitting in front of our TVs, watching the smoke rise from burning villages. As the carnage dragged on, we were distracted by the likes of O. J. Simpson and White-water—even after CNN and the BBC brought the Balkan conflagration into our living rooms.

Our consciences should be troubled by the women's accounts. We hear stories that conflict with what we want to believe about ourselves and the rest of humanity. The barbarity related in this volume forces us to ponder the source of evil that runs rampant in these stories. What was unleashed? From where? Why?[10] Is raw malevolence merely one spot on a continuum of good-to-bad, or is it sui generis, requiring that we stop and wonder at the power of the unique force before us? Such questions can become their own agenda, feeding on themselves, without compelling the asker to action. So it was with Yugoslavia. Not only the general public but also many policy shapers—including some media professionals—seemed simultaneously fixated on and confounded by the sadism. The resulting inaction was devastating. Perhaps Milosevic understood that by unleashing the strongest possible torrent of terror, he could distract world attention from his overarching political designs.[11]

The women in this book did not simply draw back in repulsion, resignation, or exhaustion. For them, ordeal was a precursor to action. To understand their work, I have tried to understand their world, including the wartime madness they experienced. The war had barreled into their lives, wiping out the known, leaving wild impossibilities. But the unexpected onslaught is only the beginning of their story. A few of the women's accounts of the chaos—the decision to stay or flee, and atrocities endured by those caught in the conflict—are related here. They are followed by a look at war not just from an external view of hell on earth but also with an interior eye, as the women described the war to me in the language of personal connections: mothers caring for children and elderly parents, lovers courting or being separated, friends sticking together or drifting apart, relationships that became a ponderous burden, and yet remained a crucial source of meaning to resist the madness.

Bus becomes barricade. Dobrinja, suburb of Sarajevo. December 1995.

1

Hell Breaks Loose

NURDZIHANA: *Serbs who left their flats just before the war gave us their keys and asked us to water their flowers and feed their fish. No one said anything about the horror to come.*

RADA: *We were like calves grazing by an active volcano.*

The story of vulnerable women has already been written.[1] The untold tale is women's extraordinary ability to survive the eruption, transform suffering into savvy, and challenge assumptions about why their worlds were torn apart. From these accounts emerges a wisdom that will startle those who believe Balkan people will always be fighting.

I didn't want to compile a book of war stories. But even though the bulk of our interviews took place after the war, and my interviewees knew my focus was on how they are rebuilding their country, the women talking with me couldn't describe their current activities without recounting memories that spilled messily across whatever else was our topic at hand. The stories weren't told chronologically: A word from me or idea from them might uncork a sequence whose logic was only in the living. Nor was the telling optional. The women's postconflict work was built on the foundation of their war experience: not just physical losses or emotional travails, but courage that emerged from the wounds of war and energy that was summoned as they responded to the violence.

The episodes the women related are burdened with desperation, terror, confusion, loss. For all our sympathy about the plight of refugees or the trauma inflicted on those who survived years of siege, those who are able to tell what happened are the lucky ones. They know they must bear witness for those who can't speak. When refugees' accounts began to trickle out, such as those gathered by my embassy staff from the tens of thousands who fled to Austria, the UN tribunal was created in The Hague to bring war criminals to justice. We policy-makers spawned a host of conferences, scores of publications, and mounds of resolutions. That process of bringing the stories to light was both necessary and hurtful. Extracting testimony from victims creates a struggle between private and public worlds. Atrocity is a necessary subject of human rights advocates and international lawyers, but even putting the experience into words can deepen the wounds of the sufferer.

Still, the pain that punctuates these pages is not the final word for any of these women. Their wartime stories are included to help give the reader firsthand accounts underlying their assessment of the reasons for the war and their motivation to transform and heal their society. The reader needs to know their stories to understand their work. But the telling was also important to the women, who are anxious to have their voices heard. Many traveled a full day to our meetings in Sarajevo. They were ready to talk—and not, it should be added, inclined to complain. Each of these women had not only survived but had taken the madness of her experience and let it live inside her, work on her, gnaw at her, energize her. In the process she'd refashioned her values to reflect a harsher reality. She'd kept her balance and remained standing in the wake of sudden aggression. Maintaining her bearings, she'd daily made the terrible decision to pack her bags, or risk putting herself and her loved ones in harm's way. The women's stories of onslaught, chaos, flight, and atrocities are told in this chapter.

Onslaught

DANICA: *We were sitting around chatting, and the next day was war.*

KRISTINA: *You learn to feel in your gut when to go hide.*

IRMA: *We couldn't . . . It was like, "Oh God, who wants to hurt us?* [She begins

to cry.] *What's happening?"*

The effect of violence in Bosnia was magnified by the shock of the onslaught. Stepping back from the women's narratives, an outsider can trace a perverse order in the acts that led to hostile conflict. But those simply trying to maintain a normal life as the world around them was warping couldn't imagine that events would develop as they did. Like much of the rest of Eastern Europe in 1989 and 1990, Bosnians were hopeful at the prospect of democracy in their country. In-

stead, they became enmeshed in the nationalist politics that presaged the breakup
of Yugoslavia. In 1991, when Slovenia and Croatia declared independence, alarm
spread among the non-Serb majority in Bosnia that they would be left as a dis-
advantaged minority in a rump Yugoslavia fashioned as Greater Serbia. A referendum over February 29 to March 1, 1992, on whether Bosnia too should secede
from Yugoslavia, yielded a 99 percent favorable response; though the nationalist
Serb political party (SDS) and much of the Serb population boycotted the vote,
leaving the decisions to 63.4 percent of the eligible voting population.[2] Bosnia declared independence from Yugoslavia on March 3, as Serb forces set up barricades
and sniper positions around Sarajevo.

Fighting erupted in the capital and across the country. Ethnic cleansing began
in early April, when the notorious Serb thug called Arkan and his paramilitaries
entered Bijeljina and Zvornik (on the Serb border of northeastern Bosnia) and
began expelling or killing the Bosniak residents. With the invasion of Vukovar,
Croatia, the year before, Arkan had pioneered the technique of terrorizing civilians into fleeing.[3] In Bijeljina, his "Tigers" set up sniper positions to terrorize the
citizens. They hunted and shot Bosniak leaders on the spot and went through
the streets indiscriminately firing their machine guns.[4] Meanwhile, in the capital,
Serb snipers fired into a peace demonstration on April 6. As Serb troops encircled
the city, the three-and-a-half year siege of Sarajevo began.

Then, all of a sudden—at least to me it seemed sudden—something happened.
FAHRIJA was shocked when her politician husband urged her to leave Bosnia,
convinced that an outbreak of violence was just around the corner. Demagogues
surfaced, making bizarre claims and promoting notions of ethnic differentiation.
*The trouble originated in Serbia. Strange political meetings were held. There was a lot
of talk about history, and accusations about terrors during the Ottoman Empire. The
theories put forward were ludicrous to us. We didn't take them seriously. I thought we, as
a people, were so strongly connected that nothing could destroy that bond. My husband
said I should take the children somewhere awhile, so he would be free to join the political
scene and fight for Yugoslavia. Ejup knew the war was starting that day, but he didn't
tell me. He knew I wouldn't leave. Arriving in Belgrade, we immediately received news
that Serb forces had attacked Sarajevo. I knew they wouldn't let us come back.*

Fahrija is a sophisticated, Chicago-trained dermatologist, raised in Serbia in
a wealthy Albanian Muslim family. She and her husband, Ejup, a former professor of engineering at the Massachusetts Institute of Technology, had returned to
Bosnia with their two small children. As the trouble erupted, she decided to go
to her father's home about 150 miles from Belgrade. Given Ejup's high profile as

a political leader, she decided to go by bus, hoping she and her two children could pass incognito. *I saw strange things during the journey. There seemed to be something everybody else had known for a long time, something I was just realizing. Groups of soldiers were at every checkpoint. The bus driver would simply wave a three-finger salute in political solidarity, and we were allowed to pass. Each time my heart would stop, fearing a soldier would board and check our papers. They'd realize that I was the wife of—and these were the children of—Ejup Ganic. We were in the middle of Serbia, and they were blaming Ejup and our president, Izetbegovic, for the war. I was trembling.*

TANJA was also politically involved, a member of the prewar Bosnian Parliament, who eventually moved into the multiperson presidency (a typical Balkan political construct). Before and after her political work, she was a professor of landscape architecture. Tanja is active, forceful, and intelligent; still, like Fahrija, she was caught completely off guard by the eruption of hostilities: *Even in the Parliament, none of us could imagine war was coming. Many of my political colleagues were thinking about what seemed to me to be an abstract idea—the division of the country—and all my being welled up against the notion. When the shelling started, I thought it must be some drunks. When we discovered it was serious, and it was ethnic Serbs attacking the city, even though I'm a Serb I decided to stay in Sarajevo and not go to the mountains—not shoot down from the hills on my friends and colleagues.*

Tanja's words challenge credulity. Surely she must have known war was brewing. But disbelief among professionals and common citizens was widespread. SUZANA's account corroborates Tanja's. She too is a Bosnian Serb, an identity that allowed this delicate young woman entrée into the sphere of the Serb military as a journalist during the conflict: *One day before the shooting broke out in Sarajevo, a friend of mine from the Yugoslav army told me I should leave immediately, because the next day the fighting would start. I was shocked. He knew the* exact day *war would break out! But of course I stayed.* As the onslaught started, twenty-three-year-old Suzana went to pick up some food from her parents, who lived a two-hour drive northwest of the capital. *I was naïve to believe the war would be over in a couple of days, so I was trapped there in Serb territory. I was a journalist for what some considered a Muslim magazine. The Serbs came to my father and tried, at gunpoint, to mobilize me for civil defense, to make me prove my loyalty. My father managed to get me transferred to the medical corps, where I was active only once—helping with a violent psychotic woman from the emptied mental hospitals. After three months, I escaped my parents' town on the first bus allowed to leave Bosnia and go to Serbia.*

Another media professional caught completely unaware was RADA, living unwittingly on the front line with her radio director husband, seventeen-year-old daughter, and eight-year-old son. Rada embodies the mixed demographics of Bosnians: from a rural family, transplanted to Sarajevo, married to a Bosnian Croat, and with ethnic Serb parents. With the onset of war, the radio station was in disarray as programming began to be politicized by the SDA, the prominent Bosniak party. Although she was in the heart of the news industry, Rada felt outside the information loop. *Nationalist leaders were appearing on TV, but I don't think anyone thought war was possible. Maybe when you're too close, you can't feel it. There were lots of nationalist Serb and Croat political party members, as well as Serbs in upscale apartments owned by the army. They left in February. Jeeps and cars picked them up, so they must have already had some warning that something was going to happen. We saw them leave but didn't attach any importance to it, because the war had started in Slovenia and Croatia, and antiarmy feelings were increasing. We thought the army people were afraid of the animosity, and that was why they were leaving for a while. They didn't move their furniture. They just left with suitcases, so we weren't alarmed. We accepted it as normal.*

From her sixth-floor apartment, Rada looked out over a peaceful, quiet neighborhood, filled with a large number of Bosniaks, as well as Serbs. *Then one evening in early March '92, trucks arrived with armed men — some in camouflage, some in blue, some with bands around their sleeves with white eagles,[5] which were the only sign that they were extremists. There was nothing strategically essential about our neighborhood. Although the Yugoslav army was all around, we didn't feel threatened. Near our area there was a water supply plant, and they took it over; but we thought that it was for some public purpose: to guard it — maybe prevent someone from poisoning us.* [She laughs sardonically.] Almost overnight, the modern residential neighborhood in which Rada lived was transformed into the front line for Serbs attempting to take over Sarajevo. *From my flat I watched armed people come in and out. Telephone lines were cut; I had no contact with Pale* [Karadzic's newly declared Bosnian Serb capital fifteen miles from Sarajevo].[6] *No communication whatsoever. We were trying to figure out what was going on. But war? No way.* [Rada laughs again.]

Rada went out to her balcony to watch the soldiers. *They started shooting at our windows, thinking we were Bosniaks or their sympathizers. At the beginning it was sort of a warning. That's what we believed — rather innocently. We weren't supposed to watch, but we didn't know that.* [She leans forward, laughing again, her hands moving constantly as she paints the scene.] *We had a fantastic view, right in front of our eyes, like a movie screen. Every day they were shooting, not over the buildings, but into our windows. After that, the military issued orders for us to put blankets over the windows — for security reasons, they said. Sometimes, out of curiosity, we tried to peep out and see what was going on. They'd shoot directly into our windows if they saw us. One morning, a sniper fired at me seven times. If I hadn't dropped to the floor, I'd be dead. My flat was completely destroyed early in May '92. It was hit by so many shells that it looked like an arsenal.*

In May or June, and even after, most journalists just wanted to get out of Sarajevo. It was mass confusion. Nobody knew what was going on or how long it would last. Everybody thought it would be just one or two months—at worst until winter, then everything would be over. Some of my Serb colleagues felt ashamed, so they either stayed at home, waiting for the fighting to stop, or they left for Serb territory or Zagreb.[7] The Bosniaks mainly remained, although the ones who had relatives abroad went to be with them. We were left—patriots who had no idea what we were fighting for, just a compulsion to do something.

As other journalists were leaving, Rada stayed and recorded stories of refugees expelled from their homes. *My brother and mother in Pale didn't want to accept reality; but I interviewed Bosniaks from Pale I'd known all my life. That was awful, listening to people who were living with their friends one day, and the next day had to flee. Their expulsion, we realized later, was lucky, because in the spring of 1992 an enormous number of soldiers from Serbia moved in, most of them wearing the white eagles insignia. Executions followed.*

The aggression led by Milosevic-backed forces was stunning. Repeatedly, the women expressed their amazement, shock, and disbelief that this nightmare could be descending on their stable, modern country.[8] ALMA, a young engineer, had been raised in Mostar, a couple of hours' drive south of Sarajevo.[9] One of two children, with a gutsy spirit, she had been a talented high school athlete. In April 1992, Alma was visiting her parents in Sarajevo for Bajram, a three-day Muslim holiday. Though fighting had started in the capital, she imagined it would be fleeting. She was concerned about missing work in Mostar, so she boarded a train to go back home. That trip changed her life forever. The track had been blown up, and she found herself trapped. *I was stuck midway, in some town where I had no friends or family.* Like any person trying to make rational decisions in crazy times, she was disoriented. *I just couldn't believe this was happening. There was still electricity. On TV I saw Sarajevo being shelled. My parents were there! I kept thinking the track would be repaired. I wanted to go back to Sarajevo or on to Mostar, but I couldn't get to either.*

Over the next weeks the war escalated. *To survive, I joined the army trying to protect Bosnia, working as a medic.* Women in the army had no training and no one directing them. *As a girl, it was hard; women had to prove themselves more and*

Along the main road from the airport to Sarajevo. December 1995.

*had to protect themselves, psychologically as well as physically. We were on our own —
defending our people.*

Some scenes were almost ludicrous, as citizens tried to protect themselves
from the violent assault. KAROLINA was in her early fifties when the fighting
started in Sarajevo. She handled finances for a local business — a no-nonsense sort
of job. Although Catholic, she lived in the old Muslim section of town. *When
blockades were put up in the streets, my son and his friend, eighteen and fourteen years
old, guarded us with two small axes. They put sandbags around the house. We were
so naïve, thinking that could protect us. The Chetniks were running up and down our
street, throwing bombs into our yards. During the night we'd hear footsteps* [she slaps
the table with her palms, making the sound of steps] *and then an explosion. We only
had those hatchets — garden tools. We were trapped by snipers with infrared equipment,
shooting at us like pigeons or rabbits. We put pillows, blankets, and mattresses against
the windows. They were using bullets that exploded into fire, but the bullets would get
caught in the wool, and we thought maybe the fibers stopped them from exploding. It was*

a psychological attack as well. During the shelling, I didn't have the strength to run. As time went on, I developed a sixth sense; I knew exactly where a shell would land. You can't explain that to someone who hasn't gone through it. You just learn; it's instinctive. Just like animals in the woods—that was how we lived.

As the tapes from my recorder piled up, so did the dramatic scenes: Fahrija, incognito on a Serbian bus, two young children in tow; Tanja, parliamentarian caught unaware as the shelling began; Suzana, trapped in Serb territory when she went to get some food; Rada, hanging blankets over her plate-glass window; Alma, leaving the blocked train and joining up with troops in the hills; Karolina's children with hatchets to protect against shelling. In the women's stories, such tales of onslaught quickly devolved into chaos.

Chaos

DANICA: *In just five hours, lifetimes were turned upside down.*

ALMA: *We'd be sitting and talking, and suddenly a shell would explode and five or six people would be dead. They'd be different ages, male and female, different ethnic groups. You see, a shell can't choose whom to hit.*

GRETA: *With bomber planes in World War II there was a warning siren, and everyone ran to a shelter. But in this war we never knew when to expect an explosion.*

Despite a pattern obvious in hindsight, Bosnians couldn't believe that the brutality they'd watched in Croatia would be repeated in their country. President Izetbegovic insisted that it takes two to fight, and his government would simply not engage. He prepared no armed defense. His unwillingness to descend to the pugilism of Croatian President Tudjman or Serbian President Milosevic left Bosnians vulnerable.[10] Tudjman and Milosevic had discussed dividing Bosnia into two parts, to be annexed into their newly defined countries. The plan assumed the forced migration of hundreds of thousands of non-Croats out of the western half of Bosnia into the Serb-dominated east, and similarly, the moving of non-Serbs out of the eastern half into the Croat-dominated west. But the swap provided no haven for two million Bosniaks scattered throughout Bosnia. They should simply leave, willingly or not.

To encourage their departure, Serb as well as Croat troops destroyed mosques and Muslim graves. Soldiers—or neighbors in the cover of night—looted, then burned homes of Bosniaks to discourage their return. But a local Bosnian army was eventually pieced together to mount a defense. Their sporadic success resulted in a continuous shifting of front lines, so that control over a community might change hands several times.

The images the women described made our interviews grueling: Bicycle wheels spinning to generate light in the cellar. Jam jars made into explosives. City buses on their sides turned into barricades. Parents in bunk beds as human shields against snipers aiming at hospitalized children. A mahogany wardrobe converted into coffins. A clock ticking on the wall next to splattered brains. The Olympic soccer field appropriated as a makeshift graveyard. Body parts collected from the market between the vegetable stalls. Park trees burned as fuel. Porch rails burned as fuel. Books burned as fuel. Running shoes burned as fuel.

War perverted the materials of everyday life into materials of everyday death. That twisted betrayal of purpose bred disorientation and trauma. Unlike Bosnian men serving in the army with some semblance of a plan, women were left behind with only their instinct as they tried to save their homes, protect their children, and, ultimately keep their own bodies and souls together. The cost of confusion was added to the toll of wartime loss. Change became the constant. No calendar was wise enough to predict how long shells would keep pounding, electricity would be off, the exile would last, hope would endure.

IRMA is the only child of architect parents of different religious traditions, both born in Sarajevo. She inherited not only their talent for drawing but also their sensitivity. *One morning I woke up and got ready for school. We heard on TV that Sarajevo was totally surrounded. My first reaction was, "Yea! I don't have to go to school!" I didn't know that was the last time we'd go that year; the teachers just handed out grades. As time passed, shelling started.* [She shakes her head at her naïveté.] *It was like what you'd hear on TV or in a movie. Danger all around, but somehow you couldn't accept it. It was so scary. Finally we started to understand what was really happening. We heard the first tanks attacking Sarajevo. . . .*

From the time I was born, I lived in a four-story building with trees all around. That was home to me, and I wouldn't trade that place for anywhere. The basement had storage spaces about six by nine feet, one for each of the eleven families in the building. In that warren, for the first six or seven months of the war, and sporadically thereafter, some seventy people set up life together. Irma's own family threesome swelled to six as they were joined by family members whose home had been destroyed. At night, with no room in the storage space, her parents slept on the floor of the corridor. When it was dark, refuse, including human waste, was gathered in newspapers and taken out and buried in the orchard behind the building. For four years no garbage was collected in the city.

Irma's adolescent recollections of the pandemonium have a comical edge. *Everyone was crowded around the radio. That was our only communication with the world. It seems funny now. And all those old people saying things like, "Oh, this is going to end soon." "Oh, my friend told me this and that and this and that." Everyone was talking, but nobody really knew anything. The panic affected people more than the shelling. Old people, young people, were grabbing their kitchen knives and saying things like, "We'll defend ourselves!" An old lady came to our cellar with her husband. She was, like, ninety. They were so sweet, you know, dressed with all these coats on. [She starts laughing.] They had their kitchen knives, too. God, they were clueless! I remember their faces. We were kids, just running around the cellar, making everybody nervous, and everybody was yelling at us. Then there was one woman who kept going upstairs, and when she came back, she always had a story: [Irma mimics her high-pitched voice.] "Oh! I saw a man with a gun!" "Oh! I saw tanks in the streets!"*

Soon enough, the war was all too real. Within weeks, Irma's family heard an explosion a few blocks away that left several people dead. Then one night, a shell hit the home of Irma's best friend. His arm was blown off. In the dark, his parents couldn't find the limb, so the hospital doctors couldn't attempt to sew it back on. Irma was devastated.

Weeks, then months, passed in the cramped quarters, and tensions in the cellar were aggravated. *It was very, very hard. As time went by there were fights, lots of fights, because people were all fed up with everything. People were . . . I don't know . . . maybe it was someone's turn to make bread, and the other lady wanted to make bread before her. . . .* Finally, Irma's family decided to take their chances upstairs in their apartment, despite the risk. After all, there was no real way to know how long the fighting would last. The plan was for everyone to rush down to the cellar when shelling resumed, but Irma's father sometimes had to forcibly pull her. *I guess the worst was when we thought we didn't have to go to the cellar anymore. Then suddenly, bombing would start early in the morning, or something like that, and you just ran down again, and you were miserable and everybody was so . . . you never knew. . . . That was actually worse than when the shelling was constant. Just when you thought you were starting to live a normal life. . . .*

The indiscriminate shelling was powerful mental torture on the part of the

Bosnian Serbs, whose president, Radovan Karadzic, was a psychiatrist. Over time, Irma's father was able, by listening, to track projectiles in the air, analyzing several seconds of sound to anticipate the arc and calculate whether his family might be blown up. With the explosion came relief. Disaster averted, at least for the moment.

For Irma, the internal stress was as troubling as the external danger. *The shelling might start at 5:00 A.M. My mom and dad could sleep through it, but I'd take my pillow and blanket and go to the bathroom — an ugly bathroom, with white walls, and dark yellow and orange tiles. I'd curl up on the toilet, 'cause that was a place where you couldn't hear it so loud . . . all those sounds of the shells coming at us, flying over our house. We were always thinking, like, "Oh, God, this one is going to hit us. This one. . . ." I spent lots of mornings in that bathroom. If there hadn't been that sound of them in the air, just a bomb, okay. But that sound . . .*

Irma found solace in letting life roll on: *A bunch of my friends would come over, and we'd all sit in front of my building. Some of the boys played guitars. We wouldn't stop, even when the shelling would start. We sang songs like "Stairway to Heaven," but also Bosnian songs: "Anywhere I Go, I'm Dreaming of You." "All Roads Lead to You, Sarajevo, My Love." During the war, that song became really popular again, because it was sentimental. There were tons of songs. [She laughs.] We were actually happy. I mean we had to be.*

A year into the war, Irma's friends came to celebrate her birthday. *I made this goofy pizza [she laughs] with whatever we had: bread and sardines in a tomato sauce. It was actually great! We were playing the guitar. Suddenly we heard this BANG! Then a flash of light. It was like a thunderbolt, so loud and so close. We all fell on the floor. People were running. Someone was crawling. We thought it had hit our building. We ran to the exit, then downstairs. After a few minutes, we realized the shell had fallen where we usually sat outside singing. We thought, "Oh, my God!" Everybody thanked me for inviting them to my birthday, because my party saved us.*

At the beginning of the war, the boys said, "Oh, great!" The only fighting they'd ever seen was on TV.[11] *They didn't even know how to hold a gun. They didn't know why they were fighting. I asked our sixteen-year-old neighbor what he was trying to prove. He had his mother and father and brother. He should be happy making them happy by being alive. Why fight? Lots of girls tried to tell the boys they were doing wrong — that fighting wasn't the solution — but they were determined. Once they'd tasted war, they understood it wasn't like the movies. Everybody said, "This is never going to end! I'm not stupid. My friends are all dead. What the heck am I doing?" A lot of them ran away from the city when they could. As soldiers, they could go through the tunnel, and they just didn't come back.* Irma sees the issue in terms of social learning. *When I was playing with Barbie dolls, the boys were playing war and shooting and something like that, because they saw it in the movies.*

In the war, women were more [she pauses] *calm. Yeah, they faced it: Okay, we're in a war now. We have to survive. We have to eat. We have to find water. We have to figure this out. My mom was much tougher than my dad. During the war I really got to know him—every little detail. He was so afraid—for me, for my mom, for everybody. I know he was doing right when he made me go to the shelter, but he made me panic because he was so upset all the time. He'd say, "Oh God, it's a shell!" He just kept drumming it in. He was angry and always yelling at us. You know, he didn't mean any harm. He just wanted us to survive. But it was exhausting to go through.*

I don't remember all the things I did in the cellar, but I remember the feeling, because war brought us together, whether we wanted to be or not. We were living on top of each other. I mean, it wasn't awful, 'cause we made it comfortable, with beds, carpets, chairs and everything. And cards! Oh, my God! We played lots of cards. Then when the grown-ups went to sleep, we started kissing—my first kiss on the mouth. Before that, we'd put a cherry in a glass and play with it with our tongues, to learn how to kiss.

Meanwhile, "the grown-ups," as Irma calls them, were constantly thinking about how to protect their children, who might bring hot shrapnel in from the street as a novelty, or go swimming in the river in easy range of the snipers—as Irma and her schoolmates did. After all, kids cope with war with the skills they have, which includes imagination and play. For the grown-ups, on the other hand, as months stretched into years and turmoil became a way of life, all sorts of assumptions—regarding education, for example—were now uncertain. Principals had to decide whether to hold school, teachers had to decide whether to stay in Sarajevo or try to leave, parents had to decide whether to let (or make) their children thread their way across the besieged town to the school, students had to decide if their fear outside would be greater than their boredom inside. *When the war started, we quit going to school for maybe three months. Then it was September—time for classes. My primary school was near where I lived, but high school was across town, half an hour on foot. It was crazy, but what the hell? We had to do something. Our teachers just told us, "When your mom and dad think it's okay for you to come, then it's okay. If not, don't come."* For Irma's parents, the worst moment of every day was when she'd leave for school. Her father urged her to run, so she'd at least be a fast-moving target. When shelling began at midday, the children sometimes stayed in the school basement. For parents across Sarajevo, those times were nerve-wracking. Still, the teachers assigned heavy homework, even though there were no new schoolbooks. Irma hand-copied old texts by candlelight at home, determined not to let war have the last word.

At least Irma could run through the city to get to school. Farther out, NURDZIHANA, an accomplished journalist in her forties, was cut off from the city as she dealt with the devastation in her neighborhood near the airport. Dobrinja was a relatively new neighborhood, built as the 1984 Winter Olympic Village, a fifteen-minute drive out from the middle of Sarajevo. *From the beginning, we were completely encircled by Chetniks. Our "line of defense" was a ridiculous notion, because we didn't have weapons. One day, people were panicking, running here and there. I didn't know what to do and didn't want to run.* Meanwhile, Serb troops were advancing across Dobrinja, taking control block by block. Nurdzihana started to run to a building about 300 yards away, set up as a makeshift headquarters. *Someone yelled, "Sniper! Sniper!" I said, "So what?" I didn't know what a "sniper" was — much less that there was one around.*

I found our "neighborhood commander," who hadn't slept for two nights. He had a band around his head. I yelled, "People are stampeding! They say you don't have anything to defend us with! What should we do?" He looked right through me and didn't answer. I shouted again, "What should we do? I don't think people should run away. Is it true you don't have any weapons?" He looked at me and asked, "Do you want me to show you?" I thought he meant he had an arsenal. It turned out there was just an empty apartment building.

Back among our neighbors, a man who had gone with me shouted to the people, "Do you think you can hide? Don't run away!" The woman next to me muttered, "Damn it!" But the people stayed. I telephoned the Interior Ministry, looking for my friend, the minister. I told him, "People are panicking! What should I do?" He shouted over and over, "Organize the people! Don't run away! Defend yourselves! Throw flowerpots on them! Make explosives with hot water and gasoline!"

For months, even years, most people from Dobrinja couldn't reach the center of Sarajevo. When the shelling and bombing started, we lost connection with many neighbors and friends, because if you stepped out of your building, you could be shot, and the telephone lines were cut. Before, I'd been in contact, trying to find out what was happening with others. Now, I was afraid for everyone I knew, and I had to take care of my mother and my brother's son, who accidentally found himself at my place when the war started.

Most people didn't stay because of patriotism. They stayed to defend their homes, their basic way of life. Although it was summer, Nurdzihana stayed dressed, round-the-clock, in pants and boots. A month into the war, Nurdzihana and her family abandoned their apartment, which was directly in the line of the snipers and shelling. They found space across the street, but Nurdzihana often ran back to her home through trenches and behind barricades. Many people were wounded trying to cross. *We were naïve, wanting to water our flowers and plants, or maybe feed our fish. I went back to try to protect my books, afraid some thugs would break in and take my things.*

My library was very important—even essential—to me. I imagined how in five minutes a lifetime collection of books—mine, or some child's, or maybe a family's photo albums—could be reduced to ashes. Nurzdihana thought she might protect her books by covering them with a blanket; eventually, she hid them under a futon in another room. *That was my greatest fear—that my books would burn. That's why I went back, although less and less frequently, because it grew more dangerous.*

I was in my old flat, with a friend, in my library. Suddenly there was an explosion, then another. Everything happened within seconds. I reached out and touched him to check if he—or I—was still alive. We were scared. After a few seconds we saw a bullet go though the lamp over my head. Another whizzed by, grazing my back, then went through the door and into the hall. They were big bullets, still hot. She returned again—in defiance, really. *We couldn't just flee—leave our homes and wait for someone to save us. Nobody knew what would happen next. If we'd known what was ahead . . .* She left her sentence unfinished. Looking back, events at least have a known sequence. It's more difficult looking forward, not knowing if the struggle will last five hours, five months, or five years.

Many sharing the uncertainty became intimate friends, because they understood the risk, the commitment, and the price. *Only one man was in my old apartment building all the time. His wife and daughter were in the other part of town with some relatives. He'd stayed behind to look after the flat. In the evening, I'd be working in the building opposite, and I could always see him from my window.*

We were using free-burning natural gas as makeshift heaters or lamps—a really dangerous, stupid thing to do. (I wondered why I was sleeping so soundly all the time. We were being asphyxiated!) Once when I was sleeping, drugged by that gas, I woke to someone yelling my name. I went to the window but of course didn't dare stand there looking. The man who had stayed behind was calling me. Then I saw my apartment building in flames. At that moment someone pounded on my door, shouting, "Your flat's on fire!" Through the window I hollered at my neighbor across the street, "Break my door, my bathtub is full of water!" (I'd been keeping water there to put out the fires that kept starting because of the shelling.)

It was after midnight. I threw something on and ran out. There was a trench crossing the street. *We crouched down going across so the Chetniks couldn't see us, and we had to be quiet so they couldn't hear us. At my building I couldn't get in through the main entrance. We ran around to the other side, through some mazes someone had made. Debris from the roof was falling on my head. When I reached the building, I thought if I went upstairs I'd never come out alive. My flat was on the third floor. Windows were burning. I was dodging burning pieces that came crashing down. When I got to my entrance, it was full of smoke. I thought, "Oh my God, I'll never get out of here!"*

As I made my way up, the smoke-filled stairwell suddenly became bright. She could see enormous flames pouring out of the middle apartment on her floor. *I was terrified—a strange feeling for me. Somehow I managed to get up to the third floor. At the door of my flat was the man who had called me, shirtless, with a plastic dish and a small glass, tossing water onto my neighbor's door, which was covered with flames. I started laughing at him. He was happy to see me, but frightened. I said, facetiously, "So, are you a fire-fighting expert?" He looked at me, scared: "Don't laugh. Everything else I've tried to use has been devoured by the fire! We can't put it out, but I'm trying to stop it from spreading." We stayed together, trying to save the rest of the building. It was horrible—the noise of crashing doors and windows, burning couches and cupboards. I brought some more water, but the fire was falling down on other flats—four were already ablaze. The fire spread down to the first floor through the balcony.*

When I'd run over, I'd asked people around me to call the fire brigade, even though I knew there wasn't any such thing! I just thought somehow others could help us if we all worked together. But that man said "If they come, they'll spoil our work." [Nurdzihana is laughing.] *Some old men actually managed—an hour-and-a-half later—to bring a vehicle with some hoses. They were amateurs and couldn't possibly put out the fires, but they drenched everything else. Amazingly, my books survived, and many of my papers.*

As it turned out, conflagrations like the one that drew Nurdzihana out into the night had an even more sinister purpose. *In the meantime, the Chetniks were shooting.* Serb troops would start a fire, then target those trying to put it out. *The fire provided light so snipers could do their work. A few days before my fire, a young man I knew—a nineteen-year-old redhead—was shot putting out a fire; we buried him the next night in the park.*

Snipers weren't exclusive to Sarajevo. Like Alma, the unintended army recruit, MAJA lived in Mostar, south of the capital. Middle-aged, married to an electrical engineer, Maja was an orthodontic surgeon working as general manager of a large medical center. As such, she was in a position of authority. In a conversation in which she had been talking about her own two teenaged sons, she recounted to me how she rescued another young man being drafted into the army. *I told the soldiers, "I'm a doctor, and this boy is insane. But if you want to risk it, I'll let you come in." They said, "No, no. Thanks anyway. Goodbye." Today that boy is in the United States. He was about twenty-one, twenty-two, just the age for the army—but he was so afraid of weapons.*

Let me tell you something. I understand fear. We have to respect fear. To get to her Mostar office, she had to cross two roads, in range of sharpshooters. *I was scared, but I kept telling myself, "You may save a life at work. You've got to go." I wasn't really surprised that some of my colleagues didn't dare. There were some moments, I must say, when I was dragging my feet, thinking: "Well, shoot me! If you want me, here I am. Just shoot!"* But when she thought of giving up, Maja also remembered that others were depending on her. Abandoning them wasn't an option.

In addition to taking care of patients or employees, in their role of primary—or sole—family caregiver, Bosnian women had to cut through the chaos to tend to parents and grandparents as well as children. BILJANA grew up in Sarajevo and emigrated as a young woman to Sweden, then the United States. In 1993, she left her affluent and stable Colorado Springs world to plunge into the war zone of Croatia, in order to be by the side of her mother, who was dying of liver failure. *The possibility of losing my mother, combined with being in a war-torn country, was shockingly difficult. Everything around me was so unfamiliar. In the past, I'd spent summers with my children in Yugoslavia. We'd always felt safe and happy. The beauty, the aromas of nature, and the sweet smell of the ocean would fill my heart as soon as I'd get out of the airplane. But not so that time in Croatia. UN helicopters, trucks, police, soldiers, horrible graffiti—"Go Home Slobbering Idiots," referring to the Muslims. My heart was ripped apart. I was scared. I didn't know what to expect.*

From the moment I'd arrived in Split, on the Croatian coast,[12] *I'd been intensely aware of the military environment, which seemed very hostile. And of course I met refugees, women at my mother's home and then on the beach.* At first the refugees streaming out of Bosnia were put up in the empty hotels normally filled with tourists vacationing on the Adriatic coast. Then male refugees were taken to fight in the Croatian army, leaving behind women, children, and the elderly. Nationalist Croats intent on annexing part of Bosnia forced the refugees into the streets—on a night, Biljana adds, of driving rain and fierce winds.

From among the refugees, Biljana got to know the woman who cared for her dying mother. *Fadila came from eastern Bosnia. She was in her mid-forties but looked like she was seventy. Her hair had turned gray overnight. Her family was like any one of us Americans living a middle-class life: two parents, two children, a TV. Just everyday Bosnians, happy with what they were doing. She and her husband were engineers.*

Exodus of Serbs from Sarajevo, alongside trenches used to avoid snipers.
December 1995.

They had a vacation home in the mountains an hour-and-a-half from the town where they lived.

Hearing that Serb troops were advancing, Fadila's husband drove up to their mountain place. *He wanted to save a few stupid things like the VCR, because he figured by the time he returned home his cabin would be destroyed. That night, he didn't come back home, and she got a message that he was killed. She sobbed as she told me how the Serb soldier said he didn't want to waste a bullet on her husband, so he split his skull open with a garden hoe. She fled with her two teenage boys—got onto a bus with just her purse, no documents, nothing, and came to Croatia.*

Biljana's Yugoslavia, a serene summer resort, had devolved into chaos: children dodging sniper fire as they ran to school; neighbors rushing into burning buildings to save each other's apartments; young men feigning insanity to escape the front lines; refugees with tales of barbarity and cruelty. Adding to the mental stress was the need constantly to guess whether it was more dangerous to stay or go, calculating the toll of flight against the danger of the present situation.

Flight

MIRHUNISA: *Many died in their own homes, simply because they didn't want to leave—so they were carried out.*

SABIHA: *Losing your country is losing your core.*

On the opposite side of the front lines from Biljana's Fadila was KRISTINA school-teacher and mother of two daughters. After her husband was drafted into the Yugoslav army (which had essentially become the Serb army), she was caught up in an exodus with other Bosnian Serbs tossed in the tides of war. Kristina's home region in northwest Bosnia was mostly Serb, with 17 percent Bosniaks and virtually no Croats. At the start of war most of the non-Serbs living there had asked to be transported to an area controlled by the Bosniak army and were allowed to leave. When Croat forces took over, the non-Croats fled. Kristina was among them.

As I listened to individuals from every ethnic group tell their stories of hardship, it was easy to understand how some outsiders could say that all sides of the conflict were equally culpable. Yet Kristina's displacement and loss were caused by a counterthrust of the Croat army, as it claimed territory that had been "cleansed" by Serbs in a scorching sweep across the land. Kristina well may not have been aware of the crimes committed in that campaign; she was focused on finding refuge in Banja Luka, which by now had been transformed from a multicultural city to a Serb stronghold.

The weight of war fell not only on political strategists, army generals, and foot soldiers but also citizens like Kristina as her town, Sipovo, became a battleground: *No matter their ethnicity, all men had to go to the front lines. Only those who managed to run away abroad saved themselves from the fighting. My husband, even though he was forty-eight, had to join the army. He was stationed on the border with Croatia. With him on the front line, I had nobody to help me, nobody to protect us. Croatian forces attacked, and the population fled. No one stayed.*

It was complete pandemonium. By the time we started packing, most families had already left. Shells were falling everywhere. My daughter and I hooked up the trailer and threw some things into the car. I got behind the wheel and just took off. Lots of people had no transportation. Everyone was looking for family members. As we were leaving, my neighbor asked me to take her children, so we had two other little ones in the car; you can imagine how that added to the situation. *They were so afraid, and I didn't know what to tell them.*

Kristina made it about 300 feet, to an intersection of roads from around her town. Cars and horse-drawn carts had come to a standstill. *But the shelling continued. It was complete bedlam. All around us, women were screaming and little children crying. Utter madness. Those were the toughest moments of my life. I've never felt so helpless. Cars were everywhere, blocking each other. The river of people couldn't move. We waited the whole day. It seemed like an eternity. I was sure a shell would hit us, or there would be a massacre. "They're going to kill us right now," I thought. People were exhausted. My whole body was in shock. A friend came up, begging me to clear a way. His father was in his car, dead.* At last the road cleared somewhat, and Kristina was able to move forward. *With my car and trailer, I started passing others. Shells were falling all around, and people were being killed. I remember thinking that every single meter we moved forward was going to save us.*

Like thousands of others, Kristina and her daughters made their way to Banja Luka, where they wandered from place to place, looking for refuge. Someone suggested they head for Sanski Most, a smaller town nearby. *But we knew how bad it was there too. Shortly after that, Sanski Most was occupied. We barely managed to stay in Banja Luka; my younger daughter begged and cried, convincing a police officer to let us stay. The enemy was only one day's distance away — and we didn't have anywhere else to go. Life was unimaginably strained. The word "refugee" says it all — how dependent we were, the kind of life we had waiting for food and clothes to be handed out, just trying to make it to the next day. People from thirteen towns flooded into that city. You can imagine the bedlam, the fear. People were shoulder-to-shoulder, all panicked. Shelters for refugees were full to the brim.*

There wasn't much of a life as a refugee. All those days were like one day — the same thing over and over. The most troubling sight for Kristina was the children and elderly. *They were tired, sick, and didn't have a place to sleep. We'd go around and try to visit them in the shelters. They were collapsing, dead, right in front of us. I was a refugee too, staying with my sister. We two families were living in a one-room apartment; still, I was lucky, because I knew where I was sleeping. We were so happy that she took us in. We had no income, of course, and no way of earning anything.*

Day after day I searched until I found the Kolo Srpskih Sestara [Association of Serb Sisters, a Belgrade-based organization]. They were wonderful. They suggested I bring together the people from Sipovo as a group within the Banja Luka organization. In every situation there are good people — and we found some who let us use their space. The people from Sipovo were suffering terribly. We distributed food and clothes to them.

Kristina stayed in Banja Luka until September 1996. The lines drawn during the Dayton peace talks positioned Sipovo in the new Republika Srpska, so Kristina and her children returned home. *Other problems started then.*

Over the months, then years, of war, the exodus of people fleeing their homes had reached biblical proportions, as over two million people made the weary progression from living in fear, to flight, to life as a refugee, to a return to ruins. Individuals agonized over the decision to move from one stage to the next. When was it better to leave behind home and memory-rich possessions to be trampled through or burned by the enemy? Bosnian identity was tied to ancestral agrarian homesteads, jobs, familial roles, community positions, and a network of friends; to flee would mean starting up again in a new place from within a crowd of other refugees, with "VICTIMS" pasted across every signpost of the psychological landscape.[13] There was little chance the refugees would find encouragement for their slow, gradual healing process. Thus leaving their homes only replaced a worse situation with a very bad one. The adversity of war was more than death or destruction of property or one-time terrible events. It also brought exhausting upheaval that, month after month, year after year, would not let up. The decision to flee meant a sudden perverse transformation, as respected, stalwart citizens found themselves begging for shelter in a mass of panicked strangers.

Suffering wasn't limited to victims of the attempted genocide; Bosnian Serb families I visited in 1996 in "collective centers" (a euphemism for refugee camps) of the new Republika Srpska were angry and bitter, blaming their own Serb officials for destroying their lives, leaving them uprooted and stripped of meaningful activity. The hardship of displacement was oblivious to ethnic differences — creating an ironically tragic common bond. The Bosnian women who added their stories to Kristina's represent a range of backgrounds: a Bosniak dermatologist, a Croat florist, a Serb pediatrician, a small-town Croat seamstress, and a schoolgirl who vehemently eschewed ethnic labels. Now all six could be described with one label: refugee.

Listening to FAHRIJA describe her trek to Turkey, who would guess that she was the great-granddaughter of the king of Albania and a U.S.-trained physician? Instead, she was a refugee fleeing Bosnia at the insistence of her politician husband, who recognized the approaching aggression: *I stayed in my father's house for about twenty days. Even though we never went out, one day my father came to me and said that everyone in town had figured out that we were there. "I can't hide you. The soldiers could come and take you. They'll just claim you did something wrong or name your husband, and I won't be able to help you. I can kill three or four of them,*

but I can't stop them. They'll take you and kill us." Fahrija's father was beloved—
and too well known—in Novi Pasar, in the Muslim-populated Sandzak area of
Serbia. His daughter had no choice but to keep moving.

Fahrija's physical challenge was compounded by emotional disorientation. *I
had to leave the second town I called home, and I knew there was no other. I had nowhere
to go, but my children and I could have been killed or imprisoned. My husband couldn't
help me from Sarajevo. I had to resist telling him how scared I was. I was trying to be
rational, but I was in denial. I thought: "This can't be happening, or at least it can't last.
I don't deserve this. We're in the middle of Europe, and it's the twentieth century. We're
educated people—the world will stop this nonsense." But reality is cruel.*

Fahrija decided her best bet would be to travel by bus to Turkey, where
she had relatives. The plane from Belgrade was too dangerous—their passports
would give them away—and driving by car would mean no witnesses should
they simply disappear. It was a twenty-hour ride to Istanbul. *We were in a crowded
bus, in May with no air conditioning and no circulation. Most of the passengers were
peasants. I had nothing against them, but when sixty people in thirty-five seats took out
their meat and pies, I thought I would die from the smell and heat and never reach Istanbul alive. I vowed that if I survived, I would never step into a bus, any bus, even the
best bus in the world, for as long as I live. I could write a book about that trip.* Fahrija's
mother, who had been on the run in past times of political upheaval, had told her
to never leave behind her most valuable possessions. *So I had all my jewels with
me, which made traveling all the more dangerous, because some guy who didn't even care
about politics might care about money. I took them, because I had a hunch that I was
going away for a long time, not just a week. I also took my diplomas, and my children's
school records. I felt, or perhaps feared, that something terrible would happen.*

At the first border, between Serbia and Bulgaria, Fahrija was worried about
being detained or robbed by the border guards. *I couldn't have stood that, not when
I'd left behind just about everything in the world that reminded me of who I was. So
I asked the people on the bus to put my jewels on their necks and hands and pretend
they belonged to them, since I couldn't wear all the pieces. Some were afraid to help me,
because it was obvious the jewelry wasn't theirs. But some of the women did help, and
the driver was very kind.* [Fahrija's voice adopts a reverential tone.] *He carried my
money and told me not to worry. He said if they tried anything, he wouldn't abandon us.
"The whole bus will go back. We won't cross the border. I promised your father I wouldn't
leave you."*

*I tried to hide my fear from my children. Emir was only six and a half. He was so
scared that he was shaking. Looking at him, I wanted to cry. As we came near the border,*

all I could do was pray to God, "If I ever did anything good in my life, let us go through safely." Two men were checking passports. My mind was racing, trying to decide which to approach. One was quite young. Maybe just like me, I thought: raised in communism and not passionate about religion, war, or politics. I went up to him. He didn't hide his surprise when he saw my passport. "What are you doing on this bus? Why didn't you fly?" he asked. I said: "A cousin of my aunt in Istanbul suddenly decided to get married, and I couldn't get a ticket yesterday, so I'm going by bus." He looked at me intensely then said, "Take this passport before those two men see you. Just run. Behind that line is neutral territory. Go!" I looked at him, grabbed my children, and ran. We made it, and the bus crossed safely. I felt like I took a breath for the first time in hours. I told my children we were safe now and promised them coffee and breakfast in Bulgaria.

When we crossed the Bulgarian-Turkish border, my little son clutched my blouse, asking, "Mommy, do they have Chetniks here?" I wanted to cry at his words. I thought, "God, he's too young to know such fear." But what could I do? How could I erase such monsters from his head? I just said, "No, baby, there're no Chetniks here. We're safe." Our lives weren't in immediate danger now—but my husband was back in Sarajevo, miles behind us, and who could say what the future held?

Arriving at her destination as a refugee didn't end Fahrija's ordeal. Uncertainty made it impossible to plan, or to start a new life. *In Turkey, every day I waited for someone to stop this madness so I could go home and resume my life. Sometimes I'd wake in the middle of the night and, for a moment, not know where I was. All I'd see was a strange room; then I'd feel a sick pain in the pit of my stomach. "Oh, God, I'm not home . . . I'm here."* [Fahrija rolls her eyes.] *Our room was small; two couches barely fit. My young teenaged daughter, Emina, slept on one, and Emir and I on the other. I don't think I'll ever forget the heat, the terrible, oppressive heat that wants to drown you in itself, negating all that you are, all that's human. With the heat came the flies. Their buzzing, and the dry breathing from my children's mouths—those sounds were my only company during the long, restless nights.*

There was a water shortage in this suburb of Istanbul, so we couldn't shower when we wanted. Even drinking water was a problem. Water was collected on house roofs in cases of emergency. When nothing else was available, we had to drink that unfiltered, dirty water. You can imagine how I felt as a medical doctor, and with my son so small. He would play with children on the street and then come running to me for money because a man was selling ice cream on the corner. But the man would be so dirty and the ice cream pots even dirtier, so I would try to explain to my little boy that he could get very, very sick. He didn't listen, because all he knew was that he wanted ice cream. So he would go behind my back and buy it along with other sweets sold on the street. Then one night he had a terrible fever. I thought I'd lose him. The hospital didn't know what to do. It was just a little town, and the doctors either lacked education or perhaps failed to take his condition seriously. Or maybe I was just too scared and wanted them to do so many things for my son — test his blood, his urine, take a throat culture, take a stool culture — when all they could do was give me an antibiotic and a few pills for fever, then send us home. He was delirious. I thought God must have been punishing me for some reason. I felt so helpless.

Emir recovered, but the enervating sense of helplessness lingered, a feeling experienced by not only Kristina and Fahrija, but almost all the women who shared their stories. Sadness flowed particularly freely from DANICA, who was living as a refugee in Croatia when we began our interviews. The daughter of a mixed marriage, she was a florist near retirement age, a gentle mother of two, and grandmother as well. Her home was in the picturesque town of Bosanski Samac in the northeast. *As 1991 was coming to an end, everything was going along with blessing and peace, and we were happy thinking of spring's coming. We in Bosnia were afraid of the war in Croatia, only a hundred kilometers away. But we said, "That can't happen to us. We're united."*[14] *Warplanes targeting Croatia from the Yugoslav National Army* [by now essentially the Serb army] *were flying that summer over our city, shattering our sense of safety and our hope that war wouldn't come to us.*

Danica had many people to worry about: her younger daughter, who lived across the border in Croatia with her family; her elderly mother, who insisted she would die in her own home; her older daughter, who refused to think of leaving the town in which she'd grown up. *I went to my Tanja's and said, "Give me your kids, I'm going to take them away." She answered, "That's ridiculous, I'm not giving you my children. Look. It's peaceful all around us. Are you crazy?" So I decided to stay, although my bags were packed.* Danica converted her basement into a shelter, with first aid supplies, just in case.

The deciding moment for Danica came when a friend's brother appeared at her door. *He was trembling all over and asked if he could make a few phone calls. He was Bosnian but was going to join the Serb fighters. I asked, "Why are you doing this? Where are you going? I was thinking of leaving; should I?" He just looked at me — that was his only calm moment, when he looked at me — and said, "Go. You have to. You gotta get out of here." I called my daughter to come over to my house, because I was too weak to go to her place, I was so shocked. As we looked at that young man in such a state, my Tanja changed her mind and went to pack for her children.*

Danica led me on through the thought processes of a middle-class merchant, deciding whether and how to become a refugee. *That night I packed. The next day*

I worked, came home at seven, and sat down for a cup of coffee in my kitchen. I decided I'd go in the morning. I thought I should call my mom and tell her to get ready. But then I thought, "She won't sleep if I worry her like that, and she'll be tired for the trip." I thought all night about who and what would fit into my car: my mother, my five- and ten-year-old grandkids, their things. I'd tell my mom to pack a small bag. I looked around my living room and took a little thing from here and a little thing from there: souvenirs from my cupboards I thought would give me a sense of home.

As a businesswoman, Danica was also thinking practically. She would need money to keep going. Anticipating inflation, devaluation, and difficulties in foreign exchange, she packed up some valuables, including a fur coat. *I opened one closet that had my nicest things and just took all I could carry, with the coat hangers: a few coats, a few skirts. I put them on the bottom of the trunk of my car. I needed shoes; I took a pair of boots because I knew I'd be cold. The trunk was full. I was so afraid. I had my rings on, and people could get their ears cut off just for an earring.* She decided to separate her resources, to be safe. *I thought, "If I have my money, what will happen at the checkpoint, if they stop me and take everything? I wouldn't have anything left."* She would leave her money at home, to come back for later. *But I never came back.*

It was a cold, rainy day. I picked up my mother. We crossed the bridge in the nick of time. The next day, the Serbs took it, and it stayed closed for years. When I called to say I couldn't get back over, my daughter, who had stayed in the town, said: "Don't come back; there's nobody here." I said I still had a delivery of flowers at the train station to pick up. She said, "Mum, we won't need anything." I begged her, "If that's the situation, please, Tanja, call for the boat and cross the river. Don't spend the night in the town." "I don't believe it's as bad as that," was the last thing she said.

Tanja did escape that night—on the last boat before the town fell. Danica's husband escaped over a different bridge; he managed to pick up his eight- and thirteen-year-old nephews, staying just ahead of the Serb troops as one town after another fell. I asked her what happened to those who didn't get away? *Accounts seeped out. Our town was occupied by Arkan's paramilitary forces from Belgrade. They entered our houses, arresting people and bringing them to the primary school for interrogation, taking over our police station and radio station.* [Danica sketches out a map of the town to orient me.] *One of our citizens was killed that first night for resisting, and others were wounded. People were taken to concentration camps near the city. Paramilitaries, with help from some townspeople and supported by the Yugoslav National Army, humiliated and terrorized those who stayed. That's how the town in which I'd lived for thirty-five years was occupied. Other towns in the region fell after only a few hours or* days.[15] *Before the war, we had the same number of Muslim, Croat, and Serb citizens. Of five to six thousand inhabitants, only thirty-three Croats and three hundred Muslims remained.*

Danica was suddenly a refugee across the border in Croatia, a country itself at war. *I've learned that the world falls apart when you tell someone you're a refugee. It's a terrible burden — as if you told them that you have AIDS.* [Danica's eyes are cast down as she speaks.] *You're treated as if you're guilty for the war, for hunger, for evil. People act like you asked for it somehow, like it didn't have to be that way, and it's your fault that it happened to you. There are lots of questions and sometimes accusations. "Why didn't you defend yourselves?" "Why didn't you stay?" "Why didn't you organize?" "Why didn't you do this or that?"*

In Croatia, Danica's daughter felt ostracized as a refugee, so she managed to cross further into Austria and create a new life working low-paying jobs that pre-served her dignity. *She wanted her children to be spared the treatment she'd received and not have kids in the schoolyard saying, "Those are Bosnian refugees — they don't be-long here." The refugees lived in centers and received relief payments. She refused all that, establishing herself instead as a normal citizen. It's a good thing, because now refugees are being forced out of Austria, even though their Bosnian houses haven't been returned.*[16]

Danica goes on to talk about her possessions, a reflection of more than simple materialism. Possessions represent home, a base, as she probes the internal di-mension of refugee life. *I can't put into words how it feels to have absolutely nothing — to lose your youth, your entire existence, your successes, everything you've built for your-self. I was fulfilled. I had three expensive cars: a Ford, a Citroen wagon, and an Opel Vectra. But if somebody asked me today, "If you had to, what would you give up: all your cars and possessions, or your telephone?" I'd say, "Take the cars." My existence was organized around people. With one phone call, I could solve any problem. I felt at home in my community. I'd achieved a certain status. Then overnight, I had nothing . . . no one to call . . . just this big book with the addresses and phone numbers of all the people I know. I could never again be in touch with them. Everybody disappeared in one day, without a trace. People lost a lot of material things — a lot of property. All that can be made up for, but lives cannot.*

Danica wept easily as she told me about new life in Croatia. *As a refugee, I had others to care for: my mother, my little grandchildren.* Still there are the long hours — with her thoughts and memories. *Every night I think of my house . . . my curtains, my windows. "I'll wash them. I'll do some cleaning." I dream of how I'll make it so pretty again. Then I wake up in the morning, realize where I am . . . and I'm so sad.* [She begins to cry.] *When you're fifty and broken, how do you start again? Who's going to hire a grandmother? Who's going to take her seriously, help her start her life again, with no record, no reputation, no friends, no money? Everything I'd earned I left behind. It's terrible. Not what I lost; that's not terrible. It's terrible that I can't continue to make anything of myself.*

As the Serb army and paramilitaries continued their push from the east across Bosnia, killing and driving out citizens with non-Serb backgrounds, Croatia's President Tudjman seized the moment to pursue his design to take over the western part of Bosnia. NADA, a Bosnian Serb, found herself in danger as a member of a small minority of Serbs when the struggle began between the Croat army and the ragtag Bosnian defenders. In addition to being a beauty, she was a hometown girl made good. The daughter of divorced working-class parents, Nada was a valuable member of her community, having just completed her specialty in pediatrics. She stayed on in Kakanj, thirty miles from Sarajevo, after the town's other Serbs (except five or six doctors) had left. *I was provided an apartment, and I wasn't discriminated against. My friends tried to convince me to be patient, to hang in. There was some psychological pressure, but I wasn't at all maltreated. I postponed leaving from day to day. If it hadn't been for the fighting between the Croats and Muslims, I probably would have stayed.*

Eventually, professional and community status were not enough to ensure her safety. *Until mid-1993, I was the head of the medical center on the outskirts of Kakanj. There were about seventy people employed there, from all ethnic groups; it was like a community center. Our population was 60 percent Muslim, 30 percent Croats. The few Serbs lived mostly in the villages surrounding the town.* When the Croats made their land grab, Nada's clinic was in the middle of the fray. *We had come to work, just like every other day. Suddenly the grenades and shooting started; we couldn't leave. Almost none of the Muslim employees from the town were there that day, probably because they knew about the attack. Every night we just washed out our underwear and slept on the examination tables in the offices. My director was a Muslim, and we were on the phone every day through that time. Two of my colleagues were Serbs, and there were two girls, nurses, who were Muslims from the nearby villages. The rest were Croats. We had no conflict among us; it was just tense. We were all scared.*

Wounded Croat soldiers and civilians were brought to the clinic. *We treated lots of ugly wounds from bullets that burst inside the flesh. You have to remove individual bits of the bullet. We were doing basic first aid, just trying to stop the bleeding. The more complicated wounds, like stomach or chest . . . those patients just died. I, a pediatrician, had to amputate the arm of a young soldier with only a local anesthetic. One of our staff, who was just starting a surgery specialty, telephoned a colleague to ask how to do it.*

Every clinic had a "war kit" packaged in wax, to use in such a time. Inside were little saws for amputations. We had to cut through the bone, just below the elbow. The soldier asked us for a cigarette, and drank a little alcohol. As we cut through his arm, he kept joking about the sound, saying he hadn't realized he was made of wood.

When the Bosnian army finally prevailed, Nada fled with other clinic staff further into territory dominated by the Croat army. *We weren't fleeing the Croats or Muslims. We were fleeing the guns. For about ten days, I was cut off from all my relatives — my mother, my deaf and mute brother, and his family. The roads were blocked, so we couldn't return to Kakanj, and we had no telephones. There were rumors we'd been killed.* Nada was able to get a ride in an ambulance with some patients to a clinic in a nearby town. *"I need a phone," I said. "You can call from my house," said one of the doctors. That's how I reached my mother. She started crying.* [Nada is crying now as well.] *She was so scared, and so happy that I was still alive. I asked her if she wanted to stay or come with me. She wanted to come. Back at that clinic, I found a refugee whose baby I had examined at my office. Now he was working for the Red Cross, so he and a colleague took two Red Cross cars and picked up my mother, brother, and his family. That's how my family joined me in Croat territory, and we took taxis to the border of Serb territory.* Anything with wheels was used to evacuate civilians fleeing the fighting. *There we got on a truck organized for Serb refugees.*

Like Danica, Nada had to decide if flight would be safer or more costly than hunkering down and staying put. In the context of other wartime losses, possessions took on meaning far beyond market value. *I had no suitcase, just makeshift bags I sewed from tablecloths, which I had kept packed with a few necessities, like winter clothes. It was difficult to leave anything behind, but I couldn't pack everything. When my mother left, in her panic and fear* [Nada is wiping away tears] *she took with her some foolish things like handcrafts, some small porcelain pieces. More important things she didn't take with her.*

As it turned out, Nada didn't even end up with the things she'd packed, since her life as a refugee started from her office rather than her home. *I fled with just my white clinic jacket, and some pants — just summer clothes. It was June, but incredibly cold and rainy. The wife of the doctor whose phone I called from (he was Muslim, and she was Serb) gave me some underwear and a couple of sweaters.* But at least Nada has the photo album that was in her desk at her clinic. *I'm so happy I had the sense to take it. I love those pictures dearly.* She brings the album from another room of her home. It's blue, with a sunny cover picture of the Dalmatian coast. The album was a birthday gift. Nada's eyes crinkle as she laughs, pointing to pictures of herself as a baby, her mother and father on a sofa, boisterous friends with waving arms, medical colleagues posed for a group photo, her prewar boyfriend (a Muslim doctor, she notes). She adds ruefully: *But I have nothing from my home.*

Ultimately, the task for refugees is to try to become acclimated, if not reconciled, to a new environment. That task was steep, even for a young, energetic, intelligent, professionally trained woman like Nada. Adjusting to refugee status may present a greater challenge when the drop into the identity abyss is from a place of comfort and accomplishment. The educated person may be better equipped to handle loss, but the loss is much greater. *I don't like to think back on that wartime. We spent lovely years in Kakanj. We had quite a high standard of living. As a doctor, I had a good salary and traveled a lot. Then all of a sudden I had nothing. We were in a tent in a refugee center — six of us: my mother, my brother, his wife and two kids, with no income, no employment, no home. I had to start from scratch. My mother was sixty-one. The children were ten and seven. My brother was, and still is, unemployed. I had to take care of everybody in the family. Several months later I left for Derventa* [a couple hours drive north] *where I started to put together a normal life.*

Like Danica, Nada, and every other refugee, VALENTINA's story is a mix of poignant personal detail and political import. Valentina insisted to me that, apart from observing Catholic tradition, until the war she never thought there was anything significant about being an ethnic Croat. From a rural family, with a husband from a rural family, her words are uncomplicated: *In the war, our village of Podlugovi, about fifteen minutes by car from Sarajevo, was controlled by Serbs; and Visoko, the larger town nearby, was controlled by Muslims. In both places, the fighting was terrible. But who was doing the shelling? We couldn't say. All we knew was that we were afraid. In Podlugovi, in Visoko, the only thing we had in common was fear.*

Valentina and her sister were given free bus tickets by the Red Cross to escape the fighting. They arrived in Belgrade. *Suddenly I was a refugee. I started to cry — not because I was surrounded by Serbs, but because I didn't know anyone. I didn't know where places were, or who to turn to for help. I had nowhere to go. I was seventeen, with my twenty-four-year-old sister and her two-year-old daughter. The little money we had was spent.*

The Red Cross was terrific. They found a Serb couple who took us in, who really accepted us. [Smiling, she describes each of them.] *We stayed there a long time, like part of their family. We ate together, watched television, talked. As we got to know them it was less difficult. At least I had a roof over my head; I had someone to comfort me. In those two or three months before our mother and father could contact us, they actually replaced my parents.* After six months, Valentina made a visit home but then returned to Serbia. *They were really good to us. They knew we were Croats, but they didn't care.* Refugee experiences don't usually have a clean, clear end. *First there was a phone line, and then regular bus lines so we could go see our family and they could visit us. Gradually, there was less war activity, and every day was a bit easier.* Easier, perhaps, but the passing time brought a profound weariness. *At the beginning, we thought the war would last for ten days—or maybe a month. As it went on and on, we stopped thinking about an end. We took for granted our new way of life. We had no choice. Before the final end of the war, we had no hope that life could be better. That's how it was: a lot of sorrow . . . and then it ended.*

Only three years younger than Valentina, IRMA, sick of the sounds of war, was not lucky enough to have the Red Cross bus her out of besieged Sarajevo. Life had become increasingly difficult. There was no fruit or vegetables, and a kilogram of sugar cost about $40. People sold jewelry to buy oil. After years of shelling and shelters, she couldn't take the mental pounding anymore. *In August '95, when I was fifteen, I didn't think things were going to be better. I just couldn't stand it anymore. I went to my parents and said, "I've gotta get out! I've waited three years, and nothing has changed. What's wrong with you? Why can't you get me out of this place? How come so many others are leaving, but not me?" One day, my mom came to me and said, "Do you wanna go in two days?" Relatives in Austria had invited me. I said good-bye to all my friends.*

In a Sarajevo suburb, a tunnel had been dug in early 1993, running under the airport. One end was apartment #25 of the former Olympic Village, a unit with nothing to distinguish it from the rest of the shell-pocked neighborhood. The other end was a private house next to a field that stretched to the base of Mount Igman, a long, flat, tree-covered mountain. Eight hundred people had been killed trying to cross the airport to escape the city before the tunnel was constructed—in four months, using wheelbarrows to remove the dirt from five meters underground. Inside, a track ran along the base, and steel supports lined the sides. Once completed, the tunnel was used to bring in military personnel, transport the wounded, or provide a channel for some small bit of supplies for the 200,000 people in the city.

My mom brought me to the apartment building near the tunnel entrance, then stood in the street, waving. A soldier took me with him. I thought it was arranged that he would go with me. But he just brought me to the tunnel and said, "You go through here." I was in there, all alone—a child, with all those soldiers around me. I was scared. I didn't know when I would see my mom again. So many things were going on in my head. There was no real light, only little lamps every ten meters. It had started raining, and water was dripping down. People were all around, stooped over as they passed through, and on every face you could see pain and suffering. The passage took twenty minutes when the tunnel was empty; but it was more like two hours with the crowd sometimes stopping and sometimes crawling though the space, which averaged four feet but was lower in some places.

Irma's father, because he was working for the UN, had managed to get transportation through the front lines to meet her at the other end of the tunnel, just below Mount Igman. Regulations forbade his bringing his daughter with him, but he had her suitcase and had been waiting for her all day. *I came out at an open trench, about a hundred meters. I didn't have an umbrella, so I was soaking wet. At the end of that stretch I saw my dad, waiting for me. Oh, I was so happy to see somebody I knew! Then Mount Igman. For two hours we climbed in the dark on the steep road. There were no cars, no buses. Then at 3 A.M. a big truck came by with soldiers, and we climbed in.* Irma and her father tried unsuccessfully to hitch a ride to the town where her mother's sister lived. The next day they heard that that town had been heavily shelled. Azra, Irma's mother, was distressed to hear from her sister that they never arrived. They stayed instead with a stranger who took them in. *I don't know what that nice man was doing out at 5 A.M., but he said, "You can sleep at our place," so we went with him, slept a little bit, then went on to Split.* After two days, Irma and her father took a ship to Italy, then spent fifteen days trying to get a visa for Austria. In Florence, they were told they needed to return to Sarajevo and get the document from the Austrian Embassy in the Holiday Inn — as if that were possible. Eventually, their Austrian relative drove down to Italy, hid Irma in the trunk of his car and smuggled her back across the border.

From there I was going . . . I didn't know where. I didn't know those relatives. I sat there in the car, looking at the people I was going to spend I didn't know how many years with. When I first saw them, it was a shock. I was happy that I was out of Sarajevo, but they were two old people. He was eighty-five, she was seventy-five. He had a big nose, gray hair, and lots of wrinkles. She was really sweet. I liked her from the first moment, because she was, like, "Oh, Irma [in a caressing voice] Hello! Grüss Gott!" She didn't know any other language, so she was talking to me in German. I knew hardly any German when I got there. So I was saying "Ja, ja, ja." It was, like, the only word I knew.

I was happy in Austria, but I didn't feel totally comfortable, because they were old, and I felt I always had to smile, whether I was angry or sad or something like that. They gave me money. They gave me a place to live. I felt I shouldn't bother them with my problems. But they were very nice to me. And, of course, I helped this old lady. Her name is Frieda and his name is Hano. I helped her with cooking and cleaning.

Back on Mount Igman I'd asked my dad, "Oh God! Am I ever coming back here again?" When the war ended, months after her flight, Irma could go back for visits to Sarajevo. She wanted to earn the more highly respected Austrian degree but missed her parents tremendously. Phone lines were undependable. Visits were many months apart. *Finally I decided, "I'm going back. It doesn't matter what happens to me . . . what kind of school there is. I'm going back!"*

Atrocities

ALMA: *We'd seen the traumatized refugees. Those girls were . . . My God, if we had been caught . . .*

GRETA: *It's one thing to hunt wild beasts, but the snipers were hunting* people. *Every day we lived in fear.*

KRISTINA: *I don't like remembering this; now as I'm telling you, I feel like something's choking me.*

As in many conflicts worldwide, the civilian population, particularly women, suffered most from the barbarity allowed by violent conflict.[17] In our interviews, the women sometimes whispered, sometimes blurted out, accounts of the horror they experienced. Their voices were usually calm, but tears often welled up in their eyes. Even as it was hard for them to articulate, it's difficult for me to write about the sadism let loose in the Bosnian war. But to ignore it is impossible.

There are many reasons not to write, or read, this section of the book. Words fall far short of the pain and terror the women experienced. At least one of the women I interviewed is being treated for post-traumatic stress disorder. That being said, journalists seeking a gripping opening paragraph for their war coverage have created an abundance of harrowing images, enough to cause that mental glazing-over known by aid workers and politicians as "compassion fatigue." As well, passionate descriptions of gore and cruelty may feed a prurient appetite in the writer or reader. Perhaps such base acts ought not see the light of day. Laying them out before the public may be a profane exercise. Their destructive nature may be so profound that even the telling should only happen in a protected place.

It was nonetheless important to the women to watch me tape and type their narratives. The one thing worse than having too much attention focused on their experience may be for their suffering, and its causes, to be ignored. But it's hard, in an interview, to step into such personal space. For example, I didn't ask any of the women if she'd been raped. It's doubtful, given the lack of anonymity in this book, a woman would have volunteered that information. But my purpose was to learn about the women's postwar work, so I didn't push for descriptions of traumas. That's the reason I include only skeletal accounts of atrocities from five women. Two worked with victims and absorbed their stories; three are first-hand witnesses. In each case, the speakers only touch on the atrocities, almost as if to say, "This experience must be referenced, but should not be reopened." But each delivered her story with passion and, it seemed, a hope that the telling itself could help prevent such evil from ever again being unleashed.

NURDZIHANA speaks with the detail one would expect from an accomplished journalist describing the events she witnessed in May 1992, on the outskirts of Sarajevo, as the Olympic Village complex of Dobrinja was encircled: *We were hiding like mice, watching Serbs moving around with their armored personnel carriers—APCs—screaming, shooting. After tanks rolled by, we organized guards at the entrances of our apartment buildings. We looked after our buildings in shifts, thinking we were somehow safe by doing that.*

Then, one day—a quite peaceful day—the explosions started. We didn't know what the shooting was, but it was horrible. Everyone ran up the stairways, or wherever there was a close place to hide. I ran into my flat. My mother was already in the hall, which seemed safe. My brother's son, Jasmin, was with us. Our neighbors Nada and Delveta joined us with Delveta's son, Sasa. It was a long, narrow hall. At first we didn't know what was going on except the shooting. Bullets went through my kitchen. There was glass all over us. I tried to protect everyone with a red wool blanket we'd been using as we slept in the hallway on sofa cushions. Sasa was eighteen and Jasmin nineteen. I thought it was most important to protect the two of them, but of course I wanted to shield everyone.

The shooting went on for maybe half an hour, but it seemed like an eternity. Then somebody knocked on our door. It was our neighbor Sveto: "Everyone has to get out! If we don't, they're going to kill us all!" We heard muffled voices on the stairs. Somebody said, "They're in!" Someone had pulled the bar out of the makeshift barricade across the door. Young men in camouflage were coming up the stairs, rifles pointed. They reeked of alcohol. They were forcing people out, using their guns.

I didn't know what to do with Sasa and Jasmin because the soldiers were taking the men away. It was all very, very fast, like lightning. I tried to hide them. I had a deep wardrobe with two doors. I pushed Sasa into one side, Jasmin into the other. I thought I'd cover them with some clothes, to save them. They were completely confused and just turned themselves over to me. I started to go out with Mother and the others. But at the stairway I turned back, saying, "This is really stupid." The boys wouldn't have a chance. "If they find you, they'll kill you." Better to lead them by the hand, Nurdzihana decided, and stay together. Meanwhile, the thugs were running up and down, pounding on doors, screaming for people to go outside. *We made our way down the stairs. Mother said to one young Chetnik, in a soft and gentle voice, "My sons, what are you doing?" He raised his rifle butt as if he were going to hit her. I glowered at him, even though I knew if I so much as lifted my hand, I would die right there and then. Seeing my eyes, he lowered his rifle and said, "Get out, Granny!"*

As shooting continued from the two APCs, Nurdzihana joined the crowd in front of her apartment house. Buildings and cars were ablaze, and people were herded into a corner. *Three hundred people, standing there like cattle. I came closer to my mother and took her hand. She was only worried about what would happen to Jasmin. Jasmin and Sasa were trembling. We were all quiet. We could hear shooting. People were pouring out from other buildings. Then a woman started screaming, "Where's my child?" Her daughter had been with us in the hall, but I didn't know what had happened to her. For a moment, there was consternation and confusion. A few minutes later, we heard the Chetniks laughing terribly, saying, "Look at this girl." Elvira was a young woman of twenty-five, beautiful, with blond hair. "Pretty kid!" they said, and started walking toward her. Who knows what would have happened to her . . . but something distracted them. They said, "Quick, separate the men from the women. Men come with us. The women can go home." That meant Jasmin and Sasa would be taken. As we started toward the entrance, Jasmin tried to come with us, but they were physically pulling the men away. Then Elvira tapped my back and said, "Jasmin . . ." She motioned for Jasmin, who was almost six feet tall, to crouch down. He bent down and hugged my mother tightly, walking with her as if he were a child. Sasa did the same, and we made it into the building.*

The Serb paramilitaries left hurriedly, with some 150 men, most of whom were not seen again. *After several hours we found out why they hadn't killed all of us. While we were all outside and Elvira was hiding in the flat, she managed to make several phone calls. She reached some young men from other parts of Dobrinja. None had guns, but they started shouting behind the buildings, banging on garbage containers. They pretended to have weapons saying, "Shoot them, now!" Later we saw where those young men had written "MINED" on one of the nearby garbage containers. The Chetniks were scared.*

Of course, we were all distraught as the men were taken away—we didn't know where. A few days later, we got horrible news from the Aerodrom neighborhood, just across from the airport. A young man came often to our cellar, to see a girl he fancied a lot. *They were young, but he liked to take care of her, and he wanted to show her how brave he was. He said he would tell us everything that was happening. If we needed to run away, he'd tell us in time. One day, he came in very upset and said he had vomited on the way. He'd seen several men butchered by Chetniks — and he said the slaughter had just started. It was the infamous Aerodrom massacre, in which over a hundred people were killed. I know a family that hid for forty days in an attic, from which they witnessed the horror.*

The impact exceeded the terrible loss of human life. *The war was such humiliation for us. Encircled, under constant attack, butchered. We buried people in the parks, using our wooden wardrobes for coffins.* Death, once again, was the great equalizer. *It didn't matter who they were — Bosniaks, or Serbs who had stayed behind in Sarajevo. They were killed indiscriminately.*

About three hours northwest of Sarajevo, on the opposite side of the front lines, was GALINA, an energetic organizer who put aside teaching deaf students to instead address the overwhelming needs of Serb refugees streaming into Banja Luka. Although hardship in the Bosnian Serb community was severe, international human rights organizations have attributed the overwhelming majority of atrocities to Serb perpetrators. Thus it was hard not to flinch when Galina told me of Serbs "liberating" Bosnian towns and when she explained that the Serb military action was in response to the destruction of Serb churches and the victimization of Serb people. Indeed the Serb press flagrantly fabricated tales of atrocities committed against Serbs, sometimes even taking an actual situation (such as rape camps or the massacre of Srebrenica) and reversing the protagonists and antagonists.[18] On the other hand, Galina denies that Banja Luka experienced ethnic cleansing, despite these published statistics: According to the prewar census of 1991, the population of Banja Luka (195,000) was approximately 30,000 (Muslim) Bosniaks and the same number of Croats. After the war, the international community estimated a population of about 220,000, with 3,000 Bosniaks and 2,000 Croats.[19] All sixteen mosques were razed.[20]

Still, at an individual level the suffering of the women was comparable, even though across ethnic groups it was not. *In '92, Odzak — an ethnically mixed town — was under the control of Croat forces (before being liberated by the Serb army). The men were either at the front line or in camps, so in the village all the peasants were women. They were under occupation for three months, imprisoned in their homes with the children, and they suffered awful trauma. They were raped in front of their children. Old women, even little girls, were raped. They killed grandmothers.* The war raged on. Extreme situations worsened. *When I asked them about these crimes, these women would pause. "There were so many," they often said.* Every day of the three-year war, they lived a new story of fear, of heroism, of betrayal, and, yes, atrocity.

The Bosnian government calculated that 50,000 women were raped in the war. Between 1993 and 1997, the German-sponsored Medica Women's Therapy Centre in Zenica examined 28,000 women for rape and other sexual abuse. Firm numbers are impossible to gather. Victims were likely not to report the crime since enormous cultural shame is attached to rape and victims are often considered unmarriageable.[21] As well, many of the women had been raped repeatedly — some for months, in bondage. Statistics couldn't do justice to their experience. Political explanations shouldn't blur the fact that men were doing violence to women.[22] But more important is the effect of war in allowing acts that otherwise are held at bay by civil order.[23]

However, most of the rapes in the Bosnian conflict were neither side effects of war, sexual aggression, nor acts of revenge. They were planned within the strategy of ethnic cleansing. Those who organized the rapes forced others to join in. Forced impregnation was the ultimate ethnic cleansing, and Serb rapists taunted their victims, telling them that now they would give birth to a Serb baby. Rape was a crucial tactic of the political-military strategy — not the aggressive manifestation of sexuality, but rather the sexual manifestation of aggression.[24] In addition, rapes served other military objectives, such as bolstering masculinity. Raping women was a way of attacking men as their protectors, humiliating them. War provided man-to-man communication via the violation of women. It was, in effect, symbolic rape of the community. Rape promoted ethnic cleansing when a woman who had been repeatedly assaulted or a witness to the raping was set free to tell the story. The remaining inhabitants in the area were more likely to flee, the women out of fear, the men out of humiliation that they were not able to protect their women.[25]

It's easy to see why many recoiled in fear or repulsion from this aspect of the war, but MIRHUNISA did the opposite, leaving academia to try to ease the suffering of the women she encountered. That choice was not obvious for a professor of accounting at the University of Sarajevo, who had written academic textbooks, had a successful ski equipment business with her husband, and was raising two children. But her life turned upside down early in the war; and, in addition to gathering data from victims seeking refuge in the capital, she began to orient her time toward aiding refugees, much like Galina on the Serb side of the conflict. *Every single day I listened to accounts from raped women. I gathered about 570 statements from children, women of all ages, even men. The most specific rape information came from eastern Bosnia, where schools had been turned into rape camps. I received a call from a mother who had been in one of those camps with her two daughters, fifteen and sixteen years old. She had made it to Sarajevo, and she wanted to tell someone that other women were still in captivity. She was probably in shock when she talked to me so openly, so matter-of-factly, because later she completely closed up. You know, most women were ashamed. They couldn't talk about this, especially if their daughters were also in the camp. They wanted to hide it, to protect their daughters. Mothers were afraid that . . . if tomorrow her girl found a boyfriend and he learned that she'd been in a rape camp, she'd never . . . you know. I was with these women every day. The most difficult was when I'd take the girls to the hospital to get an abortion. When I brought them back, I couldn't even give them a cup of real milk—just powdered.*

Mirhunisa concludes by putting a personal face on the abstraction of atrocity, with her description of an eleven-year-old whose testimony was duly taken by the UN war crimes investigators and human rights groups, before the girl left to be with her mother. She had been brought to the Sarajevo hospital by UN forces from a village near Foca, where she had been held in a rape camp with her mother and baby sister. *When men would come to take the girl and her mother to rape them, the baby would be crying. Can you imagine what the mother felt—being led out with her daughter and leaving the baby behind? At the clinic, they removed all the girl's reproductive organs because of a terrible infection. I met her at the hospital after she was operated on. She had shaggy brown hair and was extremely pale. She looked lost, traumatized. Her clothes were rags. She seemed in a state of complete desolation, of depression, as if she didn't care. When I interviewed her, she described carefully how and why things happened to her. She talked about her mother and others at the camp. She kept focusing on details—like how the baby was crying, and how difficult it was for her to listen to the baby cry. I was thinking that maybe I should be steering the conversation toward things like: How did she manage? When did they take her to this brothel? What happened to her? But she just wanted to talk about how happy she was that the baby had been spared from the same horrors. She didn't seem interested in talking about herself.*

Her eyes were penetrating. Every time she looked at me, even without saying anything, I felt as if she was asking for help, unwittingly perhaps. My daughter was about her age, so I would tell her about my daughter. She would ask me, "Was your daughter in the camp, too?" "No, she wasn't in the camp, but we went through some horrible things," I answered, trying to make it seem like it's a normal thing, just to make what happened to her seem a little bit less.

Her greatest wish was that I should bring her one particular folk singer, because her father—she had been forced to watch as his throat was slit—her father loved that singer.

So I found the singer and explained what had happened to this girl, and she came to visit. Since the girl was so poorly dressed, we brought her several pretty things to wear, but she didn't even look at them. She just stared at the singer . . . and said, "My father loved you most."

EMSUDA, meanwhile, was enduring the devastation of Prijedor, in western Bosnia, where she was incarcerated in one of 200 concentration camps that sprang up across the country. The camps were used for torture, rape, forced labor, and extermination of non-Serbs.[26] They also served as collection points as people were being expelled. In Emsuda's area, a school had been converted into a makeshift concentration camp: *In the summer of '92, we knew something terrible was brewing. My husband and I, along with the children, decided our best bet was to split into two groups. I'd go to my brother's on the outskirts of town; my husband would stay home. We asked the children who would go with whom. Our son chose me, and our daughter chose my husband. That split was a good thing. I'm sure if I'd stayed home, I'd have been killed, or something else terrible.*

A day before the shelling started, I went to my brother's. The people who lived around him weren't prepared for the war. In one day, we managed to construct shelters in the woods. We gathered the women and children. Everyone who made it to the shelters survived. Of those who didn't come with us, only a very small number stayed alive. Some were killed in the fighting, others taken to the camp and killed there. We didn't think we'd survive. Shells were exploding right in front of us. Our shelters were behind the military line, where nobody suspected they could be, and that's why we were safe. I felt good that the people had listened to me and taken refuge. The rest of my family was there, along with about thirty other families. . . . My parents lived with my brother, so we were together. We watched what was happening; we could see quite clearly that horrible sight and we thought no one had survived. Still, we didn't realize what was in store for us.

In the lunacy of that time, with people being taken to camps, everyone thought I'd been killed when my house was destroyed. Though Emsuda was alive, she had no idea of the fate of her daughter and husband. They were ecstatic when they found one another, three days later, imprisoned in the camp. As she gave me a few details from her incarceration from May 26 to July 1, I had the feeling I was in a private, sacred place in her psyche. I was reluctant to ask probing questions that would evoke memories I couldn't heal, or even bandage. But Emsuda was patient with me as I pieced together some semblance of her experience: *Some were lucky to be killed in the shelling, because later . . . children had to watch their parents being murdered, and parents had to watch their kids being killed. A brother, father, and mother had to watch their daughter being raped. Sons had to watch their mothers being raped or murdered. Or the mother and the sister would be forced to watch the brother and son being killed.*

I was trying to save as many young people as I could from being killed or tortured. We couldn't save everyone, not even most. Women were giving birth without any medical help, without any anesthetic, outdoors. In addition to the school, there was a youth center with a movie theater, and a large yard in which a few thousand people fit. Cold, hard rains fell all day long. Conditions were terrible. The yard was packed: old, young, people dying and being born in the mud, one right next to the other, without food or water. I was one of five women friends. One other and I survived — she wasn't considered dangerous enough, so she managed to make it. I personally knew twenty-nine women who were taken to the camp, but there may have been a great many more. It's hard to remember. People were in such shock, they completely forgot who they were.

There were so many rapes. Sometimes at night, the soldiers would go through the crowd, shining flashlights on faces, looking for young women. One night they took away twelve girls. Kids . . . babies . . . they were so young. They piled them onto trucks, took them a little ways, and started raping them. Only five or six came back. They were scarred physically and emotionally. We had a well-known doctor there, and also a midwife. The two tried as best they could to help these women. They put in some stitches, trying to patch them up. But then the doctor was taken to a different camp, and he never returned.

The homeroom teacher of Emsuda's daughter was tortured to death, with her students watching. *They took one woman while she was breastfeeding her baby. The soldiers came and grabbed her and gave her baby to her mother-in-law.* Often women taken by soldiers never returned. *The most horrible acts simply disappeared — they were never recorded. The witnesses were killed. We saw only a tiny fraction of what was perpetrated.*

I had thirteen family members in the camp. My brother-in-law had been a student in that school, so he knew every nook and cranny. During the day, when Serb soldiers were looking for familiar faces, we'd whisper to each other and slip off to hide in the physics lab. At night, all thirteen of us would meet there. My brother-in-law knew the door to the lab didn't work right. You had to push really hard to open it. Otherwise it seemed to be locked. When the soldiers came at night looking for people to torture and rape, they'd try the door and think it was locked, with no one in the room. That's what saved us. We were lucky. Others were outside, in the wind and weather. Serb police and soldiers surrounded the camp, which was filled with Bosniaks . . . also Bosnian Croats, who comprised just seven percent of the area's population. Romani [Gypsies] were there, too — anyone who was non-Serb. They kept bringing new people into the camp, until there was no more room. Then they allowed very old women and those with small children to go outside the barbed wire to nearby houses under the control of the soldiers. My seventy-year-old mother took my nineteen-year-old daughter, who is exceptionally beautiful. Fortunately, she wasn't good with makeup; so casual observers didn't notice her too much.

My sister left with another old woman. Then came my turn. I wanted to check on my mother and daughter. I was terrified my daughter would be taken. They wouldn't let me go because they said my twelve-year-old son could handle a gun and go to war. I said we only wanted to see my mother and daughter — with their permission, of course — and that we'd come back. That's what we did. I checked on my mother and daughter then came back to the camp with my son. I built some trust. The soldier I'd talked to before said yes another day when I asked him to let me go see them. Then I didn't come back, and we hid. We tried to find a house with some food, but we couldn't. We didn't have anything to eat. We went to my niece's house, but two soldiers discovered us. One, I real-ized from his accent, was from the camp. He seemed different from the others, more calm and settled — around my age, in his forties, medium height, brown hair, blue eyes. After I started talking to him, he realized who I was. They had lists of people they were to round up, and he remembered I was on the list. Then I mentioned his cousin. He told me not to leave the house and to hide. He promised to return within an hour . . . then went back and talked to his cousin. The cousin, from a poor Serb family, had been hired by Emsuda to design clothes for export to France, Germany, and Italy, after Emsuda convinced her husband to invest their savings in a cottage industry that allowed pensioners, jobless women, and single mothers to work from home, sewing.[27] The job had allowed the young woman to continue her studies in medicine. *She explained that I'd helped the poor — among others, her. She begged him to look after us, to save us.* That soldier became her protector as she waited for a chance to take her family and escape the area.

When she didn't return, the camp leaders were determined to find her. *I was targeted because I had a business, and they knew I have a lot of money — or I had a lot of money — and they didn't know what I'd done with it. They also knew I carried a lot of weight in the community, and they didn't like that, of course, because I always fought against violence and injustice. They knew I'd stand up to them, no matter what. They accused me of arming the green berets — our defense — buying uniforms and weapons for them. A few months earlier, I'd organized a demonstration against the war in Croatia, so they considered me Enemy Number One of the Serb people, opposing the creation of the Serb state.*[28]

I wasn't around when the camp leaders started looking for me. The Serb soldiers took all the women outside into the schoolyard, separating them from the men. They called my name. There were about twenty-five hundred there, and most of them knew me really well. Not one admitted she did, or that she'd seen me just a couple of hours earlier. My husband, brothers, and father all stood on the other side, with a lot more of my family. For two hours those women stood in the sun as the soldiers constantly repeated my name, describing me so they'd remember. At last one woman, who couldn't take it anymore, said, "Her sisters are here." They took my two older sisters [Emsuda's voice is wavering] *and kept asking, over and over, "Is she your sister?" One sister just kept repeating yes until they realized she was in shock, and they couldn't find out anything from her. So they released her. She got word to me, through a friend with a Serb name, that I mustn't show my face.*

We were so lucky to meet that soldier. He risked his life to rescue us. I thank God, and him, that we didn't go through what many other women did. The whole region was a concentration camp. Every house was watched at every moment. As we waited for the right time to make our escape, we slept in the same house every night, but we couldn't turn on a light. In the middle of the night, somebody might grab your arm and take you away. During the day we switched houses to confuse the soldiers. We'd fix food and try to organize things to survive and keep each other informed. One day I was in a village close to the camp, with about thirty women and a few older men. It was like an information center. They'd know, from word of mouth, where the soldiers were going. The soldier who had saved me came to warn me about a friend of mine who lived in a house across the road. She had three girls, one who was eleven, although she already looked like a young woman — she was so developed and she had a certain air. She was to be taken that night, with her mother. They were sleeping in a different house than ours, but I managed to get the message to her. The soldiers came that night. They made a racket, banging on windows and doors. The houses just echoed. We knew they assumed the mother and daughter would be hiding in a big house, so they hid in a small one that was barely standing. In the end, the soldiers just set fire to the house they thought this woman and her daughter were sleeping in, but because of the message we managed to get to her, the two had already left. That girl was saved, but most of them weren't. The ones they took away never came back. Where are they? What happened to them? [Her voice trails off.] *There are no witnesses.*

After twenty-four days, the soldier who had befriended us told us we had to trust him. He took us to the Serb military camp, pretending we were visiting someone. Then he told people he was going to see us off to the railway station. That's how we escaped. He knew all the checkpoints. With him at our side, we got on the train and made it out of Bosnia.

Stories like Emsuda's were revealed to the world as reporters discovered concentration camps in western Bosnia. The international community could no longer claim ignorance. Although the ultimate responsibility for the aggression rests on leaders in Pale and Belgrade, the rest of the world was complicit, by commission and omission, in the Balkan disaster. Even with hindsight, however, it's difficult to judge which political acts were helpful, which harmful. Germany's highly controversial push in December 1991 for the European Community's recognition of the independence of Croatia and Slovenia — five months before UN admission — was one step in the geopolitical square dance, as various world leaders took their positions, then turned, moved backward, forward, or sideways — even switching partners occasionally, while their domestic constituencies called the steps. The problem was, no agreement on the choreography was ever reached. Some leaders were determined to contribute to, others to remain disengaged from, a comprehensive solution to the conflict — at least until they changed their minds. As Milosevic and Karadzic fiddled, international figures were constantly bumping up against each other.[29]

Still, how could such atrocities be allowed, given the existence of the UN — itself created, after all, out of the madness of World War II to prevent just such catastrophes? The member states, including the United States, bear the greatest burden of blame for not giving the United Nations a mandate to stop the killing. But in an irony lost on few of the women to whom I spoke, the presence of UN humanitarian personnel officials precluded or excused individual countries from action. In 1991 Alija Izetbegovic urged the UN to send peacekeepers to prevent bloodshed. The UN refused. Despite encouragement from U.S. Ambassador Warren Zimmermann, the U.S. government didn't push.[30] In early 1992 the Security Council sent "peacekeeping" troops into the former Yugoslavia, where there was no peace to keep. The lightly armed soldiers were assigned to areas being shelled by tanks. Their mandate was extremely limited. For example, they could protect a specific international aid convoy or the distribution of relief packages.[31] Meanwhile, they watched civilians they had just supplied with food be shelled and massacred.[32] Intervention was deemed as "taking sides." To make matters even worse, those troops, prevented from dealing with the exigency of the situation, were nonetheless available to be taken hostage by the aggressors — most notably in 1995, providing CNN footage of humiliated UN soldiers handcuffed to telephone poles. That embarrassment led to shameful deals with the Serbs, including a purported French agreement to block the use of air power against the Serb army if they promised not to harm UN soldiers. The international protectors were thus manipulated by Milosevic through his Bosnian Serb henchmen, Mladic and Karadzic. That distortion was masked by the bravado of some UN and NATO military who parroted Milosevic's propaganda—for example, at a confidential briefing in which high-level officers informed me that Muslims were indeed firing on themselves in Sarajevo to attract sympathy.

In one of its many failed attempts to manage the situation, in April 1993 the United Nations declared several of the remaining pockets of Muslims (Bosniaks) in eastern Bosnia "safe areas," ostensibly protected by UN monitors and supplied by scant deliveries from international humanitarian organizations. In fact, these "safe areas" were some of the most dangerous places in the world.[33] The enclave of Srebrenica was swollen with refugees as Serbs overran the surrounding countryside. The prewar town of 12,000 had become refuge to around 40,000 by July 1995, surrounded by Serb forces on all sides and defended by an ad-hoc militia. Karadzic had warned the United States and United Nations that he would take Srebrenica and other "eastern enclaves" if Croat and Bosnian offensives continued. On July 6, when Serbs attacked the UN positions in the area, repeated urgent radio requests by the Dutch commander for protective air strikes were virtually ignored. The UN "forward observers" were easily overwhelmed by the Serb army. In the following days, the worst atrocity in Europe since World War II shocked the world in its scope and depravity. For the survivors, the tragedy was not political. It was pointedly individual.

Like the concentric circles in Dante's *Inferno*, scenes of war are closer or farther from pure evil. None was nearer the dark center than Srebrenica, where KADA lived with her husband, son, and daughter. Kada had grown up with the scars of war. Her father disappeared in World War II just a few months before she was born. She worked in a textile factory and was particularly proud of her husband's university degree in sociology. During the years of siege, she focused on keeping her family alive. *A long time will pass before some people are able to talk about these things, to admit reality*, she observes.

Meanwhile she was ready to tell me her story. The calmness of her words belies turbulent emotions she carries. For those who care about the victims in this war, asking women like Kada to repeat their stories one more time seems an obscene intrusion. But even as she wept, Kada insisted that I listen, that I know what happened, and that I tell others. Her account has been verified by hundreds of others, in explicit detail.[34] *We all went through hard times in Srebrenica. We were hungry. We were shelled. We didn't know what was happening. I had to walk twenty kilometers, carrying twenty-five kilograms of corn seed, to feed my family. I couldn't let my son go do it. He could've been taken by the Chetniks and killed, or he could have stepped on a land mine. I risked my life, because to me, mine was worth less than his.*

Nineteen times during the war, I went out to find food in the fields of villagers who'd come into town for safety. We went at night and gathered corn and potatoes, even though Chetniks were all around us. They set mines for us. Lots of people died. Once I almost froze. I was stiff from cold. It had started snowing and the corn was still in the fields. I went in the morning and was gone till night, walking the whole time. I was proud of what I could do—inhuman strength, really. The first year, we suffered like that, until we started receiving packages dropped by parachutes.

The Serb commanders called the bluff of the international community, advancing, without opposition, on the "safe area." When even the relative security of the safe zone was violated in July 1995, and Serb forces moved into Srebrenica, the refugees—disarmed by the UN protectors—were terrified. *We decided we'd go with the crowd from Srebrenica to the UN headquarters at Potocari, ten kilometers up the road, where we'd be safer. We were all being herded by the soldiers. But a bunch of young men figured they'd be killed if they stayed with the group. When we got to the gas station on the edge of town, they decided to make a run for it. My Samir, who was twenty-nine, was with them. When he'd gone about thirty feet, I realized I hadn't said goodbye. "Samir!" I called.* [Kada is wiping away tears.] *He turned his head. "Good luck, my son." He raised his hand goodbye. That was the last time I saw him.*

Then terror—two nights and days. When the Dutch UN battalion told us through their translators that Serb soldiers would come into the camp to get some information, my legs suddenly felt full of lead. I don't know why—fear or shock. Then suddenly I didn't care any longer. No dread, no joy, no sadness. I felt nothing. I was empty. I can't explain it. I just sat there. The sun was shining. I was there with my husband. So was one of my brothers, with his wife and children. We kept looking around us, silently, wondering what would happen. Everything was somehow bearable until the afternoon, when the Chetniks started taking men, one by one, out of the group. They went behind a house nearby. Some of our women, who were out collecting water, returned with faces white as sheets. They whispered, "Ten bodies here . . . ten bodies there. . . . Some here . . . more there. . . ." With night, horrible screaming started. I can't describe the voices that came out of people. A woman said, "UN soldiers are killing our children!" Chetniks were dressed in UN uniforms. But we knew those men—they were our neighbors. During the day, they had had a good look at who was sitting where. They were taking girls and young women out of the group. Women screamed as they were being raped. They killed mothers and children. There were twenty premature births that night. Next to me sat an old man. They took away his son. He'd call out, "Edib, my son!" The blood would freeze in our veins. I couldn't wait for morning.

Then they started transporting people to Tuzla. There were lots of trucks and buses parked in a line about two or three kilometers long. We had to get into one; I didn't care where it was going. I said to my husband, "I can't live another night like this. I'd rather be slaughtered than go through another night here. Let's push our way through." There was a crowd. Everyone wanted to get out of there as quick as they could. We spent two or three hours in this group of people who were pushing. There was a ramp with UN soldiers. They let us go through, and I felt a bit easier. Then as soon as we got past, a group of Chetniks took my husband. I watched him go. He didn't even look at me. We didn't say goodbye. I didn't expect them to take him. No one told us this would happen. The UN soldiers could've told us, but they probably didn't want to create hysteria. They wanted people to believe in something.

After the women were sent to Tuzla, in Bosniak-controlled territory, the men and boys were executed. For years after, mass graves were excavated in Srebrenica. An estimated 8,000 were killed during those few days. *I got on the bus with my brother's wife and daughters. I still had hope. I thought they'd send the men later . . . but they never came.* A few made it through the ambushes set up in the forest to kill the males who tried to run. *I kept hoping my son would manage to get through, but he never came. For two months I walked up and down the streets of Tuzla. I asked everyone who knew my son and had come through the woods, "Have you seen my Samir?"*

2

Love in the Crucible

SWANEE: *How can you do all you do?*

AMNA: *Well, I get up at six.*

SWANEE: *I know that, but where does your spirit come from?*

AMNA: [with a wide smile] *From friends. Friends. That's a lesson I learned from the war.*

NADA: *In a way, it seems less tragic when relationships break during a war. You have other crises. You see people dead. You're trying to find a place to live. You don't have the luxury to worry. Then later, time does its work. New events push the old ones into the background. But still it's difficult, even now, to talk about the relationships I lost.*

Every element of human life has its wartime version.[1] Everyday habits and happenings are transformed. Just showing up at work becomes a bold assertion that life will go on—as if dodging sniper fire en route to the university or rehearsal hall or clinic is simply a new occupational hazard. Using a cup of water to bathe is a decision to have one less cup to drink. Putting on makeup becomes an act of defiance against the ugliness. A lifetime of acquiring is undone in one shelling, but the owner may not care, for possessions seem irrelevant compared to safety. Health, religion, education—any element of life looks different viewed through the lens of war.

But the dominant element of life the women repeatedly wove into their stories was the effect of the war on their closest relationships. The women constantly referred to themselves as mothers, wives, daughters, and friends. Over

Sarajevo soccer field. December 1995.

hours of conversation, I realized how this theme was fundamental to the work they're now doing to rebuild their country. Their effort and sacrifices are motivated by their commitment to make life better for those they love.

Viewed through the lens of relationship, the cost of war is compounded. Tattered relationships added to the trauma of displacement, fear, and physical hardship. Mothers fled their homes with terrified children in tow. Worse yet, they didn't know where their children were. Or worst of all, they left them behind in graves. Often wives had no news of their husbands, who were off fighting. The men not only weren't around to protect or comfort them; the women were worried about their well-being. War took an equally huge toll on friendships. The neighbor who once had gossiped over a cup of coffee might now be shelling the kitchen of his erstwhile friend.[2]

On the other hand, the war environment clarified and intensified relationships. The elements spread across the same spectrum as that of "normal times." But adoration, protection, nurturing, sacrifice, resentment, jealousy, betrayal all were intensified. Every Bosnian had relationships destroyed or burned pure by the heat of the conflict. The dozen stories I collected represent millions—each with a value never computed in the cost of the Bosnian war. Mother to son, father to daughter, daughter to mother, wife to husband, friend to friend, neighbor to neighbor, colleague to colleague—they are all here, inviting the reader to imagine what it would be like to have our most precious relationships jeopardized. What was the toll on Irma's neighbor, whose husband was killed when he went out to buy cigarettes—for his wife? "Better it was him than the children," the wife said plainly, as if that platitude could somehow halt the moral hemorrhage.

Relationships are intrinsic to identity. We know ourselves as individuals only as we experience our connection to others in relationships,[3] the loss of a loved one is a loss of self. Furthermore, living in a war is dehumanizing, I realized, as the women described feeling "caged" or "trapped" or "hunted"—like animals. Relationships, on the other hand, are a mechanism for feeling fully human, for belonging, for fulfilling the psychological need of human beings to be part of a group. Repeatedly, the women rejected the notion that ethnic or religious affiliations are the boxes within which they live. But family and friends—that's a different matter, and those ties reach across conflict lines imposed by others. That's not to say these close relationships didn't shift or change; in discrete moments or broad sweeps of time, war impacted every relationship these women held dear. Death was the ultimate alteration, leaving the women with only memories when even photo albums were claimed by the war. But months or years of separation took a toll as well, and marriages had to be reassessed and realigned—if they held together at all.

The fearful accounts of mothers with their sons were stark against the backdrop of the panicky, out-of-control nature of war. MEDIHA has had multiple careers: a university professor in Sarajevo, a promoter of affordable orthodontics, and member of parliament in the party that, after the war, insisted on a multicultural platform. But she insists: *There's no greater thing than being a mother.* Divorced early in her marriage, she is from a family of professionals, connected to the former Muslim aristocracy—a past of distinction that pervades her present and is obvious in the breadth and depth with which she understands herself and her society. *As a doctor and a professor, throughout the war I decided to stay in the capital with my patients and my students . . . and my son—a young man, really—who wanted to stay with me. The fear of dying was exhausting. Death hung over our heads. Everyone lived the same life, not just I. When I think about those four years of prison in Sarajevo. . . . The city was a huge concentration camp, with no electricity, no water, and constant shelling. I still have nightmares today, and I can't stand the sound of fireworks.*

In my dreams, I still see some small sequences so gripping they remain in my life. My son and I used to leave home every day at the same time. When we reached my university, we said goodbye. We didn't know whether it was the last time. He went to work in one direction; I went the other way. He'd always look back, and I'd watch him and pray to God I'd see him again. Those were long, long days, since there was no telephone communication. I used to arrive home earlier than he did. My apartment building was in total darkness and silence. There was nothing to do, so people went to bed early. I'd sit in the dark. From time to time, I could hear the entrance door slamming, and I'd hope it would be he. I waited there, wondering who would knock on the door and bring what kind of news. If I heard the knock on my neighbor's door, I felt pain and relief at the same time. Then the next set of footsteps . . . the next knock. Finally, at my door. Frozen with fear, I'd ask who it was. I'd hear his name: "Bojan." I'd open the door with tears in my eyes, but he couldn't see them. I felt first relief . . . then a knot in my stomach, knowing we'd go through the same tomorrow. Then I'd make him something to eat in the darkness, and when he'd had enough—he wouldn't have eaten the whole day—he'd ask if I'd had something. "Of course I have," I'd lie. "Have some more." Then if he left something, I'd eat it . . . in the same darkness.

Anyone who has listened for the footsteps of a beloved can identify with the twisted gut, the spontaneous tears, the white lie. Like Mediha's, MAJA's suffering was quiet, in keeping with her professional role as a hospital administrator. One of her sons was twenty-three when the war broke out—draft age, even though he had already put in his required time of service. *At the beginning, he was with me in Mostar. But he was very affected emotionally by the situation. He wouldn't accept that he was divided from his friends by a street down the middle of town. For his sanity, I had to send him away, but it was an extremely hard decision.* Maja's relatives, first in Italy, then Cyprus, took in her two sons. She deliberated whether to keep the younger, the sixteen-year old, with her in Mostar, hiding him; but she decided the risk wasn't worth it. *When we were seeing him off, it was pouring rain. The skies and I were crying together. I told him, "Please take care." And do you know what he said? "Mother, when we land, I'm going to travel on a train! I've never traveled by train!" He was too young to travel the world. On that huge ferry, his head looked like the tip of a match.*

As Mediha waited for the return of her son each night, and Maja worried about the well-being of her boys abroad, KAROLINA's anguish for her son had a strong moral element as well: *I taught my son—and I'm not saying this because he's mine—I really taught him to be good. But he had to take a gun and defend himself. Why should they take such a nice young man and make him a killer? I kept telling him, "Don't shoot anyone unless you have to." The very idea is horrible. Who are we to take another's life? But he had to defend himself. I didn't bring him up to kill. It was forced on him.*

At the beginning of the war, he was eighteen. When he went to the most dangerous part of the front line, my husband couldn't bear it. He died from a heart attack. We had so many problems. First, finding food. Then basic hygiene; it was terrible, since toilets didn't work. And water; at 4 A.M., I'd go out and fetch all I could. We were constantly afraid of infection, because we had to use the same water for drinking, cooking, washing our clothes and ourselves. I took in two other refugees from Dobrinja. They didn't have anything. One girl, my daughter's twenty-year-old school friend, was orphaned. There was also a seriously wounded boy, a friend of my son's. I had to feed everybody. As years went by, the war became fiercer. Once my son was gone for two months. I didn't know what was going on with him, whether he was alive or dead.

Mothers sometimes describe the urge to protect their children as more primal than learned. The terror seems to flow from her son through her as Karolina describes his time at the front. *I went crazy. All those horrible times, when they were leaving Sarajevo, breaking through enemy lines. . . . There was open fighting outside the capital, in the mountain area. A shell landed on the cave where they were having breakfast. I was a wreck before I got word he'd survived. Really, beyond myself. There was another time when he was on reconnaissance. Four of them were hiding in the cellar of an old house, surrounded by Chetniks. The Chetniks unleashed search dogs. It was January and snowing. Four days and four nights they stayed in that cellar with no water and no food. My son wanted to commit suicide with his rifle. He tried to escape through a trench. Enemy trenches crossed each other in several places before Sarajevo. One night he crawled out, then jumped back in, but landed on top of somebody. Neither spoke, and neither boy could see. They waited for the moon to come out so they could tell who they were, not knowing if they were from different sides. When the moon came out, he realized it was a schoolmate who actually had started out to look for him. Neither knew where they were, but they managed somehow to get back.*

He had a nervous breakdown after that and spent three months in the hospital. He can't speak properly now, and he has emotional problems. He can't stand injustice, or stories about the war. He's very easily hurt. He lost a lot and doesn't like talking about it. He seems at least ten years older than friends his age. Of his classmates—fifty or sixty probably—only five survived. [Karolina's eyes filled.] *All the others are dead.*

For mothers with sons in the fighting, the strain was obvious, but there was also a tremendous tension for anyone raising children in a war setting. RADA describes her family's narrow escape from the front lines, where her apartment was being shot up, into the center of Sarajevo, with only the sweat suits they were wearing. *I was never afraid for my life. I knew I had to live. But I feared for my children and husband. God alone saved us. We didn't have a cent with us. Nothing.* Living with her sister-in-law for two years, she and her husband continued going to their jobs at the radio station. They thought constantly about the safety of not only their young son but also their teenage daughter, whom they called the wonder of their lives and who after high school found no options, despite her excellent English. When the young graduate begged her mother to allow her to start a career as a journalist, Rada at first said no, afraid she would be killed. But with no idea of how long the war would go on, she decided she couldn't keep her daughter locked up.

ALENKA, meanwhile, was trying to keep her two children safe, against a backdrop of carnage that terrified parents in Tuzla, the multicultural city about two hours north of Sarajevo. She carried the weight squarely on her shoulders; her husband had been killed in a car accident just before the war. But in addition to the basics of physical safety, she bore the burden of knowing the war was being perpetrated by members of her own ethnic group. *For four years, from May '92 till the Dayton Agreement, we sat as if we were in a prison. There wasn't that much shelling, but we knew that any single moment a shell could drop anywhere, so the oppression was more mental. The sense of dread was horrible. My children had to live like . . . like dogs, tethered close to home. Can you imagine, keeping an eleven-year-old boy cooped up all the time? It was just terrible.*

Apart from the social impact, Alenka sees the war through an engineer's eyes. *The beginning was hardest. Everything was new. I didn't know anything—like how much could be destroyed by a single shell. I thought when a shell hit a building, it was like a bomb; everything was destroyed.* But her steepest learning curve had to do with psychological survival. *At the start of the war, I was mad. It took some time—the first month—to accept that this was a war that would last for God knows how many years. The worst was, not knowing anything about how to survive shells. And then we always think bad things happen to everybody else, not to us. The idea that people were shooting at us took some getting used to, to say the least! It was much easier after a year, even though there wasn't any food. We got used to it and somehow adapted. You know, you can adapt to almost any situation if it develops step by step.*

Alenka insists that, no matter how bad the shelling was, others in Tuzla didn't pressure her family, although they were Bosnian Serbs. *It's hard for outsiders to believe. They get such a different story from the media. And speaking of the media: I have a cousin, who's lived in New Jersey twelve years. He called during the war and asked what the children were doing. I said, "Well, they play; and they work on the computer." "How can they work on a computer? They have computers?" I said, "Of course." "What kind?" "You know. Pentium." He was completely confused. I said, "My dear cousin, this is a modern war: you have shells and you have computers, you have cameras and you have slaughter."*

In the evenings, we'd sit around the TV *watching the shelling and burning of our country. Then some hit song or latest new movie would come on. . . . There was always this disconnect between the nightmare and real life. Sometimes, in the middle of the night, the electricity would suddenly start up. Everyone would plug in their electric cookers, radios,* TVs. [Alenka laughs at the memory.] *You'd step out on your balcony and, in the quiet of night, hear vacuum cleaners humming throughout the neighborhood.*

Alenka and her children live on the edge of Tuzla, separated from town by a soccer field and river. *No buildings. Nothing to hide us. When you looked from the town in our direction, you'd see the hill with a* TV *tower. We knew there was a tank next to the tower. You'd think, "If a shell comes, would I see it or not?"* Given the uncertainties, a mother anguished over when to let children risk their lives. *There were lots of interesting activities going on in Tuzla. Some humanitarian organizations started children's playrooms, some youth centers, training for this or for that. But I didn't dare let my children try to get there. For four years, they missed out on sports, guitar lessons, English courses—all those youth groups.* The signing of an agreement by politicians doesn't undo the damage of war on youngsters. Like mothers across Bosnia, Alenka was left to sort through the difficulties of parenting, wondering which behaviors were attributable to the war, and which were the normal stresses of adolescence. *My daughter's a teenager now, and there's pressure—she's trying to catch up. She wants to be out with her friends all the time, because all those years she didn't have the chance.*

Was Alenka overly protective? The times in which she was raising her children were filled with uncertainty. Perhaps that was the greatest challenge for parents, figuring out when healthy independence crossed over to dangerous carelessness. Every parent in Tuzla remembers May 25, 1995. *It was 9 P.M. I was watching TV. They interrupted the movie and said, "Special bulletin, blah, blah, blah." I'd heard the shell, of course, but that was happening every night. Nothing so special. Then Tuzla TV said a horrible tragedy had happened. The shell had hit the center of town and killed—I think they started with thirty people, you know, a few minutes after it happened. Then we saw everything: the kids' hangout, dead bodies, people who came to help move the corpses. . . .*

All night we watched death on TV. It was unbelievable: seventy-one teenagers. I remember one girl without a head. Four helpers, each picked up one arm and one leg, as they put her in the van. We saw a lot like that. It was a live program, interrupted by calls from panicking parents. "This is my daughter's name. She was there. Have you heard anything about her?" Then bedlam at the hospital in Tuzla, with all these corridors full of corpses, and about two hundred injured young people—almost all of them teenagers—lying there like logs. The nurses and doctors . . . it was a mess all around. Our cleaning lady at work, her daughter's boyfriend was killed there. My father's friend learned about his son when his second son called from Canada, saying he'd seen his brother on TV, lying dead at the hospital.

Alenka's concerns about raising children in wartime were picked up by KRISTINA, whose narrative began with two moments from the harrowing, chaotic flight from Sipovo. The first was in the car, caught in the jam of vehicles, trying to escape as the shells were exploding all around: *My daughter was begging, "Go, Mom! Please go!" I had to protect her. I looked at my beautiful girl: dark eyes, olive skin, curly hair. "She's the reason I'm doing this," I thought. She was panicking, so I had to be calm. I don't know where I got the strength, but throughout the madness I kept thinking, "I have to stay sane." In the middle of that hell it's almost like you're hallucinating when you tell yourself those things. It sounds completely surreal and seems impossible to find the strength. But while you're thinking that it's impossible, you're still doing it mechanically. It just kicks in . . . sort of a mother's instinct.*

My husband was somewhere fighting. I had no idea if he was dead or alive. My older daughter was gone. I didn't know where she was or if she was OK. I was just trying to save my baby, but I didn't know where I was going, what I was doing, how to help her, how to calm her. Everything was on me. I thought, if I don't know where the two other most important people in my life are, I've got to take care of this one. She's here and depending on me right now. I just kept repeating, mechanically: "Don't be afraid. . . . We're going to be okay. . . . I'm going to take care of it. . . . This is just a little stop, and we're going to get through. . . . Look! The crowd is moving. . . . We're going to make it. . . . Everything's going to be fine."

Kristina leaned forward as she drew me into her story: *My older daughter had come from another village, knowing we'd have to be coming that way. She was searching one car after another, filled with screaming women and children — asking everyone where her mother was. No one had a clue, and she thought she might've lost us. Eventually she came to our car. You can imagine, when I saw her . . . and when she saw us. We started crying, tears of relief.*

As the crisis cooled, concerns changed. Life settled into endless war-weary tedium. *The war interrupted my older girl's studies. My younger finished her senior year of high school in Banja Luka, where we were refugees. We were in this one-room apartment; she piled her books on the washing machine and studied in the bathroom. Before, we were the luckier ones. We lived a very good life. Then the war came, and I was struggling for my family's survival. What else could we do but just manage? It wasn't simply that we were afraid, or that we intellectually understood something bad was happening. It was under our skin. My girls' lives were turned upside down — not just circumstances, but their entire way of life. Everything was shaken up. They were almost grown. They were proud. They'd lived well. They were used to dressing nicely. Suddenly they not only couldn't have something but it was wrong to even think of it. With no warning, they'd lost everything. That wasn't their biggest problem. Just staying alive was. I tried to give them some things, to pretend life wasn't that different. I wanted to convince them this would all pass. I made them some clothes, gave them lipstick, shoes, a book, anything I had, just to help them feel a bit better.*

Amid the confusion, the women were determined to create stability for their families. Many were activists responding to the crisis while juggling their responsibilities as mother, wife, or friend. Sometimes those external and internal roles diminished each other. Other times the women's familial roles enriched their work, creating empathy that impelled them to engage in some of the toughest scenarios of the war. MIRHUNISA describes how her roles of mother and wife affected, and were affected by, her war-related relief work: *Before the war — when refugees started coming in from Croatia — I thought, "What if something like that happens here?" I had a son almost fourteen at the time, and my daughter was ten. I kept trying to think of what I could do that would be useful, but at the same time, I didn't want to leave my children alone at home.* Eventually, Mirhunisa had to flee her apartment on the outskirts of town. *Like the refugees with whom I work, I know what it's like to lose your home and take your family into complete uncertainty without any explanation. You can't explain it to yourself, so how can you explain it to your children? I remember my daughter asking, "Mommy, who's sleeping in my room now? Why did we leave my roller skates at home?" My husband could not tolerate my wartime activity, and we divorced. Now I live alone with my children.* But Mirhunisa cannot speak of her own family's struggle without then telling me about the greater hardships others endured. She describes her interviews with women and girls forced into bordellos in concentration camps; there, her private and public worlds blend. *As a woman, as a mother, I couldn't imagine what they had endured; but as the days passed, and more young girls arrived, I began to understand.*

Understanding translated into action. Despite — or perhaps because of — her feelings as a mother, Mirhunisa pushed farther and farther into the flood of refugees being airlifted into Sarajevo from eastern Bosnia. *They arrived without arms, without hands, without eyes. Most had to be hospitalized. Nobody came in one piece.* The refugees came by helicopter from Gorazde, an enclave about two hours east of Sarajevo filled with Bosniak refugees and surrounded by Serbs.[4] The town straddled the main road, separating two chunks of Serb-held territory. *It was like an island, and you couldn't reach it by land. When I heard they were arriving, I went to meet them. I asked people in Sarajevo for help — for example, a shoe factory owner, because they all came barefoot. They'd cut strips of fabric from their camouflage uniforms and tied them around their feet, like shoes. It was hard to look, because most of them were missing a leg. When we gave them shoes, they were so funny. Humor always kept them going. They joked, "Hey, you don't need the right shoe! Let's give it to somebody else." "No! What's my prosthesis going to wear?"*

Mirhunisa adds one more vignette, all the more poignant given that her marriage was falling apart: *The refugees arriving were mostly men, but among them was a woman with her husband. They and their children had been running through the woods behind the retreating army as the Serb soldiers advanced. Then a blast. The father turned and saw the corpses of his two children. From that moment, he was mute. I'll never forget it. That woman was so dedicated. She worked with him every day. He would draw a picture for me of something he needed. Then his wife would draw a picture of what she would give him. It was a picture of a baby.[5]*

The women confiding in me were not only mothers fearful for their children but also daughters, worrying about their parents, even when they themselves were in extreme danger. Unable to get home to Mostar from Sarajevo, ALMA joined up with the army as a paramedic, but despite the shelling and snipers, she remained focused on her family: *It was on Mount Igman that I was first injured.*[6] *I was part of an ambulance team and we were going down to Ilidza. My mother had begged me by phone, "Come here, darling."* Alma didn't realize that that suburb of Sarajevo, near the airport, had been devastated by Serb attacks. *I couldn't wait! I'd be able to go to my parents' home!*

I was exhausted, so I was lying almost prone in my seat, slumped down, daydreaming about seeing my parents—and that's what saved me. The Serbs started shooting. Every vehicle coming down the mountain road was hit. [Her hand becomes the vehicle winding down the road.] *We had a lot of dead and injured that day. Luckily, the bullet hit my helmet. We had quite a time getting out of there. Our car was disabled. The driver and other medic bolted out, but the stretchers were across my door. I managed to crawl to the other side of the car then jump out. There was barbed wire in front of us. I wasn't sure if that meant we were in Serb territory. I was frozen with fear. My only thought was, "I mustn't be caught alive!" There was a thunderstorm. I was totally disoriented, even though during the peace I used to jog on that mountain path. Now I didn't know where the hell I was.*

Eventually, Alma made it down the mountain. She managed to get within half a mile, but there was no way to reach her parents. Ilidza had been totally destroyed, and she had no idea if they'd survived. *What we saw on TV, as well as the reports we received, gave me no hope they were still alive.* Hospitalized, she could think of nothing but her parents. She checked herself out. *Then after half a year, came the greatest happiness a person could have. In April of '93 we were reunited for ten days. Then I went back to Mount Igman to help my fellow soldiers. The situation in Sarajevo was very bad then—shelling all the time. In June '93, I was injured again. I tried to hide it from my family. But seven days after surgery, I learned that my brother, my only sibling, had been killed. My family was in Mostar. I decided to travel there—on foot. My nose and knee were broken, my ligaments were torn, but I felt no pain. I just wanted to get to my family.*

Frequently during the war, I listened to grown daughters like Alma, distressed that they couldn't provide the comfort their parents needed. As FAHRIJA was trying to support her politician husband in Sarajevo and figure out how and when to make her escape with their two children, her concern also turned toward her elderly mother. *She was not really sick. She just had high blood pressure, and the political crisis made her condition deteriorate. When war started in Slovenia and then Croatia and threatened to engulf us as well, it brought back memories of the Second World War, when she lost her first husband and escaped on foot from Sandzak through the mountains carrying a bundle hiding her one-year-old baby, my half-sister. That was when she was very young, and for the rest of her life she bore the memories of her father and husband killed by Chetniks. With this new war, she was scared that her four sons would be taken from her. Her blood pressure was out of control. She died in January '92. There are twenty doctors in our family, and none of us could save her.*

The public face of war is often that of terrified soldiers, refugee women, or hungry children. But as each woman layered her story on top of others', I began to understand the devastating effect of conflict on the elderly. DANICA's mother grew up in a wealthy Slovene family but moved to Bosnia to be with the man she loved. Life in Bosnia was difficult for her as a farmer's wife, raising four children. But Danica speaks reverentially about her mother's attitude during the war that gutted her final years. *I started packing for our escape, thinking of my daughter and my two young, helpless grandchildren. Then I thought, "I have to take my mother."* Setting up life as a refugee in Croatia, Danica struggled with depression. *But my mother didn't make a scene when we fled, and even as a refugee, in her appearance and in her soul there was always peace. She just seemed to adapt to her new situation and fit in again, as happy as before. We didn't have much income, but there was never a problem. That was because of my mother, who kept us all stable.*

Danica's story of her mother is more than a tale of stoicism. Tens of thousands of parents and grandparents found themselves unable to provide for their dependents in wartime. Being on the receiving end of humanitarian assistance created a shift in their identities, robbing them of the satisfaction of being a provider. *I took her back to Slovenia, where she became very ill with intestinal cancer. She had a difficult death, but I don't think it was the cancer that was most painful. It was that she had only her purse with her when we fled, and she felt devastated that she no longer could give us things, or make something pretty for us.* [Danica is crying.] *During those days of dying, she kept saying, "It's so hard when a person can't give any longer. People are giving us things, taking care of us, when I want to be the one taking care of you."*[7]

Beyond family, the war took a tremendous toll on social relationships, many of which cracked under the political strain. GRETA reflects on life maneuvered within the cross hairs of snipers. She is, after all, an authority on survival, having endured internment in Auschwitz but then returned to Yugoslavia, where she was a government minister and professor. Her description of Sarajevo under siege has the stark edge of someone who knows war intimately. *I can't understand how snipers could take aim and then shoot women and children. In Sarajevo more than ten thousand people died. More civilians than soldiers were killed by snipers and shelling. With no fuel or electricity, we had no buses or trams, and of course no cars; then when electricity started up in 1994 or so, we had a few streetcars again. At the intersection in front of the Holiday Inn, a bus would have to stop because of the tram, and that's when the snipers would shoot. On one street near a small Catholic church, it was impossible to leave your house without snipers seeing you. People had to go out through their back-yards.* Greta has pondered war for sixty years. *It's even worse than with the Germans. They were foreigners to us, but these were people with whom we'd lived. We had mixed marriages; we were neighbors. I had over a thousand students over the years. Those may have been my former students shooting at me. Who knows?*

A story from KAROLINA, in Sarajevo, conveys the same unsettling theme of insiders turned enemy: *I have lots of Serb friends. For the ones who stayed here and who love this country, it was really hard. Just the fact that they were here, and they had cousins and relatives on the other side. . . . That was very tough.* At Karolina's firm, almost all senior managers were Serbs who joined the aggression. *They were on the other side, in the hills. To get to my office every day, we had to cross a park full of big, old trees. Chetniks would shoot from the surrounding hills, and we'd be caught in the crossfire between the two sides. My new Muslim director and his deputy were fighting on the front lines, but once a week they'd come to the office to keep business going. Three of us were walking together across the park one day. A sniper started shooting at us. My director asked, "Shall we run, or should we walk slowly?" I was recovering from a heart attack. My feet suddenly felt like lead. There was no way I could run. I said, "You go. I have to walk slowly." They said, "No, we'll all walk. Nobody run. If they're going to kill us, they can kill all three of us together with one shot." The bullets were flying all around, not directly at us, but beside us. When we were halfway, one of the directors said, "Who's shooting at us? Milan, Goran, or Slavko?" We were sure it was one of our former colleagues, and he knew exactly who we were. He wasn't shooting to kill us—just frighten us.*

These weren't stories of colleagues working in a climate of distrust, mothers anxious about children getting in with a bad crowd, wives seeing husbands waste away with cancer, or friends drifting apart. One cataclysmic day the war broke out, and everything changed. The suddenness of the assault added to the social chaos and traumatic loss. MIRHUNISA has two vignettes: *There was a well-known woman who, before the war, was in the government. She wore thin, metal, spiked heels, and she'd hit the captured men in the stomach with those heels; they showed me the marks. That was a* woman. Repeatedly, I heard reports of longtime friendships becoming casualties of the war as unexpectedly as the first shell in a barrage that blew away half the living room. Mirhunisa, again, described a schoolroom with some seventy men sleeping on small cots. She asked one, who had a cross cut into his back with a knife, *"How could seventy of you be captured? I don't understand physically how somebody captured seventy grown men."* The answer was: *"They were our neighbors. We trusted them."*

Ultimately, the women were left to try to close the wounds of betrayal. There is no greater healer than EMSUDA, determined to realign her life, despite her concentration camp experiences at the hands of members of her own community. *Everybody was in shock. They simply couldn't understand what was happening. They couldn't grasp it. It just didn't penetrate. It's especially hard now, since the war, as people are returning to places where the crimes took place. They have flashbacks, or they simply remember what it was like. Then they finally have to face it again, after these years, and realize it really happened, that it's true.*

It was difficult for us to understand then, and it's still difficult today. I sometimes think it's a dream. One day I'll wake up, and it will have been a nightmare. But unfortunately I'm wide awake, and it's all absolutely true. Our friends we loved—loved like a brother or a sister—turned out to be cruel.

3

Reasons for the War

NURDZIHANA: *People descend to such an unbelievably low level, trying to justify themselves by saying the war was for some goal — that someone demanded it of them. But there was no reason for the war — except robbery.*

KRISTINA: *War wasn't caused by simple people. This wasn't a popular, national movement.*

VALENTINA: *I don't think smart people, even professionals, can explain why all of this happened.*

"What caused the war?" I'd ask, trying not to be too leading in my question. I wanted to give the woman across from me free rein, invite her to tell me what she really thought. Twenty-six times I asked, each time waiting for some version of the sigh of resignation ("That's the Balkans!") put forward by many international leaders and repeated by obedient bureaucrats and soldiers. Looking for corroboration, I was consistently disappointed. These women had a very different perspective.

Just trying to survive, they weren't listening to policymakers' declarations I heard of how this was an age-old and inevitable conflict the rest of the world had best stay clear of. In fact, the international community, represented by the so-called Contact Group, was paralyzed by opposing allegiances that reached back to World War II and by the dual key agreement that required UN approval before the use of air power. In short, the United States was part of an international response mechanism that virtually guaranteed no confrontation of the Serb aggressors. This was "alliance" at its lowest form.[1]

But in our conversations the women didn't list the ineptness of the international community as a reason for the war. They didn't have access to the newspapers delivered to my polished desk in Vienna, some of which parroted the partitionists' explanation about intractable hatred—the tidy justification for the tidy restructuring of the country being proposed by many columnists and editorial writers in too-simple synchronicity. Nor were they privy to the classified reports and analyses of the United States intelligence community, which frequently warned of worst-case scenarios that served to frighten off would-be helpers.

In discussions far removed from Sarajevo, many political observers laid the blame indirectly on Marshal Tito, the architect of the fifty-year history of Yugoslavia. The Partisan leader led the first defense against the Nazis, then maintained a communist state independent of the Soviet Union (no small feat, for which he was amply rewarded with American aid—ironically, supporting the creation of a powerful Yugoslav army, which the Americans later bombed). Tito also led his country through a transitional period following atrocities committed by Nazi-sympathizing Croats, not only against Jews but also Serbs. Half Croat, half Slovene, he was well positioned as a uniting leader, but his early methods were repressive. His achievement died with him when he failed to put into place a stable plan for his succession. His death in 1980, at eighty-eight, was a critical variable in the onset of the conflict. Tito had watched Serb domination during the monarchy lead to internal conflict. As leader, he assiduously suppressed those tendencies. With his disappearance, there was no strong leader to counter the propensity of leaders in all parts of Yugoslavia to pursue their own interest—that political vacuum allowing Milosevic to try to turn Serb numerical dominance (as the largest ethnic group) into political dominance. Over the next ten years, given the shift from a strong centralized government to the "ludicrously feeble collective presidency" that was left in place,[2] local politicians vying for power cut into the seams Tito had so carefully stitched. The garment unraveled.

A different hypothesis about the cause of the war is the split between rural villagers and urban sophisticates. (The majority of the pre–World War II population lived in or around villages. By 1991 Sarajevo was the largest city in Bosnia, with 500,000 people, but most of those city dwellers had strong rural connections as well, either with family or friends.) Although there were some urban/rural dynamics that figured into the war, only two of the women I interviewed mentioned the notion of the war being village-based. NADA, a physician from a small town, said the war was started by villagers, who seemed more extreme and more nationalist. *Towns had more mixed marriages, so we were shocked by the war. Villages are more homogeneous; their population is more or less one ethnic composition.* AMNA agrees. *This was a war of village against town. There were soldiers on the hill, shooting into East Mostar. They got a new machine gun from abroad, and they didn't even know how to aim it. Then one soldier said "I'll do it," and he simply began to fire. And they said to him, "How do you know how to use this gun?" And he said, "I don't know how to use it, but any shell will hit Mostar." And the other soldiers said, "But there's an East Mostar and a West Mostar, and East is Bosniak and West is Croat, and we're shelling the Bosniaks." And he said, "It's all the same to me. They're all city folk."* RADA, on the other hand, who had a rural upbringing, insisted that country folk were more tolerant, not less. Living close to nature teaches an acceptance of differences, she claimed.

A broader geopolitical theory regards the Bosnian war as a fallen domino after the collapse of communism. The connection is indirect. Polish and Hungarian societies were opening. After exploiting its role between superpowers, Yugoslavia was no longer the buffer between East and West. Thus U.S. policymakers could voice more criticism about internal issues such as human rights abuses, especially in Kosovo, where the basic civil rights of the ethnic Albanian majority were being quashed.[3] The political shift had economic repercussions. No longer the favored child of the West, Yugoslavia's economy was plummeting with the rest of Eastern Europe. The internal unrest fed into the hands of the demagogue, Milosevic, who was playing to nationalists for support. What some may regard as historical inevitability — as if lifting the heavy lid of communism allowed ethnic tensions to rise to the surface — should not eclipse the fact that nationalism was already rising before the breakup of the Soviet Union, and Yugoslavia was relatively free from Soviet dominance. (Tito broke with Stalin in 1948.) The end of the Cold War may have been a factor — but in a different sense, in that it marked the end of vigorous attention to Yugoslavia by the West just as a new tyranny was on the rise.[4]

A more psychosocial theory of the cause of the war holds that weak core values and civil structures in Yugoslavia couldn't withstand the changing times. Bosnian political leader Haris Silajdzic, raised in a devout family, remarked to me that communism stripped people of their core religion and left a vacuum. That space was filled by nationalist fervor after Tito's death. Given their relative affluence, citizens weren't miserable enough to form strong opposition to an ever more untrustworthy group of political leaders. Apolitical young people didn't rise up against Milosevic's nationalism. They were after all free to travel. A policy of encouraging workers to emigrate was used to suppress unemployment. There was relative openness in the media. Products were freely traded, both East and West. But as communism broke down, Yugoslavia's political and economic structures dissolved. Profiteers, fearing for their privileges, fomented rage and hatred. There was no strong cadre of upright civil leaders to save the nation as old nationalist ideas emerged.[5]

War is a flood fed by many streams. It's reasonable to assume that these myriad ideas about the cause of the war — the death of Tito, the rural/urban split, the end of the Cold War, lack of solid values — have some degree of merit. Still, while the women might nod their heads at one of these theories, their narratives, which determined the content of this book, describe prewar Yugoslavia as a well-run society with an engaged populace — not without challenges, but certainly not heading toward dissipation and ruin. What, then, do they say is the confluence of factors that can turn a citizenry into a maniacal mob? Leadership. Slobodan Milosevic emerges instead of Vaclav Havel, and a civilized nation goes careening off course. There are further variables. The leader must have a vision, a dream, a goal — which may not be apparent in early political speeches or on the airwaves. To create the war cry, bits and pieces of ideology can be dug out from the historical trash. Existential urgency builds as masses are told, and told, and told again that they're in grave danger. Their survival is at stake. It's kill or be killed — not just themselves, but their families.

This is the backdrop against which Bosnian women described what they saw in the day-to-day unfolding of the war. Responding to my questions about their experiences, the women didn't attempt or pretend to provide a balanced, carefully constructed analysis of what caused the war. Their opinions and anecdotes give a ground-level view of what others were saying, and what they themselves surmised. Just as important is what they didn't name as a cause of the war: ethnic hatred or religion. They leave such theories to academics writing in their offices. But historical analysis should be informed by the experience of people on the ground. Those who disagree with the women may dismiss them as mouthing popular misconceptions, but the onus is on analysts observing from a distance to explain why their interpretation is more valid than those experiencing the situation firsthand. Observers who would particularize the war as some sort of regional cultural experience — as if the Balkans are more prone to violence than Germany or the United States — miss the point. Even as World War II was not caused by hatred of the Jews, ethnic hatred was a theme, but not a primary cause, of the Bosnian war. This conflict, according to those who lived it, was strikingly similar to others: with greedy politicians exploiting an imbalance of privilege, using a media machine to whip up fear among the citizenry.

Those Greedy Politicians

SABIHA: *Politicians led us into war. They committed horrible crimes and must be punished.*

EMSUDA: *One lie built on another. The politicians created social problems then manipulated the citizens by giving out money at critical moments.*

SUZANA: *The killing was all in the service of politics. The big powers could have stopped the fighting before it began. Then the politicians divided Bosnia, cutting it up, town by town. In that treachery, no side is innocent.*

IRMA: *Politicians started it.*

How could such a relatively prosperous country on the Adriatic (where Westerners brought their families for Dalmatian coast vacations), with ample trading partners, rich resources, apparent political stability, thriving arts, an educated citizenry, and international attention as an Olympic site fall into want and ruin?[6] The women insist repeatedly that the sickness didn't come from within their community; the contagious conflict that swept across their country was the work of individuals. Yugoslavia did not die a natural death. It was deliberately and systematically killed off by men who had nothing to gain and everything to lose from a peaceful transition from state socialism and one-party rule to free-market democracy.[7] In a socialist country, with limited private economic or civil society activity, politics is not just a high stakes game; it's the whole game. For decades in Yugoslavia, a government position had been a person's easiest route to housing, employment, health care, travel, education, even a car. As in many countries around the world, politics was a breeding ground for corruption. It allowed unbridled greed.

The women had strong negative opinions about their political leaders in general. But I was surprised to find a general sentiment that no current politicians could hold a candle to Marshal Tito. The honor, respect, even laud afforded their former leader make more sense when he's juxtaposed with the politicians who led Yugoslavia into ruin. Tito's mixed Croat/Slovene heritage was rarely mentioned by the women with whom I spoke — and rightly so, since one of the hallmarks of his tenure was his purging of individuals or groups who flirted with nationalist politics. Similarly, the practice of religion was discouraged (although not prohibited), which tended to limit it as a differentiating characteristic among peoples. Granted, in 1969 Tito allowed Bosnian Muslims to identify themselves as a nation (like Croats or Serbs), for the purpose of political representation on councils or committees.[8] But the designation was more ethnic than religious, and the communists consciously repressed Islam, as a religion and even more as a political factor.[9] In addition, nationalism (meaning ethnic egocentrism, rather than patriotism) could bring harsh prison terms. The most notable example was the incarceration of the future president of Bosnia, Alija Izetbegovic, as punishment for his philosophical *Islamic Declaration*, which called on Muslims around the world to support each other. At the 1983 "most famous trial of the decade," the piece was described by prosecutors as a manifesto for the creation of an ethnically pure Muslim Bosnian state, even though Izetbegovic pointed out that the text said nothing about making Bosnia ethnically pure, and in fact made no reference to Bosnia.[10]

Thus when Tito's would-be successor, Milosevic, played a nationalist/religious trump card to incite the war, it was both predictable (since nationalist sentiments had been Tito's great fear) and shocking (since such thoughts had been severely repressed for decades). The rise of Slobodan Milosevic has been documented not only in several outstanding historical works but also by observers from the media and his interlocutors within the diplomatic community.[11] The world sleepily watched the step-by-step progression by which he chose an idea that was culturally gut-wrenching—alleged ethnic Albanian "terrorists" in Kosovo victimizing the Serb minority. It was a well-known ploy of tyrants. To respond to this terrifying prospect, he then transformed the multiethnic Yugoslav National Army into a force loyal to him, with Serb commanders, and unloosed them on the Albanian Kosovars. The other Yugoslav republics saw the handwriting on the wall.

How astounding to think that Slobodan Milosevic will vie with Marshal Tito for the place of the most influential Balkan leader of the past century.[12] It took Hitler about ten years to be named Germany's chancellor. Milosevic rose twice as fast, marked from his rabid "No one will ever beat you again" speech to Kosovar Serbs in 1987. Both used power politics: media takeover, ruthless military and police force, fear, and the hateful labeling of another people.[13] In contrast to Tito's straightforward if heavy-handed leadership, Milosevic led his people into a paranoid frenzy, built around the historic Serb banner of victimhood, with media tactics straight out of Nazi propaganda.[14] But what conditions allowed such a figure to win the confidence of the Bosnian Serbs? Partnership was essential.

Milosevic had his political lieutenant in Bosnia: Radovan Karadzic, president of the Bosnian Serbs, who actually hailed from Montenegro, not Bosnia.[15] The psychiatrist/poet promoted a radical agenda and blatant racism toward non-Serbs, asserting that Serbs had a right to any territory where they were living, or where their ancestors were buried. He envisioned a Berlin-type wall across Sarajevo to satisfy an apartheid that was more extreme than in South Africa.[16] The relationship between Milosevic and Karadzic was symbiotic, with each denying—with great conviction—any influence over the other.

Meanwhile, Franjo Tudjman had stated publicly that the alternative to an all-out war in the tottering Yugoslavia was a separate state for Croatia, and he schemed to divide Bosnia between Croatia and Serbia.[17] At the very moment that Germany was lobbying for recognition of Croatia, citing the principles of self-determination and inviolability of borders, Tudjman was advocating that these lofty ideals be ignored in the case of his neighbor.[18] But Tudjman and Milosevic weren't acting in a vacuum. In the period leading up to Bosnia's first multiparty elections, dozens of political parties formed, including several claiming to represent the interests of Bosnia's different ethnicities. Three of these nationalist parties won the majority of seats in the November 1990 elections. They were euphemistically named the Party for Democratic Action (SDA), which appealed to Muslims; the Croat Democratic Community (HDZ), a branch of Tudjman's party in Croatia; and the Serb Democratic Party (SDS), formed with the backing of Milosevic and nationalist intellectuals in Belgrade.

The coalition government formed by the three parties was rife with divisions and internal contradictions. The governance structure required the sign-off of all three nationalist groups. As a result, in eighteen months, not a single law was passed.[19] While publicly weighing questions such as the future political structure of a confederated Yugoslavia, the three parties were privately dividing up Bosnia's resources among themselves. Prime positions at the head of publicly owned firms or in the police departments went to party allies, and ethnicity mattered more than qualifications. In parts of Bosnia that had Serb and Croat majorities, political leaders took the carving up of Bosnia's assets one step further: to the territory itself. Following the model used earlier in Croatia, Serb autonomous regions were created in Bosnia in the fall of 1991 under the guidance of Belgrade and public leadership of Karadzic and Momcilo Krajisnik, who eventually declared the creation of Republika Srpska in December. The HDZ followed suit, declaring the Autonomous Region of Herceg-Bosna, the chunk of southwestern Bosnia they intended to be annexed to Croatia.

In the discussion that follows, imagine six women around a table, holding miniature cups of strong, muddy coffee as they tell stories that confirm or contradict the analysis of outside observers. Those who still claim the Bosnian war was rooted in ethnic conflicts may note that it's virtually impossible to guess ethnic backgrounds based on the sympathies expressed by the women in this discussion.

JELKA survived the Mostar nightmare with her artist husband and two sons as the Croats relentlessly pounded what they considered the Bosniak side of town, where she lived. *Although I'm a Croat, I have to confess: Croatia, as a state, directly supported the division of Bosnia. They wanted Mostar to be their center. But to turn Mostar into a pure Croatian town, you'd have to throw out almost 70 percent of its population. It was a dark idea. Maybe those words are too soft. It was fascist.* She doesn't accept the argument that local hard-liners were the primary culprits. *Tudjman's political party shaped opinions and attitudes in Bosnia and carried out policies hatched in Croatia.*

Whether as a reactionary but logical political strategy, or because of the natural contagion of avarice, the grab for power eventually spread from the Serb and Croat parties to the Bosniak. SUZANA has investigated political corruption, support for terrorism, and drug trafficking: *It was devastating to see how, after 1994, the SDA started doing similar things, like the ideological purging of the Bosnian army and other institutions of power. They colluded in negotiations on the division of Bosnia.*

Three more women—Serb, Croat, and Muslim—reflect on the politicians' responsibility. In the Republika Srpska town of Sipovo, KRISTINA will have none of the back and forth about one political party or another. *In each group there were extremists who fueled the war.* She'd rather lay the blame on leaders. *This was a political game, and the politicians were the ones responsible, with their fights and their ambitions. They tailored it.* Kristina doesn't interpret recent history as the result of Serb and Croat aggression. Is her unwillingness to attribute responsibility to any one party simply generous and conciliatory—or because she's a Serb assessing Serb responsibility? *I can't really say what side is to blame for the war. I don't want to divide Serbs, Croats, and Muslims in three parts and say only one group. A lot of men had to join the army, not because they wanted the war, but because they were drafted. That happened with my husband, and it happened on all three sides. Simple people—who just want to live, work, and provide for their families—aren't to blame. They were sacrificed in this game.* As proof, Kristina describes her work on the cusp of restoration, welcoming back students of diverse backgrounds to a town from which Bosniaks had been forcibly expelled. She recounts a reunion of teachers. *My Muslim colleague in Sipovo had become a refugee in Sarajevo. When she ar-*

rived at the gathering, we all hugged and kissed her. Everyone cried. I think that says it all.

As if to respond to Kristina, KAROLINA wonders if anyone really gained in the Bosnian war. Having endured years of shelling in the besieged capital, she ruminates: *You can't explain this war to anyone—why all this happened. Who is the villain? Who is the loser? Nobody knows. We were misled. Our beautiful country was so splendid before the war. Now our parks, where young people used to play sports, are filled with their gravestones. Why? Just because a few people wanted to plunder our land.* Karolina isn't talking about the spoils of war, but a get-what-you-can mentality that creates and is created by war. *Even in Sarajevo, where there were no Serb armies, there was still looting. Flats and shops were broken into.* In addition, led by many of the politicians themselves, black markets across the Balkans have flourished. Karolina ponders the forces that led to such hardship and heartache. *Something evil emerged in our young people. And what was the result? The Serbs raided our factories, but the Serbs aren't better off now. I recently visited Bratunac, near Srebrenica in the Republika Srpska; I saw Serb people there with rotten teeth and tortured faces. You can't say any one of us is better off with this war. Now we're all miserable and poor.*

That may be, but some are more miserable and poor than others; and perhaps a survivor of carnage has earned the right to the final word regarding those who planned and carried out the war. As usual, KADA's account cuts straight to the quick: *Very often I ask, who were those "brains" who destroyed the life we had before the war? They brought poverty. Misery. Hatred. Somebody did this on purpose. Somebody put a virus inside us. They made promises and then misled us. We were all cheated. I don't want to talk about what made the attackers of Srebrenica do what they did. It's clear, and everyone knows it. Someone hatched this idea of having a war.*

Unlike Kristina, whose husband, after all, fought in the Serb army, Kada is quite ready to lay blame on one side; but she confines responsibility to the leadership. Although her son and husband were executed by Serb soldiers, she refuses to extend the burden of blame to those who were carrying out orders. *As far as I know, the Chetnik leaders promised their soldiers they'd get all sorts of things. They told them they were in danger. The soldiers didn't know what that meant. Who was threatening them? They were told they should fight against that threat. Then religion got mixed in. God would favor people who fought. It was the same on the other side.*

Kada concludes by echoing Karolina's theme of the futile losses in war. *Did anyone gain or win? Did Chetniks get rich and make everything around them great and beautiful? No, they didn't. First, they lost their authority. Whatever they gained is now gone. They had casualties. They lost property, and now they're in one narrow territory.*

For Kada, whose family was destroyed in the conflict, the senselessness of war is particularly tragic. To die for an important cause is one thing. But to lose her son, husband, brother, home, career, friends, identity for nothing? *The leaders were just plain stupid when they let this happen.*

Preservation of Privilege

FAHRIJA: *We just thought from time to time the Serbs liked to reassert their superiority. It was like an old joke—tasteless, but nothing to get so worked up about.*

RADA: *They planned everything very cleverly. We knew our colleagues at the radio station were members of the SDS, but somehow we thought of it as a game; we used to joke about it.*

Violence in response to deprivation is not uncommon. Riots erupt among oppressed people who become enraged enough to act. But a component of conflict is also the transformation of privilege into a victim mentality, bred by and breeding distrust, then fear, then violence. In a circular pattern, privilege, rather than instilling a sense of security, becomes a position that must be ruthlessly defended.

Milosevic not only tilted the balance of power toward Serbs in terms of positions and privileges. He also understood the power of fear as the ultimate motivator, stimulating self-preservation, an instinct so powerful it can overwhelm the civilizing norms that regulate society. So it was in Bosnia. First Serbs in Serbia, then Bosnian Serbs were fed a stream of reports that Orthodox churches and cemeteries were being defiled and Serb girls and women were being raped. In response, curfews were imposed in the villages, house-to-house searches of Bosniak homes ensued, and weapons were confiscated.[20] In an environment hauntingly reminiscent of Nazi treatment of Jews, in some areas in the north Bosniaks were forbidden to meet in groups of more than three or to travel by car. Some began to fly white flags from their balconies, indicating that they would leave.[21]

This was not the first time victimhood had been introduced in Serb culture. Milosevic was playing on an old theme in his campaign to whip Serbs into a fear-fed frenzy, then call for preemptive action. Many Serbs felt they had not been adequately rewarded as victors in World War II, when Tito, half-Croat, half-Slovene, made Kosovo and Vojvodina autonomous regions. An anti-Serb conspiracy theory grew throughout the 1960s and early 1970s.[22] The depth of this victim mind-set is evidenced in the statement signed by two hundred prominent scholars and writers in Belgrade in January 1986, declaring, in language laced with hyperbolic claims, that the noble Serb people had been vilified and were being persecuted by the majority ethnic Albanians in Kosovo. The reality was that Kosovar Albanian professionals had been literally locked out of their jobs for several years.[23]

It is difficult to sort through accounts of ethnic-based privilege or lack thereof, because of the prevalence of "statistical oppression . . . and bogus ethnic history."[24] Still, it seems the Serb victim theme is ironic in that, although Marshal Tito went to great lengths to impose proportional leadership, Yugoslav society was politically weighted in favor of ethnic Serbs.[25] That privileged status was reinforced by the overly high esteem with which many spoke of their heritage.[26] Despite an ethnic key imposed to require proportional appointments to public jobs in Bosnia,[27] the practice of stacking positions with people who had Serb names was carried out on a widespread basis, laying the groundwork for Milosevic's campaign for "Greater Serbia." Milosevic fired anyone deemed not loyal to him, from factory workers to local officials.[28] As nationalism spread, the practice of purging according to ethnicity was mirrored by Tudjman in the parallel Croatian institutions that developed. Serbs were fired, for example, from the Croat police force, which was then refashioned into an army.[29] Within Bosnia, in Tuzla, Serb citizens received threatening phone calls, and many were fired without explanations as the Serb army and paramilitary took over large portions of the surrounding area.[30]

The women in these pages are, of course, not only firsthand observers but also subject to influence by propaganda promoted from all sides of the conflict. A postwar critique of prewar Bosnia by those who suffered personally from the violence can hardly be assumed to be untainted. However, the women's accounts confirm two streams of ethnic-based discrimination that, with hindsight, they judge to have blended into a slow poisoning of the society. The first was the social bias that intensified under Milosevic, elevating Serbs into positions of authority exceeding their representation in the population. Second was a mirror response by other groups. As conflict spread through the heart of multiethnic communities, ethnic identity was suddenly pertinent. Minorities of any stripe came to be distrusted, resented, and sometimes forced out of their homes, jobs, and even relationships. In the first case, ethnic discrimination was a cause of the war. In the second, ethnic discrimination was an effect of the war.

Many non-Serbs resented what they believed was the political and economic domination of Yugoslavia by Serbs, who then used their dominant presence in federal institutions as a means for cultural hegemony, manipulating political and administrative structures to secure their interests at the expense of the other republics, particularly Croatia and Slovenia. Not surprisingly, after Tito's death, political decentralization was advanced by those two republics, which resented their income being absorbed by the federal government to subsidize less developed areas closely affiliated with Serbia. The perception of Serbian expansionism under Milosevic contributed to Croatian nationalism, which in turn confirmed Serbian fears.[31]

Many of the women went on at length explaining to me their perception of how leadership positions were heavily weighted toward Serbs.[32] A businesswoman, EMSUDA was quick to give numbers to support this claim and point out how the same was true throughout the management structure of government-owned factories and other enterprises. But her intent wasn't to complain. Instead, she was making the connection for me between the systemic favoring of Bosnian Serbs and their subsequent support of Serb aggression, spawned in Belgrade when Yugoslav leadership was up for grabs at Tito's death. *When the multiparty system was to be implemented, those Serbs knew they would have to stop living at the government's expense. They knew there would now be regulations, fines, and the like to constrain them.*

According to Emsuda, Bosnian Serbs benefiting from the status quo had much to lose if a political breakup meant their capital would now be Sarajevo rather than Belgrade. They would shift from being in the plurality among Yugoslavs to being in the minority among Bosnians. The Belgrade government had a lot to lose as well, as viewed from Emsuda's position inside industry. *I saw how petty cash boxes were dipped into. All the funds went through the Yugoslovenska Banka, directly to Belgrade. In '91 and '92, the factory workers received minimal salaries — paid in coupons that could be spent only in certain shops. When the war started, we realized those shops had Serb managers.* War also meant the Bosnian government needed to mobilize an army to defend against the well-equipped and well-financed Yugoslav army, which, through Milosevic's manipulation, now had almost exclusive Serb leadership. *The government of Bosnia and Herzegovina didn't have any funds, since they all had been diverted to Belgrade. Citizens weren't able to withdraw their personal savings from banks from around 1991 forward.*

DANICA, like Emsuda a businesswoman, but of Croat heritage, believes Serbs dominated Bosnian culture. But her tone isn't bitter. *Sure more Serbs ruled than their proportion of the population; they tried to dominate. But we were still happy. Serbs fought for governing positions more than the rest of us. If I'd done the same — who knows? Maybe I'd be the head of something. We let them govern. Maybe Tito is to blame, but only because he was head of state. He fought for equality across Yugoslavia and put everything in one pot. All weapons and technology went into the Yugoslav National Army. Everything that belonged to our country was concentrated in Belgrade. The Serbs owned us. Yugoslavia had six republics. If we'd acted like a family and divided roles: "You're going to have this many weapons, here's some capital, and here's some . . ." Instead Tito centralized it. If he hadn't, we probably wouldn't have had this catastrophe. It's just like if a father gave it all to one son, then died, and the son was terrible and mistreated everyone else.* Compounding the danger, Yugoslavs were told that their army was one of the most powerful in Europe. *They thought, "Why not? We can use these weapons."*

Danica begins to speak longingly of the past, her eyes welling up with tears. *Ours was a beautiful little town, with two big rivers and two bridges. The people in the surrounding rural area were Croats, but in town there were more Muslims.* Her nostalgia takes a turn as she tells how the incremental discrimination against non-Serbs crescendoed into runaway social pathology. *During the war, non-Serbs were arrested, sent to camps, or killed. Some were exchanged, but pretty much everybody had to leave. Of the five to six thousand people of our town, only Serbs remained.* She mentions other towns, where only a few Bosniaks and Croats were left after the ethnic purges. Largely the elderly or those in mixed marriages, they were humiliated in a style reminiscent of Germany five decades earlier. *They had to wear ribbons around their arms and do forced labor. Teachers had to mop the floors. Doctors and lawyers were made garbage men, forced to clean in front of the police station or the city hall, so everyone could see them.* [Danica pauses for a long time.] *All their rights were taken away. One of our more prestigious lawyers in town was cleaning the streets. Suddenly, from one day to the next, he was branded. Other people were simply gone. Those who had stayed behind were sent to Serb work camps. They dug ditches and trenches for soldiers or cleaned institutions, like slaves.*[33]

Addressing the gnawing question of how a well-functioning social structure, led by highly trained and educated professionals, devolved into sadistic ruin, FAHRIJA connects her recent experience of Serb violence with the past: *The more I've thought about it, the more I've realized how there's a centuries-old wish for domination and removal of the Muslim people by the Serbs. Suddenly I wondered: How come we have relatives in Turkey? We're ethnic Albanians. But after the Second World War,*

Muslims—especially in Sandzak [part of Serbia]*—were pressured, harassed, told that they were "Ottomans," and that Turkey's their country and they should live there. They left their houses in Yugoslavia or sold them for nothing. Once they arrived in Turkey, they weren't accepted, because they weren't Turks. The relatives I found when I was a refugee spoke to me about this history of hard times. In the suburb of Istanbul they lived in— and where we stayed—the whole town shares that same history. A very small percentage of its population is actually Turkish in origin.*

BILJANA also reaches into the past to understand the current conflict. From her U.S.-based perspective, she measured the changes in her country in much larger units of time. *I was given a beautiful video of Muslim nuns singing. I was struck with how different it was from when I grew up. Then, you weren't known as a Muslim or a Catholic. No group would do something so public as making a video of services in the mosque. Religion was always very private. So when this came, I was shocked. Why was it all of a sudden important to be known ethnically? That wasn't the statement we made as a people. My cousin told me that all the Muslims were being removed from public positions. She said we needed to make some kind of statement as an ethnic group, because nobody else would do it for us. She said we were being pushed aside, and everything was being taken away from us through legal maneuvers. The Serbs wanted a "Greater Serbia." They were methodically preparing their takeover long before the war, removing non-Serbs from important places where they could make a difference.* Like the other speakers, Biljana supports her political assessment with personal examples: *My cousin was director of intelligence for Bosnia and Herzegovina before the war. He was removed from his position by the Serbs and placed in an unimportant job, then totally expelled. He ended up in Norway as a refugee.*

Biljana has another example as well, from 1989, when her mother was on her deathbed in Croatia. A homeopath came from Belgrade. He was a very intense, extremely bright, charismatic figure—reminiscent of Rasputin, to hear Biljana describe him: *He had a natural power to heal, and we had a soul connection.* Biljana spoke candidly with him about the turmoil in Kosovo: *The Serbs said the Kosovars were giving them problems, but it was really the other way around. So I made a very innocent remark like, "Why don't you just leave those poor people alone? I mean they live there. You can't just say that it's your country; it actually belongs to the ethnic Albanians." He was absolutely shocked—and so self-righteous. It was unbelievable to me that he could act as if the land were his. There was a sense of Serb entitlement that allowed them to go into the home of the lady that worked for my mother, kill her husband, expel the family, sleep in her bed, and say that was OK.* Biljana moves from the concrete to the broad lesson: *There were no moral standards. The Serbs—and the Croats, in the end—were bullies. It was greed. It's that simple. It wasn't philosophical. It wasn't that intelligent. Not some ultimate, wonderful, idealist view of life that you want to impose on others.*

In case I'm missing her point, Biljana adds an important historical element: *Those kinds of attitudes came only after Tito died.* In his decades of rule, in addition to political maneuvering, the strongman had not stopped short of secret police, summary executions, imprisonment, or whatever else he deemed necessary to maintain a unified state. Some historical analysts contend that this repression was based on Tito's correct assessment that if the tight lid were removed, prejudice and intolerance would boil up. Others insist that Yugoslav society was no more divided than most, where one group dominates others.[34] Be that as it may, in the heat of war, discrimination, like a social virus, spread through many (although not all) Bosnian communities. Vesna and Amna make the case from their personal experiences. VESNA had worked fourteen years in the world of finance. *Then, in 1992, I was fired just for being a Croat. Everybody else was Muslim. My husband is Serb, and he was fired too. We're not isolated cases.*

On the other side of the Croat-Bosniak divide, AMNA describes a mirror image: *While I was in Split, my parents and sister were in jail in Mostar—fortunately just ten days. One Croat put them in the jail, and another Croat let them out. I stayed in Split to finish my fourth year at the university. But in 1993, war started between Muslims and Croats back home in Mostar. Since I was a Muslim, and I was a student in [the newly declared state of] Croatia, I suddenly became a foreigner. They started to use special ID cards so only Croats could go to the university. One day they posted a list on the dorm wall: who could stay. I wasn't on the list, so I had to pack all my stuff, and I was expelled from student housing. The dorm director suggested that since I was Muslim, I should go to Turkey! Fortunately, my friends offered me a place to stay. It was hard for me but also good, because now I knew who my friends were: All those from before the war stayed my friends during the war—and they're still my friends.*

Similar to Amna's account, KADA, in rural eastern Bosnia, describes: *A belief rooted deep in the old people around here. The Serbs put themselves above everyone else and want to take over more territory. They think everyone belongs to them.* In her typically straightforward manner, Kada speaks of "Muslims" instead of "Bosniaks," insisting that she's not interested in "political correctness." *We've always been Muslims. Why should we change?* That same pride helps her not be cowed by Serb attempts to dominate. *They think Muslims are here by mistake. But whoever knows Bosnian history knows that's not true; that's just how the Serbs justified their crimes.* This isn't an ethnic slur on Kada's part. After all, Bosnian Serb President Karadzic actively advocated dividing Sarajevo into ethnic sections, claiming that any development on what once was farmland populated by Serbs now rightfully belonged to them. Muslims were regarded as converts who had abandoned their true identify as Croats or Serbs.[35]

Ugly policies have a source. Lawyers don't spontaneously decide to go into garbage collecting. Jobs don't disappear on their own. Lists don't tack themselves to the dormitory wall. Pernicious policies are born in the hearts and minds of individuals in key positions of leadership. The ultimate irony of this Serb-weighted social discrimination is that it didn't result in the beneficiaries feeling more secure. Like those whites in America who adamantly fought the civil rights movement that would distribute basic privileges among all, those who were benefiting from an uneven distribution of power easily slipped into a victim mind-set. From another historical parallel, GRETA, as a Holocaust survivor and Jew remaining in Europe, is intimately acquainted with the power of cultural stereotypes to instill fear. As she was growing up in multicultural Vojvodina, she didn't think about ethnic imbalances. *Wherever you had bosses, you had a lot of Serbs — not just in Serbia, but in Croatia, Slovenia, Bosnia and Herzegovina. Still, to hear the politicians tell it, the Serbs were always the victims, facing intolerance and injustice. Milosevic made this big speech in 1989 about Prince Lazar losing the battle of Kosovo in 1389.*[36] *Lazar's remains in his coffin were displayed. Milosevic began talking about how the Serb people always lost the battle, but never lost their identity.*

RADA, an ethnic Serb herself, describes the power of those stories: *Serbs have had a kind of awful, permanent tragedy stretching from decade to decade, century to century. That woeful tale has been transformed into myths, with stories of sufferings transferred from generation to generation. It's become pathological: They prefer being tied to suffering than to something positive. The need for tragedy becomes a means of evading reality. The child in the cradle is taught that the Serb people have been through tragedy, individual and collective, and there's no way to escape that destiny.* Rada isn't so much concerned about refuting the Serb view of history as understanding the roots of Serb political attitudes. *The tragedy may be a pure fiction, but it creates a victim position from which Serbs react.*

Serbs haven't learned from history. We love epic narratives — tales and songs about heroes. Many of these stories have great artistic value, but politics manipulated literature. In every story, someone who used to be a victim becomes a hero. They wake up one morning, changed, and then they take revenge in the name of the rest of the Serbs. So the only way to become a hero is to start as a victim. There's a huge power in being a victim. People identify with the victims in the stories and hold tight to their victimhood. In normal life, a victim becomes a perpetrator. It's cyclical. Historically, it's true that Serbs have suffered. But how does that justify what they did?

So the tragic myths became a catalyst, turning an imbalance that actually favored the "victims" into a fear that they would lose their privileges. This shift from the ease of abundance into the "dis-ease" of violent self-preservation is traceable in the words of GALINA, speaking from an enclave awash for years with propaganda broadcast from Serbia—the "cleansed" city of Banja Luka, which was 55 percent Serb before the war, 95 percent after. First, to counter the demonization of the Serbs, she's determined to normalize what occurred. *It's not true that people didn't love each other. Look how many mixed marriages we have. It was like a family splitting up, with brothers going to court. In spite of their love, they may even shoot each other. The problem was a few psychopaths, very extreme nationalists. Normal people didn't want to have this war. There were dangerous nationalist parties, and ethnic cleansing occurred on all sides.*

I find it difficult as an outsider, not having been subjected to brainwashing reports in Banja Luka every day, to castigate the Galinas of Bosnia for the discrepancy between their accounts and those of observers. Is her view wrong but understandable, given the information she had? Is her unwillingness to lay blame on her own group a psychological defense among Bosnian Serbs (especially outside Sarajevo), feeding on the tragic myths described by Rada and Greta? Galina fingers many culprits, not only among the Bosnians but also among propagators of the divisive message. *The international community . . . talks about "Serbs, Muslims, and Croats." But people are just good or bad. You always have bad people who don't have faith in God, and that's why there's war.* But the bad ideas of bad people can be furthered by the bad policies of outsiders, she insists. *The international sanctions were unfair and didn't work.*[37] *The people are the ones who suffered. That policy fed the idea that the world is against us. We had to fight or the world would destroy us.*

Ultimately, that view among Serbs that they were victims grew into a drive to preserve what they had. *In these parts there's always this idea that someone is threatening someone else. Even business people and highly educated people feel like they're in danger. Then when there was a real threat, real danger, when it was a question of whether there would be war, people—not me—thought if something ought to belong to Serbs, then Muslims had to leave, and vice versa. People thought they had to grab a cut for themselves.* The Serb "cut" turned out to be bigger than their proportion in the society. Bosnian Serbs, who represented one-third of the prewar population, ended up after Dayton controlling 49 percent of the territory. Galina doesn't note the inequity, but adds, instead, a critical distinction for those seeking to understand the reasons for the Bosnian war. *I don't think it was hate. It was fear—and the need for our own piece of land.*

Biljana Plavsic, during her sentencing at The Hague, admitted, "In our obsession that Serbs should never again become victims of their neighbors, as they were in World War II, we allowed ourselves to become victimizers."[38] Still, it's too easy to say that war was the result of a Serb victim mentality, which fed into a fear of losing their political and economic position if they became minority members of an independent Bosnia rather than Yugoslavs. That political situation was stoked with extraordinary virulence and effectiveness by the media. *When I heard the rhetoric that started overnight on TV, terms like "Chetniks" and "Ustashas," I recognized war. Some people didn't have radio or television. Maybe they heard by word of mouth, but they all repeated like parrots "Chetniks," "Ustashas," "Mujahadeens."* As the masses drifted with the flow into what they perceived as the inevitability of war, Galina read as many newspapers as she could find and tried to listen to Voice of America and the BBC. But it was a struggle, as the local papers continuously reinforced the Belgrade message. *Someday I'll cut out the headlines. Whoever looks at them will say, "These people hate each other. They can't live together."*

The Media Machine

SABIHA: *Ninety percent of the stuff they were showing on TV was rubbish. Most of what they were saying on the radio was propaganda, preparation for the war, to incite hatred.*

VALENTINA: *We didn't have newspapers during the war, and TV depended on electricity, which we didn't get all the time. There was a Bosnian and a Serb channel. Both sides claimed killings. They might have lied; I wasn't there to see.*

KRISTINA: *The politicians used the media, which of course had enormous power over people in a communist system. . . . You know, we were used to listening to doctrine.*

MAJA: *Violent people controlled the media, but that was the source from which we had to extract the truth.*

Imagine a political climate around you is being created. Somebody is suddenly telling you somebody did something they didn't do. Or this was said, which wasn't said. And

you see this huge fight erupting. Then you start to feel you're about to lose something, be-
cause your politicians are saying you are. They're fashioning a political happening that
doesn't exist, but is about to exist. You're caught up in something that's actually in the
making. There are interminable parliamentary sessions broadcast live on TV. Suddenly
people begin to hate, fighting some enemy who, they're told, is threatening their way of
life. That enemy, as such, doesn't exist yet, because the people who are supposed to be
the enemy feel exactly the same way you do. It's just a political game, created through
TV and other media.

That account of the psychology of media warfare is all the more gripping coming not from an outside analyst, but from KRISTINA, a small-town Bosnian Serb schoolteacher. Her words give a graphic account of how the wartime news media didn't have the primary function of providing unbiased information to the people. Without a tradition of independent media, politicians started up radio and television stations and used print media to twist real events into powerful propaganda or even create stories from whole cloth.[39] The tactic was so successful that, after the war, Bosnia had the double-edged distinction of having the highest number of media houses in Europe, with over 400 print and broadcast media outlets for a population of fewer than four million.[40] It was a tactic Milosevic used until the demise of his political career.[41]

The disintegration of the former Yugoslavia was a product of, and in turn produced, arguably the most effective manipulation of media in Europe since Hitler's Third Reich. Like that campaign half a century before, the politicized media blitz that led to the Balkan wars of the 1990s stretched over several years before the shooting started, becoming progressively more virulent. Milosevic's goal was to create the perception of distinct—and incompatible—identities among people for whom such distinctions either had not existed or had not been important. Even as Hitler strengthened and evoked Aryan identity by creating an "other" (the Jews), the nationalists in post-Tito Yugoslavia launched media campaigns that reduced a complex, multicultural society to distinct nations (ethnic groups), with Serb and Croat politicians arguing that their ethnic group was entitled to dominion over land that had long been shared. Different events and periods of history could be invoked to "prove" the rightful owner of territory, ignoring migration and intermingling, as well as changes in political structures or the evolution of culture and religion. The inconsistencies, and sometimes bald-faced lies, promoted by politicians using the media for these purposes were astounding.[42]

Each nationalist leader sought to establish control of local media—perhaps most effectively through television and radio, although print was not exempt. In some cases, international media picked up themes being promulgated locally. As nationalist leaders used the media first to separate and then unify their subgroup (as if these were people separated by culture and language), the international press carried stories of a citizenry who could not conceivably live together in harmony—forgetting that they'd been doing just that, with few exceptions, for the most of the past several centuries.

While President Tudjman in Croatia and President Izetbegovic in Bosnia were also guilty of manipulating the media, the women telling me the story of the Bosnian war, regardless of their own ethnic identity, refer most pointedly to Slobodan Milosevic, who by the end of 1987 had achieved control of Radio-Television Belgrade as well as *Politika*, the largest circulating newspaper in Yugoslavia. Several Belgrade media outlets were known for high-quality journalism even under the communists. These outlets were transformed—through purges, personal threats, and other pressures—into sources of disinformation that sowed seeds of fear and intolerance.[43] In his bid to take over Croatia, Milosevic created a ministry of information that achieved pervasive media control. Likewise, the Yugoslav National Army helped Bosnian Serbs take over TV-Sarajevo repeaters across the country and reprogrammed them to carry TV-Belgrade.[44]

The media success of the political architects of a fantasized Greater Serbia is illustrated in two accounts, both by Bosnian Serb women who could contrast their Sarajevo life experience with misinformation the Serb media was feeding the public. As RADA says: *The Serb nationalists were phenomenal in their manipulation of the media. First they created a wonderful staff, taking the best journalists. Some of my radio colleagues were members of the nationalist political party, the SDS. The Croat nationalists followed suit.*

The Serbs used the media in the most terrible way, isolating their coverage area. They "cleansed" the region so they could do whatever they wanted; radio and TV signals were provided from Serbia for their territory in Bosnia, and all other relays were destroyed so other media couldn't reach them.[45] Take my mother, who—with all due respect—even after the time we spent in Sarajevo, still can't believe that someone was shooting at the city from the outside. During the war, she was in her mid-seventies, listening to the broadcasts from Serbia about how "those Muslims" were destroying the capital. She lives only seven kilometers from Sarajevo. She heard the roaring of the shells. She's not a nationalist, but still she can't believe it! For her, it was "the Muslims" who were shelling Sarajevo. Then she asks me, "Why don't you have a flat?" [Rada laughs.] *I tell her my flat was destroyed. She asks me, "Well, who destroyed it?" And I can't tell her "It was Chetniks."* As a Serb, Rada's mother might be offended to hear her daughter using a term that had acquired a derogatory meaning against all Serb people. *So I tell her, "Mother, my flat was destroyed by Rajna." Rajna is a Serb who lived opposite my building, where the paramilitary White Eagles had their sniper and machine gun nest, which faced my building directly.*

Sarajevans were shelling themselves? Who could believe such an outlandish notion?[46] Yet Rada's account is confirmed by TANJA, university professor turned politician: *Today I meet people from Serbia who really didn't know Sarajevo was destroyed, and they're amazed at what they see. They actually thought we Sarajevans were shooting at ourselves! And after a market massacre in the center of Sarajevo, the Serb newspapers wrote that those sixty-eight bodies were dummies!*[47] The twists were sometimes diabolical, such as footage of Serbian soldiers raping Croat and Bosniak women, shown on the news in Serb-controlled Banja Luka, described as Serbian women being raped by Croatian and Bosniak men.[48] Tanja goes on to reflect on the lessons of those years, and the damage that continued after the shooting stopped. *State media control is a dangerous thing. Now the nationalist political parties, which brought about this war, are in power. Using the media, they keep setting one ethnic group against another. Their propaganda is disastrous.*

"Disastrous" is a strong word. Disinformation is certainly disorienting. But in and of itself, how dangerous can it be? Dangerous indeed, when it emboldens fear and demands action. The Serb media, in particular, became a weapon of war by communicating an impending crisis, a threat to the very existence of the Serb people.[49] But all three nationalist parties were guilty of attacks on the independent media. The director of Sarajevo TV was forced to resign when he insisted on broadcasting daily newscasts from Zagreb and Belgrade, as well as Sarajevo. All three nationalist political parties demanded that Radio-Television Sarajevo stop transmitting the meetings of the All-National Parliament, in the first week in April 1992, to protest ethnic divisions.[50]

Fear, in turn, begat fear. Several women described the cycle of terror as an essential element in the mobilization of people to fight or flee. FAHRIJA relates how, just as the war was about to break, she escaped Sarajevo by bus with her two small children. *The radio was on full blast. The speaker referred to Ejup* [her husband] *and the president* [Izetbegovic] *as propagators of war who wanted to turn Bosnian people against Serbia and rally Muslims to kill them — like in the Ottoman times. It was ridiculous, of course. The Bosniaks weren't even armed. The driver was cursing my husband out loud while he patted my little Emir's head. I prayed for Emir to be quiet.* For Fahrija and the bus driver, abstract notions of "the enemy" were suddenly strikingly personal. People who had been neighbors for fifty years now feared death at the other's hands. Media had become a weapon of war, with myths promulgated by greedy politicians now popularized and disseminated among people who began to see themselves as threatened.

So how did Milosevic pull it off, this dramatic rewriting of current affairs and history?[51] ALENKA's answer packs a wallop, a blunt but effective antidote to the gentility of academic policy analysis: *Masses are just stupid — really easy to influence. Hitler was a genius at manipulating crowds. Many of these crazy politicians were psychiatrists, so they probably knew how to sway the people.* But Yugoslav society was peaceful, multicultural, and relatively well educated. So how did those "crazy politicians" gain such influence? *The campaign was composed of small bits. We didn't recognize the whole picture, because it came in tiny, invisible pieces. Propaganda filled the air. Here's a typical jewel from an extremist Tuzla newspaper: "Every good Muslim should kill at least one Serb." Sure the people in Tuzla knew this was junk. But that's what was out there. And from other sides, disgusting examples: "We're the best; others are worthless." A year or two before the war, some newspapers started with horrible propaganda to drum up support for Greater Serbia; they called for revenge from World War II atrocities. The campaign produced fear, which is the mechanism that runs war. They tell you, "Kill them, or they'll kill you!" Then you have a chain reaction.* Alenka goes on to distinguish between rural and urban people, saying that the extremist message resounded in the hills around Tuzla, but not in the city itself. She cites election results to prove that her town didn't succumb to the nationalist craze that swept the nation. Still, she's very wary of the power of the mass media. *You get so used to it — the propaganda, step by step — that you can't recognize it anymore. That's why you need someone from outside to analyze everything and say, "This is bullshit." And it is bullshit because, if someone tells you lies all the time, you forget it's a lie. And it becomes the truth.*

4

The Lie of Intractable Hatred

ALENKA: *What happened here never was about ethnicity or religion. That's a fake excuse used by the politicians who started the war.*

SUZANA: *During Tito's time, ethnicity wasn't an issue.*

KADA: *Why did they destroy mosques?*[1] *If we believe in God, we basically believe the same way—Orthodox and Muslims. Before the war, it wasn't like this. Did somebody create that feeling? I wonder.*

NURDZIHANA: *I've never accepted ethnic divisions! The way I was raised, we didn't say someone belongs to this or that ethnic group. The atrocities I witnessed had no ethnicity, no religion. We lived together until the day before.*

KRISTINA: *I've never in my life wanted to divide people into groups.*

"Those people have been fighting for centuries." We read that sentiment in Washington newspapers. We heard it on the streets in Vienna. We listened to it in London speeches. We watched it tragically acted on by key leaders in the international community. "Those people" obviously had a problem—and it was their problem, their decidedly Balkan problem.

Some saw in Yugoslavia a basic impossibility: people of different religious faiths, languages, and alphabet building their lives in harmony. Others pointed to the multicultural successes of Yugoslavia:[2] Per capita, Bosnia has many more ethnically mixed marriages than the United States has racially mixed ones; and Bosnian society doesn't suffer the gross inequities by which, in America, income, education level, life expectancy, and even prison terms are linked to race. In short, although marred by historical distortions that were an extension of conflict experienced across Europe in World War II, Bosnian society under Tito didn't ex-

Remnants of better days in Mostar. July 1997.

perience the sort of rage and distrust among social groups that led, for example, to riots in Los Angeles and other U.S. cities.

In lengthy conversations with former Foreign Service officers posted in Yugoslavia, I've discussed this issue of ethnic divides in Bosnia. One has opined that the women I've interviewed suffer from Yugo-nostalgia, evidenced in their refusing to admit that prewar Bosnia was a smoldering volcano of ethnic tension, waiting to erupt. The next has insisted that the women's portrayal is accurate. The reader will have to decide whether the first Foreign Service officer's objectivity as an observer or the women's subjective experience is more valid in this debate. My role is to relay the voices I heard; and, strikingly, as different as they were in every other way, the women were united in the assertion that pre-Milosevic Bosnia was not a society in which ethnic hatred festered—above or below the surface. Instead, they described—for hours on end—events and relationships that belied the notion that their country was doomed to divide. Historical ethnic grievances? Clearly, yes. Intractable ethnic hatred? Emphatically, no.

How did this idea of deep divisions gain a foothold in the foreign policy world? It was difficult, caught up in the progressive pandemonium, to see the step-by-step rational design behind the conflict, led by the man with whom diplomats were now dealing as they went about their political assignments.[3] Intractable hatred was also an undemanding stereotype: dramatic, simplifying, and easy to understand—even if wrong. But more insidiously, the notion that "those people are always fighting" provided an excuse for officials who, often for institutional or personal reasons, didn't want to become involved in the Balkan conflict.

A Most Convenient Excuse

TANJA: *Before Dayton, we Bosnian political leaders held a press conference in London. We tried to tell the international community what was really happening . . . but they weren't interested.*

A grand success of Slobodan Milosevic was his propagating the notion that Yugoslavs had been fighting each other for centuries and always would be. In foreign policy jargon, a "fault line" ran straight through the Balkans, dividing Roman Catholics, Orthodox, and Muslims. A "clash of civilizations" was inevitable, and woe to those idealistic helpers caught in the tectonic ethnic crunch.[4] That policy paradigm, which might as well have been crafted in Belgrade, became a most convenient excuse for those outside the Balkans looking for justification not to get involved.[5] Since their concern was ensuring that a military intervention or political strategy would be precise, well-defined, and delimited, U.S. and other international leaders were reluctant to get involved in trying to rectify what might be a basic part of the Bosnian society.

In times of social change, such as that being experienced in Yugoslavia with the implosion of communism, identity conflicts among groups proliferate.[6] In the stressful time of change, Milosevic, an opportunist more than true Serb nationalist,[7] rose to popularity by dredging up old nationalism — not so unlike the practice of some right-wing U.S. politicians playing on long-standing racist sentiments to insist on an "English only" policy in the States. Flowing across Europe, at the same time, was a worrisome, far-right resurgence epitomized by neo-Nazis in Germany, Le Pen's xenophobic appeal in France, the separatist Lombard League in Northern Italy, and Joerg Haider's antiforeigner campaign in Austria. In fact, some in the European right regarded Slovenia and Croatia as a healthy expression of anticommunist attitudes. In Hegelian terms, if the expansion of the EU and NATO represented a new thesis of European integration, the antithesis was represented by right-wing movements demanding separation. What form the synthesis might take was anyone's guess.

Perceptions of the Balkans in the late 1980s were as different as the contexts of the observers. While Washington policymakers were observing a new geopolitical era unfolding, Bosnians were experiencing their lives unraveling. AMNA says: *I was living like a princess. I had everything. I just made a wish, and my parents would fulfill it. Then 1991 came, and suddenly I had to take care of my whole extended family. In 1992, there were twelve of us living near Split in a house with three rooms, including the kitchen. We were refugees — three families of us. Six slept in each room. I worked in a humanitarian organization, just to have some food to bring them at the end of the day. At the same time, I kept going to university.* Meanwhile, Americans, oblivious to Amna's plight, were still celebrating the long-awaited fall of communism. The United States was suddenly the lone superpower — and most of us were decidedly unsure of how to fulfill that role.

Some were concerned that the demise of Soviet tyranny had uncorked a vessel of fermenting nationalism. In response to the Serb aggression, the Western world mustered just enough outrage to impose trade sanctions. Whatever good might have come of that move was outweighed by the arms embargo the UN imposed on Yugoslavia in September 1991 at the request of Belgrade, which effectively froze the military imbalance in which Serbs controlled the fourth-largest army in Europe, and non-Serbs were essentially unarmed.[8] This was one of a long series of unfortunate unintended consequences, sparked by the actions of would-be international helpers. That enormous war-making advantage emboldened Serb nationalists and, ironically, rather than decreasing the violence in the region (the UN aim), most likely intensified it. Throughout those months, the U.S. government stood back. President Bush, after all, had been advised by General Colin Powell, Chair of the Joint Chiefs of Staff, not to get involved in Yugoslavia.[9] Better to end his presidential first term (and hopefully enter his second) riding the crest of the "clean" Gulf War.[10]

The U.S. attitude toward Milosevic and the Yugoslav National Army (JNA) in early 1991 was intensely conflicted. The American ambassador, Warren Zimmermann, was initially a strong supporter of Yugoslavian territorial unity, although he condemned Milosevic's tyranny and demanded democratic rule.[11] In June 1991, tanks from the JNA barracks in Slovenia were ordered to "defend the border" from the Slovene separatists who had proclaimed independence and taken over the Slovene customs facilities. But it wasn't until mid-1992 that Secretary of State James Baker advocated multilateral military intervention in Bosnia to ensure the delivery of humanitarian aid. Although he won George Bush's go-ahead, Baker was not in a position to oversee the implementation, being immediately pulled out of the State Department to run Bush's flagging reelection campaign. His successor was Lawrence Eagleburger, a former ambassador to Yugoslavia in the late 1970s, who supported Bush's reluctance to intervene.[12]

In summer 1991, Europeans sent a clear message to U.S. officials that they saw this as a European problem. Soon afterward, Nurdzihana was faced with keeping her elderly mother safe for months on end in a crowded cellar. Galina was helping refugee children streaming into Banja Luka find their lost parents. Kristina was frantically worried about her teenage boy on the front line. Irma was holding her hands over her ears, cringing as shells exploded. But across an ocean, life paraded on. The lack of early U.S. leadership in opposition to Milosevic didn't disturb an American public usually generous in spirit but woefully ignorant of international affairs. A bipolar global struggle was comprehensible to Americans. But without the "Evil Empire" of the Reagan/Bush foreign policy, or the "Axis of Evil" on which the future foreign policy of George W. Bush spun, Americans couldn't be roused to support U.S. leadership in a place most would be unable to locate, even on a map of Europe. The "CNN factor" was shorthand for the power of the press to shape foreign policy, exemplified by gruesome footage of U.S. soldiers dragged through Mogadishu streets, which led to the pullout of UN troops from Somalia in 1992. When it came to the Balkans, such news reports of atrocities were ineffective in forcing intervention. President Clinton was slow off the mark in the foreign policy arena. He was notably indecisive on the Balkans, caught in a tug-of-war between his own high-level officials advocating or discouraging intervention. Instead, he poured his effort into wooing a Congress preoccupied with domestic and economic concerns.[13] That was well and good for Milosevic, who continued, unabated, to employ his powerful media machine in tandem with his aggressive military plan.

Similarly, given that "force protection"—no American body bags—had become a preoccupation of the Pentagon, Milosevic's propaganda about intractable ethnic hatred served two functions. First, it provided a framework for understanding the violent expulsion of millions of non-Serbs from their homes. Second, by painting the conflict as a natural consequence of local culture, it also provided noninterventionists, including the American military, the cover they needed to stay out of the fight. Those who raised questions or dissented were told that there was no political will in the upper echelons of Washington to back military intervention. Ambassadors Bob Hunter, Madeleine Albright, and Dick Holbrooke made clear their views that intervention was the correct course; but the prevailing voice was a powerful choir of key analysts, intelligence experts, and policymakers across Europe and the United States who sang of the deep-seated hatred in the Balkans.[14]

The international community could thus excuse itself from getting involved. Never mind that the last time there had been an intra-Balkan conflict (between Nazi sympathizers in Croatia and communist Partisan resisters), Germany was also at war with France—again. Did anyone in 1992 talk about a hazardous hatred between those two leading European states, dooming them to a future of perpetual violent conflict? Could anyone imagine standing back as observers during an expulsion of German speakers from Alsace at the end of the twentieth century? As in the Balkans, the Franco-German conflicts led not only to boys and men lost in battle but also to a citizenry suffering homelessness, fear, hunger, and economic devastation. In addition, there was another sad similarity to the situation fifty years earlier: The noncommittal stance of the United States from 1992 till mid-1995 was reminiscent of America's isolationist response before Pearl Harbor, as Hitler advanced across Europe.

Despite outsiders' beliefs about endemic ethnic hatred, scores of people I've interviewed insist that few citizens of Bosnia, the most ethnically diverse of the six

Yugoslav republics, could imagine an ethnic struggle in their land.[15] The women were quick to cite examples of multicultural values intrinsic to their lives. They pointed out that given the large number of mixed marriages (more in the cities, but in rural areas as well), it was impossible to identify many people by ethnicity. Repeatedly, as if to counter the claims disseminated from Belgrade, the women expressed in clear, articulate terms why they could never have anticipated the divisive nationalist cancer that spread over their land.

Unfortunately, their resolute spirit was in bold contrast to the indecisiveness of the international Contact Group, which frittered away months with one unproductive meeting after another. Often split along historical lines,[16] these countries couldn't accept leadership among themselves, and thus they failed to reach consensus — even as Serb forces burned their way across Croatia, then Bosnia. While the world stood back and waited, many of the women in this book were being terrorized.

Of all the women I spoke with, GRETA, as a European Jew, is uniquely qualified to address the question of whether an ethnic war was inevitable. She is acutely sensitive to implications of genocide and the importance of confronting prejudice. While her story is the one most dramatically linked to World War II, she isn't swallowed up by the comparison of the times. Even as she recalls events fifty years earlier, she's unwilling to conclude that war is somehow symptomatic of the Balkans — a potent reminder to outsiders who merged those wars into one bellicose cultural stereotype and then threw up their hands in resignation.

Twenty-year-old Greta was deported to Auschwitz in 1944, where she lived on the edge of death. *Then one morning, they told everybody who could walk to come forward, because the camp was to be evacuated and burned. The gas chambers and crematorium had already been destroyed, because the Nazis didn't want people to know they had existed. I went to the "hospital" — which took some courage. If you said, "I'm sick," you never knew where you'd end up. I simply had no strength. To everyone who could walk, they gave a blanket and loaf of bread. I said to the girls with me, "You know, if they burn this place* [she laughs under her breath], *at least it will be warm." They didn't even have time to set the camp on fire, because the Russians came in about two hours.* She made her way back to Yugoslavia, one of a tiny proportion of Jews to have lived through the deportation to camps. At home, she found herself in a quandary when it was time to get an identity card. *Even though Israel did not yet exist, I said, "My nationality is Jewish." They told me I could not say that, because there was no such land. I said, "That may be, but I was in a camp because I am a Jew, I have a number on my skin because I am a Jew, and I lost all my family because I am a Jew. So I'm* remaining a Jew. I am a Jew, never mind where. I can be a Jew anywhere. Do you know how to write or don't you?" [Greta brushes the air with her hand, as if dismissing the bureaucrat.] So my identity card said "Jew." Nobody else's, only mine—because I demanded it. Later on, Yugoslav identity cards had no nationality—which is another way of saying we could not imagine something like this war.

Moving between reminiscences and the present, Greta juxtaposes the improbability of both wars. Yugoslavia was a solid political state. For fifty years, I experienced no trace of nationalism. I still can't explain World War II, because we did not feel animosity among us. Returning from the concentration camp, I went to Belgrade to study. There was no hostility among people. In '52 I came to Sarajevo—an entirely different surrounding, because I'd never lived around Muslims. Even the Jews are different in Sarajevo [she smiles]: I'm Ashkenazi, and they're Sephardic. But in all this time, I've never felt any difficulties, any difference. I speak a dialect, but nobody has said, "Why do you talk like that?" Then all these years later, suddenly [her hands demonstrate an eruption] it began again. Public meetings were held every week: Should we have a confederation or some other arrangement? Still, we didn't think there would be war. A friend of mine told me at the beginning, "Did you hear them say everyone will be killed?" I said, "How can you repeat such things? Remember, in '45 we said, 'Never again.' " Greta shakes her head, trying to understand why "again" did, in fact, come to pass. Then like Nurdzihana, her thoughts move on. There were Serbs who had lived in Sarajevo for years and years and years. They didn't stay, but went away and fought against us. I cannot imagine! I had relationships with those people, and I never thought they held anything against anybody else.

Greta can understand outsiders being unprepared for the emergence of nationalism in Yugoslavia even as she was, but she has no patience for the tendency of those outsiders who shrink from involvement. Once again, she reaches across decades as she critiques the myopic mistake of the international community, reluctant to intervene earlier in Bosnia. Like many who endured the Holocaust, she recognizes danger for all in the targeting of a few. In the beginning, the war was against Muslims, but it would have spread to Jews. And who next? After all, the ethnic lines were already blurred. According to Greta, many Bosnian Jews were fully assimilated and, like many other Yugoslavs, didn't hold on to a separate identity. People from mixed marriages call themselves "Yugoslav," and my son says he's "Yugoslav," because he's from Yugoslavia. My daughter-in-law, she says "Yugoslav," too; her father was Macedonian, but her mother is a Jew—which I didn't know till well after I met her![17] For Greta, assimilation of Jews is not a response to danger due to anti-Semitism. She describes how upset the citizenry was when, in 2000, Sarajevo's Jewish cemetery was vandalized. On the other hand, she tells with pride how La

Benevolencija (a Jewish charity with members from Britain, the Netherlands, the United States, and Germany) contributed to the wartime Sarajevo soup kitchen, which served about 350 people a day. Only a third of those helped were Jews. In fact, Greta recalls how, in spite of the shelling by Serb forces, food and garments were delivered to a Bosnian Serb professor of biology. And when a group of Jews collaborated from inside and outside the country to evacuate some of the elderly and children from the besieged city, they included non-Jews as well.

Even if the status and role of Jews was exemplary, perhaps the international community was prudent to delay entering a "religious war." Nonsense, according to Greta, who draws a firm line between religion as a passion that is a source of division and can compel war, and religion as a key ingredient of culture. To debunk the first notion, she describes how, as a child in pre-Tito Novi Sad (a major city in northern Serbia), she attended compulsory Serb Orthodox religion classes; but outside school, Roman Catholics went to their churches and Jews to the synagogue. She adds, a bit ruefully, that although she was considered Jewish enough to be shipped off to a concentration camp, her family did not practice their faith. Her father never went to the synagogue. *I learned a lot of prayers, but the practice of religion wasn't important to me. Then, after the Second World War, there was no study of religion, which is a pity. Under Tito, religion was a private matter. For a devoted communist, you can say that ideology took the place of religion, although for most people a trace of religion remained. You could go to church, but you had no right to proselytize.*

It's difficult to square accounts of the rich mix of religious traditions in Bosnian culture with Tito's periodic brutal repression of religious expression. After World War II, intellectuals who were believers were summarily executed. In 1946, the courts of Islamic sacred law were suppressed, education of children in mosques was outlawed, and women were forbidden from wearing the veil. Muslims in the military were forced to eat pork, and communist officials were warned against having their sons circumcised. Both the Roman Catholic Church and the Orthodox Church were at times persecuted, at times infiltrated. All this was in spite of the 1946 constitution proclaiming freedom of belief and separation of church and state.[18] This background helps explain why, in Greta's social critique, religion was too weak to be a cause of conflict. In an unusual twist, having just endured three years of a war others thought was religious-based, she expressed regret at Bosnians' lack of religious interest. The notion of religion as central to culture is consistent with basic Jewish tenets, but at the most practical level, this professor of architectural construction feels strongly: *Even if not as worship, religion should have been taught as history.* Her reasoning? Without an understanding of the society's core set of beliefs and values, intellectual activity suffers. *When I took my students on architectural excursions to churches, I couldn't really explain what they were seeing because they knew almost nothing about religion.* That notion was reinforced by a young Sarajevan man who remarked to me that all the religions had one thing in common: The Muslims didn't go to the mosque, the Catholics and Orthodox didn't go to church, and the Jews didn't go to the synagogue.[19]

While many of the women acknowledged the historical roots of violent conflict in the Balkans, they kept history in context. No one can (or should) erase the evidence of past massacres and other atrocities that took on ethnic features, but just as clearly history must not be distorted into an all-too-easy determinism. The international community could have intervened early in the Bosnian war and, in doing so, saved a huge number of lives.[20] It chose not to do so for a variety of reasons, often primarily its own domestic considerations. In meetings at NATO, the White House, and the U.S. State Department, I was privy to some of the internal back and forth regarding whether the U.S. should lead an intervention against the Serb forces ravaging the Bosnian countryside. State lined up against the Pentagon and CIA—and lost. The United States failed to intervene more because of the situation in Washington, D.C., rather than the situation in Bosnia. Among the people of Bosnia in the late 1980s and early 1990s, there were certainly differences. But apart from providing a convenient excuse to policymakers who didn't want to get involved in the political conflict, those differences were neither dangerous nor destructive. In fact, rather than creating divisions, the diversity blended in a rich multiculturalism that Bosnians either took for granted or celebrated. Continuing on, Greta's discourse on religion is developed by women from every tradition lauding the complexly textured lives of Bosnia and Herzegovina.

The Richness of Multiculturalism

BILJANA: *I was born "Sabiha," but when I was about two, my sister began to call me "Biljana," just because she liked the sound. Soon everyone, including my mother, picked it up. Nobody cared that I was Muslim with a Serb name.*

TANJA: *I didn't even know my neighbors' ethnicity. My friends and I cared about character.*

Sarajevo was a perfect setting for the 1984 Winter Olympics. What better backdrop to the parading array of athletes than a city that prided itself on an extraordinary amalgam of cultures?[21] The swirl of musical styles, historical backgrounds, culinary traditions, and distinctive costumes combined in a delightful cacophony of sight and sound. Mosques, Orthodox and Roman Catholic churches, and a synagogue shared a few square blocks.[22] Bosnia was a trade crossroads where people from different traditions not only mingled but also married.

That social blend bore international political consequence: Bill Clinton, who was raised a white boy with black playmates, had a particular appreciation for a society that discouraged ethnic divides. In 1995, when he addressed the nation to explain his decision to order military intervention to stop the genocide, the president was not able to convince the American people. He moved forward without public support to protect a society across the Atlantic that exemplified the tolerance, equal rights, and inclusion he was trying to promote in the United States. His decision to intervene in the Bosnian war was consistent with his emphasis on race relations in America. The Bosnian war was, for Clinton, an affront to the values that had made America great.

The women I interviewed told me hours of stories demonstrating those values. For these twenty-six, regardless of whether they were from cities or villages, not only was the mix of ethnicities not a problem, but multiculturalism was appreciated as one of the great strengths of their society.[23] Diversity was based not only on indigenous traditions; it was also a mix of Balkan and modern Western culture. Yugoslavs were not as restricted in their travel as most other citizens of communist countries. They needed no visas from their own government to study in the United States, shop in Italy, or vacation in France and Spain. In return, cities like Mostar were tourist destinations for other Europeans, and the locals spoke German, Italian, and Spanish for the sake of their customers. Given that flow of people and ideas, it's no surprise that in the former Yugoslavia, compared to other communist states, objective news was remarkably available. I found *Time* magazine at a Belgrade newsstand in the mid 1970s.

It's not difficult to find Bosnians like MEDIHA who speak both concretely and abstractly about the importance of multicultural values: *My best friend, with whom I shared a school desk for eight years, was Catholic, and I was as happy during Christmas as she was! I used to wait for her in front of the church when she sang in the choir. Our parents were friends. She'd stay at our house; you couldn't pull us apart.* Mediha becomes reflective. *Difference shouldn't be a source of conflict, just of richness. After all, other people can't make you poorer; they only let you see problems from another angle. There's no reason for people who think differently not to be able to coexist — even under the same roof. My mother had three children. We're totally different. The same people raised us the same way, but our political views developed through literature, theater, rela-*

tionships. . . . We have distinct ways of seeing the world, but we don't love each other less for those differences. Although Mediha is a member of parliament, her only child has joined a different political party—with his mother's blessings. *I fully respect his political stands, as well as his views of life, love, science. . . . I love him more for our differences. I learn from him because he has his own vision, and we can augment and enrich each other. Forcing single-mindedness results in a horrible deprivation of values for every one of us.*

Mediha is wonderfully facile at applying personal lessons to professional situations, and vice versa. *As an orthodontist, over the years I've looked at thousands of children's mouths, and I haven't seen two the same. That doesn't mean this mouth isn't pretty, or that smile isn't beautiful. The difference is part of the beauty.* From the dental chair to the halls of parliament: *I'm convinced people can find a mutual language for every issue. That's how I approach my political work. I'm sure we'll rebuild and find a way to live together, as we always did. I can't remember feeling negative toward anyone because he or she was "this" or "that." I approach people based on their thinking. If I can accept it, I build a friendship with those people. If not, I move away. But I would never consider destroying that person. I'm certain the majority of people think the same way.*

She ends with a light touch. Just before the war broke out, the father of one of her close friends died. She went to the funeral service, which was being held at a local cemetery with a large plaza, surrounded by seven chapels: for Jewish, Orthodox, Catholic, atheist, Protestant, Adventist, and Islamic services. Mediha stood, in a respectful pose, at the back of the crowd gathered in the Orthodox chapel as the funeral went on and on. Finally, someone who'd been at another chapel saw her and came over to tell her she'd been at the wrong service. In all the years, she hadn't realized her friend's family was Roman Catholic. *You see, in Bosnia, religion just didn't matter.*

Given the reality, from where she was living abroad, SABIHA could hardly believe the news of a so-called religious war breaking out back home. *People weren't prepared for this war.* In fact, even now Sabiha is not prepared. As she tries to sort through the categories of identity that surfaced during the war, she stumbles. *Especially Bosniaks, the people I belong to—although I've always felt I was a Yugoslav, a Bosnian, a European, and a citizen of the world. . . . This war has damaged Bosniaks—the Muslims—a lot, but it hurt Serbs and Croats too. Well, they're not Serbs and Croats—just Bosnians of a different religion.* Her own family is a case in point. *My brother's married to a Croat. My uncle, to an Austrian. My second husband was French. My daughter's married to an American. My aunt, to a Serb. One cousin is married to a Hungarian, another to an Italian. So who am I? There are seven nationalities in my family. What could be more beautiful? Bosnia has four religions and multiple ethnic groups. No one can convince me we can't live together, have tolerance toward each other, understand each other, love each other. We're like a meadow filled with different flowers — a mixture of the Orient and Europe, and something else that comes just from this soil.*

The connection in Bosnia between ethnicity and religion is not straightforward. To speak of "Croats" doesn't indicate practicing Catholics. The same is true of Serbs (who have a Serb Orthodox background) and Bosniaks (associated with Islamic tradition). Was this a religious war, built on religious passion? Hardly. Yugoslavia was a communist country for fifty years. Religion was underplayed, and at times downright discouraged. The war in Bosnia was no more about religious faith than the Troubles in Northern Ireland are about the authority of the Pope. Certainly the exigencies of war drove some people toward religion, either for solace or group identity. To paraphrase Greta's comment about her Jewish identity, if villagers were Muslim enough to be driven from their homes, they may well have felt an increased identification with Islam.

The temptation to develop a thesis of prayers devolving into war cries is repeatedly and resoundingly quashed by the women, who assured me that religion didn't guide most Bosnians in their decisions or actions. That being said, religious institutions took on a prominent position within the new nationalist movements throughout the Yugoslav republics, with priests appearing at pre-election rallies and often using (or abusing) religious ceremonies to urge their flocks to vote a certain way in the elections. Despite this, although they spoke extensively of religious differences, not one woman of the twenty-six named religious identity as a dividing element in Bosnian society or as a cause of the war. In addition to pictures of Tito and family members, one home might have the Virgin Mary on the wall, another a picture of a girl in a head scarf praying. In both cases the female symbol of the religion was significant, because rural girls were less pulled than boys into the public, secular Yugoslav world.[24] But religion in Bosnia had its strongest manifestation not in credos but customs, many rooted in Slavic folk traditions transformed to fit contemporary religious practice.

For Sabiha, the mix of religions evoked much more than tolerance. Appreciation for diverse traditions was distilled in the sounds of faith. *When I was in Sarajevo at Christmas, even though I wasn't Christian I went to church for midnight mass. Wherever I travel, I love to listen to a church organ and hear the bells. But to hear the voice of muezzin from the mosque at the same time — that's really something! It's fantastic! You hear an echo, as if it's coming from the sky. I never understood why Serbs wanted to destroy mosques, because this is wonderful music — the muezzin's voice asking people to pray and to respect God, nature, and each other. Who's so crazy that they hate church bells? It's priceless . . . spiritual food. You'll never hear the organ and bells and crier together anywhere else. This makes Sarajevo a very, very special city; but you had this also in Banja Luka, and in Mostar. It's uniquely Bosnia. That blend of sounds taught me to respect and embrace all religions. I thought people living next to each other and knowing all those cultures were so fortunate. That's why I was crushed when the war started and one community attacked another. I thought we loved each other. I couldn't understand how they hated . . .* [Her voice trails off.]

Not only is the notion of a religious war impossible for Sabiha. She goes further to stake out a claim for Bosnians as the European paragon of tolerance. *It's not true that Bosnians have always been fighting each other; we've known how to live together for centuries. When Jews were forced out of Spain, Bosnia gave them refuge. There's a beautiful story about how Jewish people came with the keys to their houses, hoping one day they'd go back to their country. They never returned, but the key became their symbol. The Sephardic language they brought with them still exists in Bosnia, and they still sing in the Ladino dialect.*[25] *I've been involved in many Jewish activities; they're carrying their culture across generations. A valuable copy of the Jewish Haggadah was kept in Sarajevo through the First World War, the Second World War, until today. It was saved by a Muslim man, who hid it from the Nazis.* Sabiha recounts how Jews inside and outside Bosnia organized support during the recent war through political, intellectual, and humanitarian actions.[26] Perhaps, she imagines, this was the result of the Bosnians taking in Jews during their expulsion from Spain, or protecting and hiding them during the Nazi era. After all, she muses: *What goes around comes around. We had a great community of Jews in Sarajevo. Bosnia may be the only place where Muslims and Jews are working together toward peace and cultural preservation. It's not happening in the Middle East.* Then she adds, with a smile: *Maybe we should go to Jerusalem — Bosnian Muslims and Jews — to help them out.*

It's a challenge to reconcile the women's tearful accounts of cross-ethnic cruelty with these stories of multicultural diversity, recounted with smiles and laughter. But then reconciling American lynchings with contemporaneous jazz clubs also requires some mental gymnastics. Staying with the comparison, American society hasn't seen intermarriage among Hispanics, Asians, blacks, and whites comparable to the Bosnian mix across ethnic lines. As in countries worldwide, a continuum of social tolerance existed in Bosnia, with countervailing forces of integration and division. I learned not to be surprised when the same woman shifted from telling me how Croats did this, or Muslims thought that, to emotional stories demonstrating unity among people from different religious traditions.

That theme comes through in Biljana's description of herself as a schoolgirl struggling with Latin and math. *The Catholic seminary for students preparing for the priesthood was close to my school. I went there for free tutoring, and no questions about my religion were asked.* A priest-in-training, Metodie, was assigned by his professor to be her tutor; he was from a small, distant village, so he often went home with Biljana for meals with her family. Biljana lights up when she describes him: *He had a round face, tiny round glasses. I loved his gentleness. And he was always smiling.* When it was time for Metodie to leave for his parish assignment in Germany, Biljana's entire family escorted him to the train station. *He'd adopted us–or we'd adopted him.* The tutoring had ended, but Metodie was part of the family. His leaving was an emotional occasion for all. *Metodie was a big influence in my life. I asked him one time how could he exist in a communist state with such a strong belief in God. (I was really nowhere, because I wasn't committed to God, and I wasn't committed to communism. I was just having a good time, I guess.) He told me, "What's most important is that I respect you as a person—who you are, what your beliefs are. As for this communist state, I expect them to feel the same way about me. So, if they believe there is no God, that's their choice. I'll respect it, but I won't believe it." He appeared to be comfortable with that arrangement, very much at peace with it.*

Biljana credits her mentor with teaching her tolerance, not only of atheism but also of other faiths. The tolerance, she insists, was not based on ignorance. Everyone knew everyone else's religious tradition and even helped them celebrate the holidays. Although she knew everyone in her Sarajevo neighborhood, she says: *I truly cannot tell you that I knew a communist, because the Communist Party forbade their members celebrating religious holidays. I don't remember any family in my neighborhood that didn't celebrate those holidays.* In Biljana's family, that meant new clothes for Ramadan. But no other celebration compared with the Catholics'. *We were so happy for the Catholic girls, in their white dresses, with white gloves and a little white cloth, like a hankie, on top of their heads. We would wait outside their homes. Although we didn't go to Mass, we walked alongside them on their way to church, holding their hands—so proud they were celebrating their first Communion. The excitement was infectious.* She has an Orthodox version of the story as well. *My neighbor would fill my little skirt with colored eggs. Eggs were a rarity, unless you had your own chickens. I walked home with a whole skirt-full! We were happier than the people celebrating Easter!*

The argument that the Bosnian conflict was essentially an age-old religious war wears thinner and thinner as Biljana speaks, comparing other cultures with the Bosnia she knew as a child. Years before the conflict started, she would ask her American friends, *"Why do the Irish have problems? Where I grew up, all people were respected."* And the United States? *In Colorado Springs, someone comes for a facial, looks up at me, and asks "Do you have Jesus in your heart?" That would* never *have happened in Bosnia.*

I realized, as I studied the transcripts of the interviews, that the women's accounts almost exclusively concerned religious holidays rather than the content of their faith. In contrast to a scholarly theological taxonomy or an index of creeds, the women's personal stories provide a wealth of understanding of community life. The stories were so similar across rural and urban spheres, age groups, and ethnic/religious lines that the tales became their own litany. Biljana's skirt-load of eggs spilled into similar stories from Galina, Jelka, and Karolina, tumbling willy-nilly across geographical regions as well as faith traditions.

Like Sabiha, from a Muslim family, RADA, Serb Orthodox, did not only tolerate cultural differences. She cherished them. Like others, her memories reach back to childhood with her best friend, Kika, the younger daughter of the family next door. *We were always at each other's house, and she's remained my friend all my life. When she and her husband were expelled from Pale* [the Bosnian Serb stronghold just outside Sarajevo], *my mother and brother took them into our home. It was an awful risk for my brother, because he wasn't a member of the Serb nationalist party. One night he transported the furniture from Kika's house into ours. That could have meant death, because our house was surrounded by the strongest Serb extremists.*

We never had religious-based problems. I developed a love for Islamic culture and tradition in Kika's house. Something silky runs in my veins. In my mother's house, coffee was always gulped down, then everybody left. But I'd go to Kika's home . . . [Rada's face lights up as her hands describe every aspect of the scene.] *Her mother made coffee and served it on beautiful copper trays. We'd sit for hours on the "sinija"—the settee that goes around the walls—and drink that coffee.* That something "silky" in her veins is the Islamic-oriental influence on Bosnian life, whether rural or urban. Every district had its own mosque. Guests were invited to enjoy their coffee with dignity, while servants tended to the water pipe.[27] *Kika's family never said things like, "Don't lean against that cushion 'cause it's been starched and ironed." The setting was always warm and quiet, typical of Muslim homes, where life was slow and peaceful. There's a local saying, "No worry, no hurry." In those houses there were rooms upstairs called "chardaks," with high windows so there's a view all around. When I had my own flat, my house was full of all that oriental furniture, as well as copper plates, prayer beads, and other typical Muslim things.*

Given the disconnect between such personal experience and the wartime propaganda, Rada—who is, after all, a documentary filmmaker—goes on to reflect on the meaning of cultural differences. *Before the war, different ethnic groups co-*

existed. Especially in the rural areas, people knew who was Serb, Croat, or Muslim. But it was just for identification purposes. The differences didn't affect our living together. Sure, the most important thing was that a Serb girl not marry a Muslim boy, or a Croat man [Rada is laughing]. *But young people did marry whoever they wanted, the world survived, and everybody was happy later and accepted it.* Just how thorough that acceptance of others was is reflected in Rada's experience later, in the heat of the war. *As a Serb staying in Sarajevo, sometimes I heard people say, "There's that Chetnik woman."* She tosses off the insult with a psychological interpretation: *I could somehow understand. People who were suffering so terribly had to express at least a bit of resistance. Apart from the Serbs, there was nobody toward whom they could direct that feeling. I didn't let it get to me.*

IRMA is not so gentle. *Who cares about these categories?* She asks defiantly. As a young adolescent on summer break just before the war started, she remembers hearing about the conflict brewing in Slovenia. *They were talking about "Serbs," "Muslims," "Catholics," and "Croats," and I couldn't understand it. Then I started to learn among my Sarajevo friends: he's Muslim, she's Serb, she's Catholic. I'd never thought my friend's name wasn't Muslim or Croat or anything else. And of course with mixed marriages, you have mixed names.* And now, after all she's been through, Irma has a simple request: *I just want to respect my friends who have another religion, and I want them to respect me, too. We're all just human.*

As difficult as it's been, Irma's life stretches before her. She hasn't yet raised a family or launched a career. In contrast, there's DANICA, from a town not a city, expressing the same theme as the girl fifty years her junior: *Before the war nobody thought about what ethnic group they were. I never understood what Serb, Croat, or Muslim meant. I grew up in Slovenia and spent forty years in Bosnia as an adult, but we never experienced intolerance because we weren't Bosnian. People wanted to be closer to us because of our differences. People today are saying we didn't live together. I can tell you: People in our region lived side by side happily, regardless of religion or ethnicity. I'll never, ever believe this was a religious war.*

Some would say Danica must be idealizing the past. After all, if life was so copacetic among ethnic groups, how could the society have shifted so suddenly and exploded in war? Danica could only clutch at her carefully constructed life as it was dragged off its trajectory. I saw in her face the psyche of a weary state emerging from years of terror. *When the war came* [Danica's voice is much lower, more subdued], *everything suddenly changed. There were no more "Croat," "Serb," or "Muslim," but "Chetnik," "Ustasha," and "Mujahadeen"—insulting names for people who'd lived together for years. We were still the same people, but nobody could see it anymore.* Considering that she's been living in exile, unable to return to her Serb-controlled town, her measured words are particularly remarkable. *Sure, there were always differences. But we didn't hate each other; that was the most important thing.*

Danica closes with another emotion, even stronger than her sadness: *I'm just so afraid the war might start again.* For every woman in this volume, a return to that madness is a powerful threat, but the conflict is not necessarily linked in their minds to hatred among groups. Ironically, many of the stories of multicultural life they chose to tell me are drawn from the war years. Below, three more women describe experiences of cross-ethnic support that prevailed in spite of the exigency of war, although they may be couched in past memories. KAROLINA begins with a declaration: *Sarajevo has always been "multi" in every way. I married a Muslim from an old family. The house in which I live is hundreds of years old, and I entered as a young Catholic girl. According to my husband's family tradition, for religious occasions they'd slaughter a sheep. But we also had Christmas trees. I bought eggs for coloring, because I wanted my children to know my customs and my religion. When my husband died, I buried him according to Muslim customs. That was his life and origin. But I made sure our children knew both religious traditions, and then the choice was theirs. My son wanted to be a Muslim. He wanted to continue where his father left off. That's how he feels, and I respect that. If I go to the cathedral, that's my choice.*

Karolina lives in the old part of town, where she's one of the only non-Muslims. *During the war, we shared a basement shelter. Across the street from me there was a Hadjija—a well-off Muslim who has made the pilgrimage to Mecca. Somebody from an Iranian organization visited him.*[28] *It was the month of Ramadan, when Muslims fast until sundown. They were writing down names of people to be given food in the afternoon. As a gift, he put my name on the list, saying "You're part of our family. You mustn't be hungry. When we eat, you have to eat with us, even though you're not Muslim." Of course the organization took my name off the list. I didn't belong to Muslims or Catholics, so I didn't get anything from their organizations. But my neighbors didn't forget me, even though the Hadjija was killed in the marketplace slaughter.*

While the war was going on, my daughter got married, then had a baby. It's the custom here that when you give birth, people bring presents. My next-door neighbor came in the afternoon. He's from an old Sarajevan family. He was in his mid-fifties, too old to be drafted into the army but still active in the local community. He called me "Lina Hanuma," using the Muslim title for the lady of the house, and said, "I can't buy anything, but every day at six o'clock, I'll bring twenty-five liters of water for the baby." The neighbor had difficulty walking because of problems with both hips; Karolina's home was on a steep hill. *It was really far for him. He had to go down, cross the river, fetch water, and come back up the hill. It took more than an hour, but every day he'd bring that water for my granddaughter.* And then, giving me time to let the meaning of these impossibly conflicting loyalties soak in, Karolina adds an understatement: *Life is interesting.*

Interesting indeed—and baffling in its blend of goodness and evil. Stories like Karolina's turn conventional wisdom on its head and debunk the image of a hate-filled population, even as gruesome ethnic cleansing and barbaric shelling of the capital continued. Like Karolina's daughter, Ana's child VALENTINA married and gave birth in the midst of political upheaval. She tells of their time in Belgrade, trying to escape the danger in her Bosnian village. In the heart of Serbia, Valentina found a doctor who gave her the finest care she could imagine as her pregnancy progressed. Beyond the medical help, she's still moved by memories of that care. *If he could have, he would have shared my labor! It didn't matter that they were Serbs, and I was Croat, and we were at war. The whole hospital—all the nurses and doctors—were wonderful. They probably took even better care of me than the other patients.*

As a doctor who fled with her children just as the war we breaking out, FAHRIJA chafed at being on the outside of the need as her husband served as one of the seven-member, multiethnic Bosnian presidency. From the Albanian royal family, she insists that growing up in Yugoslavia meant having friends of different religions, both at home and at work. *Ethnic distinctions were never an issue, to me or my children.* She describes a project she undertook while a refugee in upstate New York. *I went to the hospitals and spoke to my colleagues, asking for donations of medicines. I told them that earlier, when I worked as a volunteer in a public hospital in America, I never cared whether a person was black, Hispanic, or Irish. I helped everyone. Now my people needed help. I asked for samples of medicines you get from drug factories. I hadn't known what to do with them when I worked as a doctor in the U.S., but now my people needed them badly. You wouldn't believe how much we were able to collect. One colleague wrote a check for $10,000. Some brought instruments and other medical supplies. Twice we collected several tons of aid. We paid for two doctors and four nurses to come to the U.S. to learn cardiac surgery and brought over children needing medical treatment that couldn't be provided in the war situation, making it possible for many to have surgery on their eyes, arms, and legs—giving them another chance for a happy childhood.*

Fahrija managed to recruit forty doctors to go to Sarajevo. *My husband made arrangements with our Ministry of Health, but the doctors ended up stranded outside Sarajevo with tons of equipment, unable to enter the city because of the constant bom-*

bardment. They could have waited months, so I told them to give the equipment to the hospital in Zagreb, Croatia, and come back—even though at the time we were fighting the Croats. I just made sure the people in Zagreb didn't know I was behind it. I figured the medications weren't for politicians; they were for people who were victims of this madness, no matter what group they belonged to.[29]

In our interviews, there were as many such stories of cross-cultural experience as we had hours to spend. Each reinforced the other, adding to a compelling argument that for most everyday Bosnians—whether educated or not, rural or urban, Orthodox, Catholic, Muslim, or Jewish—life at both public and private levels was not built around differences. Such a statement is much more than a negative. It's an affirmation of the richness of coexisting or blended traditions.

II

To Heal History

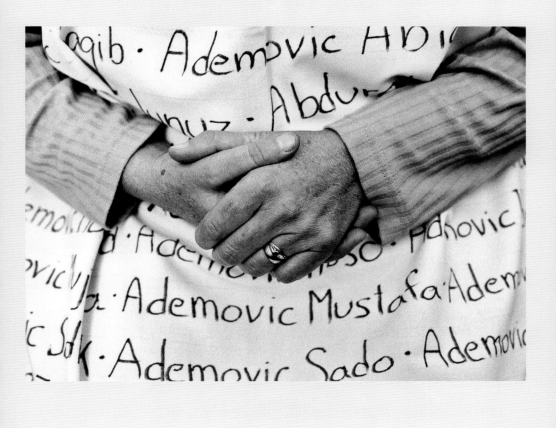

Shattered blessing. December 1995.

II

To Heal History

GRETA: *I never thought about ethnic categories before, and my parents didn't think of them. But now, when I read a list in the newspaper, I immediately start analyzing who is who. I've changed. War does that. It's an infection we constantly have to fight.*

ALMA: *My mother was the pillar of our home, with us when we were ill to make tea or put a compress on our foreheads. When we were older, she'd check on us a hundred times, as if we were little. I could confide in her. In her, I see thousands of mothers. If all soldiers were women, there wouldn't be so much bloodshed.*

VESNA: *War caused this hatred among people, but we can overcome this. Time will heal. First the economy will bring us together. But just think about it: Even after all we've endured, we have new mixed marriages. You see, love has no borders.*

MAJA: *Women never would have started this war, and if they had, they would have completed it much less painfully and faster. As a doctor, my profession is to love people. Our town is divided, but love doesn't know borders.*

MEDIHA: *I died millions of times during those years. Every one of us did. I was humiliated as a human being. But now I speak as a doctor. We have this gray brain matter, and all our abilities are there. We have to share them with others, out of gratitude. And those of us most gifted must do more.*

The wartime experiences recounted in part 1 were followed by the women's fiery convictions as to the causes of the war: the unabashed greed of politicians, a policy and practice of privilege that tilted the social balance, and media transformed into a powerful machine, churning out fear for political purposes. They ripped apart the idea that age-old, intractable, ethnic-based hatred made war inevitable. In fact, they described that reasoning as a convenient excuse championed by Milosevic and misguidedly adopted by many within the international community.

It's easy, from the outside, to see the failure of the international community to respond, particularly when thinking about Kada waiting for her Samir to come stumbling out of the woods around Srebrenica, or Maja, crying as the boat left harbor with her two teenage sons, or Emsuda, tending to the psychological scars of her family after their ordeal in the concentration camp. Our failure to respond was a failure of political leadership. A critique of the international community, however, must not shift the blame from those who caused the war.[1]

But analysis of the causes and identification of the culprits is not enough. There's rebuilding to be done, for the sake of the women's families, their communities, and their country. In chapter 5 in this second part, the women assess the formidable challenges before them. They move on, in chapter 6, to describe a few of the many projects they're doing to stabilize postconflict Bosnia despite those challenges — work wrapped in down-to-earth wisdom, rooted in basic values of compassion and fairness, and fueled by hope against seemingly insurmountable odds. The war in Bosnia is not sui generis. However local the women's efforts, there are global lessons to be drawn. Part 2 ends with reflections on the basic building blocks of reconciliation: getting the truth out, establishing justice rather than revenge, and humanizing the enemy — principles as applicable to Colombia, Congo, or Cambodia as they are to Bosnia.

5

Challenges

MIRHUNISA: *There's such a concentration of evil, and not a lot of good. Women do a noble job just existing in this dirt. Coming out of it clean is very difficult.*

MAJA: *Democracy is coming in, as we say, through very narrow doors.*

DANICA: *We've got a long, long road ahead of us.*

Danica's metaphor struck me as particularly apt. That long road stretches into uncharted territory for Bosnians, into a democratic political system and free market economy propelled by advancing information technology — all three new phenomena. The travelers are already traumatized as they begin the journey to a place unfamiliar and which they can't see. In many cases, they're on foot as others speed by. Some — the most attractive — may be able to hitch a ride. Others may simply drop by the side of the road. With the opening of the new democracies, the first out of the cage were the predators.[1] The journey, then, is even more dangerous for those not prepared to defend themselves along the way.

History can be transformative, but only when its wounds are dressed by healers unwilling simply to move on to the next crisis. Learning from the past for the sake of the future is an organic process, often birthing new concepts and institutions. The Great War spawned Woodrow Wilson's attempt at a League of Nations. The failed League was revived in the United Nations, when the War to End All Wars was followed by World War II. The atrocities of that war birthed the Anti-Defamation League, which applied its fight against anti-Semitism to dangerous stereotyping far beyond explicitly Jewish concerns. Highly respected humanitarian groups such as the International Organization for Migration and International Rescue Committee had a similar origin. The Marshall Plan grew out of the assessment of a U.S. general-turned-secretary of state that a new foundation for the European economy had to be built from the ashes of war. And members of the North Atlantic Treaty Organization responded to their disastrous experience with the Soviets following World War II by not only creating a defense structure, but also making unlikely allies of France and Germany, and eventually Turkey and Greece.

The same principle — looking to the past while building the future — applies at an individual level. What is foul must be uncovered, acknowledged, and examined so that new life can grow and replace the decay. Postwar Bosnia faces a long list of immense challenges as it emerges from not only the war but also decades of communism. Its controlled economy resulted in a lack of entrepreneurial experience and no intrinsic incentive for testing new ventures. A political power structure that quashed opposition produced a passive electorate. A network of state-run social programs bred psychological dependence. Fear of an extensive secret police force discouraged citizen-led initiatives. A tradition of political favors created a society in which marketeering and corruption are rife. Add to these challenges half the population displaced; 60 percent of the housing stock destroyed; utilities, factories, and transportation systems heavily damaged; and the tremendous toll of war trauma. It's remarkable that Bosnians are moving forward as well as they are.

Open Wounds

EMSUDA: *A wife or child wants something, and the husband can't get it, so he becomes violent. The wife covers it up. Then the sons become aggressive toward girls and other boys in the classroom, as they've seen their father. It's a chain reaction.*

TANJA: *After any war there's violence in the family, because people are psychologically wounded. Even we who could be called "normal" have been traumatized by the war; there isn't a single family in Bosnia that wasn't touched.*

ANA: *Let me tell you, our war was bad for those who didn't lose a family member: mother, father, brother, sister. . . . But those who lost someone in the family will remember this war forever. Forever.*

VALENTINA: *When we came back home, we were still afraid, but at least the shooting was over. You don't know who to be afraid of in wartime. Sometimes I'm still afraid.*

MEDIHA: *Why did we need to suffer so much? Did that satisfy someone? Did it help us progress?*

The challenges of postconflict Bosnia are at the same time public and private, a complex blend of loss and love that the women must accept and integrate, more than overcome, as they create a new future. Families are subject to enormous strain in postconflict situations, and the communities that would otherwise support them are often dispersed. Women are dealing with rape, dislocation, an eroded ability to trust, and a longing for loved ones. Many men are psychologically and physically injured from battlefield experiences, often leaving the care for other family members to the women. In addition, difficult transitions occur when women become heads of households while their men are away, then again when the men return home, usually unemployed or underemployed.[2]

VESNA's story is not uncommon. When the war started, she was in her late thirties, a life stage that should represent consolidation and stability. Instead, her mixed marriage—she's ethnic Croat, he's ethnic Serb—went through trial by fire. *In our town, at the beginning of the war, the worst thing was to be a Serb, so my husband and father-in-law had to go to Belgrade.* Such a self-imposed exile was not uncommon. Serbia's population swelled with Bosnian and Croatian Serbs who felt unsafe in Bosnia and Croatia, as those newly independent states tried to withstand attacks by the forces under Milosevic's direct and indirect control. When Vesna's husband returned, he wanted to protect and provide for his family and to make up for time missed because of the war. That created new tensions at home. *My husband is a sports journalist. He still hasn't found work. My father-in-law lives with us, and the two of them are trying to give our daughter gifts to make up for those years in Belgrade. They spoil her. Love can't be bought. Those years can't be made up.*

Vesna moves back and forth between frustration and appreciation. *I wouldn't want my worst enemy to go through what we've endured. My husband is a great man. When he catches a fly, he lets it go. In this war he was deemed guilty not because of anything he did—just because he was Serb.* But regardless of his innocence, the damage has been done. *He told me that when he was in Belgrade, he saw how Serbs in so-called pure marriages, Serb-to-Serb, had a lot of divorces. Mixed marriages like ours had even more. When he came back, he asked me to decide whether to stay in our marriage or to divorce, and he would accept it because he'd been away throughout the war. It wasn't easy to start over. We were two strangers starting over at living together, and with a child. But my daughter adores her father, so I'd sell my soul to the devil before I'd get divorced.*

Like Vesna's family, Bosnian society has been torn apart. It will never be as it was; too much is lost. Psychological shock is the least visible result of war, yet it's felt at every level of the society. UNICEF and other humanitarian agencies report long-lasting war effects on Bosnian children. Psychiatric care for Sarajevans in the first postwar years was virtually nonexistent; and broken marriages, suicides, extreme emotionality, paranoia, flashbacks, and sleeplessness were reported across the former Yugoslavia. The irony, of course, is that several of the war planners were psychiatric practitioners. Perhaps their background gave them particular insights into tactics that were, literally, maddening for the victims.[3]

The world is a violent place for women, whether in war or peacetime.[4] But a war context allows for violent behavior that is otherwise tempered by civility. The violence is more a symptom of the war environment, rather than just bad behavior on the part of soldiers. For example, women and girls have been brought into Bosnia as sex slaves, and many of their clients are members of the international community. Trafficking is a booming business for organized crime rings. That social blight carries over to the way Bosnian women are treated at home.

Many activists point to a connection between domestic violence and war. The Belgrade war protesters called Women in Black insist that "when violence against women ceases, war will cease."[5] Not only are societies with high domestic violence a breeding ground for warfare, home violence also generally climbs as soldiers return, shaped by experiences at the front lines. Sex roles become accentuated, as men become warriors. Although quieter than the clamor of battle, a surge of domestic violence has been reported as soldiers returned home to a shattered economy and relationships under high stress. Alcohol aggravates the problem.[6]

None of the women I interviewed described herself as a victim of home violence (although I didn't ask directly, which was my oversight). But several had comments on the subject in the context of the lack of counselling services just when they're needed most, and the emergency hotlines now appearing. SABIHA gave me an example: *One night last week I couldn't sleep as I listened to a man beating his wife. She's a wonderful woman, taking care of the house and family. He's always drunk, and when he wants to go to bed with her she refuses, and then* [Sabiha makes the sound of a neck being broken]. *I beg her repeatedly: "I can help you. I'll call the police. I'll arrange things for you." And she says, "Please don't, because this place belongs to him. I've never worked. Where would I go if he decides I'm against him?" I say, "This flat is government-issued, given to him because he has family. It doesn't belong to just him."* But she says, *"No, no, no, I'll keep quiet."* The story is not anomalous. *Many, many women are not only beaten up; men rape them or call them horrible names. Communication between men and women has become ugly. It's worse now because of the war trauma and the horrible economy.*

Violence permeating Bosnian society is not only physical. Those who had to flee the war endure a constant emotional battering, as everyday tasks require titanic effort without support systems that have long since imploded. As courageous as they usually are, several of the women confessed to me moments of severe depression. DANICA describes her life as a refugee, longing for her home and stripped of her professional identity. Though able to organize and comfort others, she seems beaten down by years of frustration and discouragement. Her depression is almost palpable as she looks back on the tolerance—celebration, really—of different cultures coexisting in Bosnia during the past fifty years and compares it to the current situation. *Now everybody's blaming someone else for something. What is this evil that happened among Serbs, Croats, and Muslims?* No answer follows, so she tries to imagine the future. *After so much wickedness, after so much dying, after so much killing, if someone were to say, "We're going to recreate Yugoslavia just as it was, where we were happy and worked hard, where our children grew up . . ."* Danica has no end to her sentence. She begins to cry. She tries again to reconcile the irreconcilable. *Was our life together fake? Self-deception? I don't think people could have been so free and happy, so equal, if it were all a lie. But look: atrocities . . . so many dead people . . . even children . . . so much suffering. Now something has changed inside us.*

I know it's not "politically correct," but I'd be happy if miraculously there were three separate regions. A united Bosnia, but within it three areas—Serb, Muslim, and Croat—each with its own customs, habits, culture, religion, but everybody respecting everybody else. I know it's impossible. Everybody fights against ethnic separation. But if we could divide Bosnia into little squares and just put all Croats here, and all Serbs here, and all Muslims there. It would almost be a good idea. Everyone would know, "We live here. You live there. Let's not touch each other." A remarkable statement from a woman who, for years, has been focused on returning home, since her pipe-dream solution would require much of the population to move from their homes. Danica knows her idea doesn't make sense. She's just speaking as a woman who has for the moment despaired of alternatives. *As we are, I can't see the way out. It will take a very, very long time to feel as we did before. I wonder if I'll live to see that day.*

As if in a direct conversation with Danica, KRISTINA picks up her words. *All people really wanted was enough money to live — you know, to get up in the morning and go to work, take their family to the coast in the summer. They could have had that, but they were told they couldn't. Do you understand?* This schoolteacher, surrounded by the paranoid propaganda spewing from Belgrade across Bosnia, can look back now and say: *It was a big lie.* Lies can take on a life of their own, and Kristina surveys the ruin caused by a powerful idea like Greater Serbia. She describes how, immediately after the war, she brought humanitarian aid to her devastated hometown. She was grateful that her volunteer work gave her an excuse to return. *But to be honest, we didn't feel like moving back to Sipovo. It hurt too much, and there was nothing to go back to. Suddenly it was like a foreign place. Everywhere we looked, there was a reason to cry. Our flat was burned, and everything in it. I thought, if we're going to start over, we should go to a place not burdened with so many memories. But my husband was stubborn. Nobody was going to kick him out of anywhere.* [She laughs.]

For hundreds of thousands like Kristina, even after the war, simply making it through the day has meant a struggle to rebuild a life out of memories. *We came back, because he wanted it so much. But we had absolutely nothing. Nothing to sit on. Nothing to sleep on. I don't know if you can understand. We didn't have a spoon — nothing but our pride. Little by little, with help from friends and through perseverance, thank God we're making it now. Even in the thick of all the problems, we were always a happy family in a sense, because we had each other. But I hope we don't have to be tested like that again.*

Kristina and her husband returned to their home, two competent adults rebuilding their lives. But as teachers, they know the fragility of young psyches. Many Bosnian children went to sleep for years listening to bomb blasts after spending a day in a cellar where war was the constant topic of the adult conversation. But the damage began even before the war officially started. IRMA's father remembers how fifteen days before the shooting began, they saw their best friends, Bosnian Serbs, not allowing their young daughter to play with the granddaughter of Izetbegovic, the Muslim political leader. He and his wife were appalled, but looking back, he realizes how the seeds of distrust were spreading.

Irma herself, with a teenager's honesty, reflects on the lasting effects in her internal world, where trust and distrust vie for space. Despite thick resentments that must have developed during six months in a crowded basement, she puts aside the negatives as she compares the intensity of wartime with the pale mundanity of postwar life. *During the war, there was more love, because we were forced to be together and be friends. When you have so much time, you get to know a person — to like him, or fall in love with him. But now people are going their own way, thinking just about themselves. There's lots of pressure, and everybody's changed. Take my neighbors. I know them like I know my own face. But now, after all those days and nights together, it's just "Hello" when we pass in the corridor. During the war, we used to sit around, playing the guitar. Now I don't even see those people. They're all here, but it's like they've just disappeared.*

Irma has a difficult time talking about her friends. She starts and stops repeatedly, trying to find the right words. That difficulty seems related to the inconsistency she's experienced in her relationships. *As I'm getting older, it's becoming very hard for me to find friends that I . . . You know, when I was little, I could be friends with anybody. Now it's a little different, because I can be . . . I can know a lot of people, but friendship has a different meaning for me. I appreciate a friend more, because during the war I lost a lot of them. Now—and this may be left from the war—I often think something bad is going to happen to one of my best friends. Lots of my friends died. I was sorry they died, but you forget. And now, when I remember, I think of them. That's what hurts me, how people just disappear, just . . . It's so unfair.*

A psychologist wouldn't be surprised by what follows: *I don't trust too much any more. Before the war, some of my closest friends just left and didn't say a word to me. Why? One phone call wouldn't have been so much trouble.* Then she tucks in a statement about ethnic identity, a cue for me to the fact that her friends' leaving was more than betrayal or abandonment. It was Irma's first experience as the victim of a political act. *I didn't even know what "Serb," or "Muslim," or "Croat" meant before the war. I couldn't believe they just left without saying a word to me. I mean, they didn't say* anything. *Now I don't go around trusting just anyone.*

Irma goes on to a brief reflection on one of the deepest scars in postconflict Bosnian society: the split between those who stayed and those who left before or during the war. *Anyone can be my friend, no matter if that person was here during the war or not. But there's a difference. You know, sometimes when we sit and talk about the war, I get the feeling that my friend who's come back feels bad. She's uncomfortable. I'm not judging her. Maybe if I'd had the possibility to leave Sarajevo, I would have gone too.* It is an unusual statement. After all, Irma did leave, escaping through the tunnel under the airport during the latter stages of the war. However, she draws a distinction not only in terms of how long a person endured the siege but also between those who fled for safety reasons and those who left for political reasons, having been tipped off that the siege was about to begin. *Those friends who left before the war and didn't tell me anything . . . if I saw them on the street in Sarajevo, I wouldn't say "Hello." I wouldn't say anything. I'd just go right by. It's not hate. I just don't want to have anything to do with them.*

Beyond shooting, hunger, or refugees, war is about memories melted in the heat of firebombs, hopes crushed beneath the weight of tanks, and plans ground into dust by combat boots. The loss may be material or intensely personal. Sometimes it helps to sit with an interviewer and sift through a past now in ruins. I felt a sense of the sacred in my hours with KADA, who vacillates between grief and numbness in the aftermath of the loss of her brother-in-law, two brothers, husband, and son. *A person can't live with these feelings . . . but we have to.* Her words struck me as both contradictory and complete. Indeed, all the women I interviewed described thoughts and feelings that crisscrossed the lines of logic. An outsider like me could only absorb their lessons intuitively, not account for them linearly.

Given the barbarity she experienced, Kada's words seemed markedly tame. *Looking back, I'm disappointed with people and with our leaders. Before the war, I thought government officials never made mistakes . . . never told lies. But now I know they lie. I don't respect them any more.* Beyond her disenchantment and distrust of the political system, Kada has serious worries about everyday life, including concerns about her daughter and son-in-law, both unemployed in the postwar society. But at another level, she wears the wounds of war. *We had a good life—calm and peaceful. I used to be young in spirit. But what I've gone through has shaped me. I'm not that happy woman I used to be. I'm old. If it hadn't been for the war, I wouldn't be old now. Sometimes I wish I were standing in the shade of a man. It's the traditional way for a Bosnian woman. Sometimes I wish I had someone to protect me, at least for a minute.*

Kada wonders at the damage done to the society at large, then returns to her own experience. *Before, Serbia existed on myths. They applauded and supported "Slobo." And they believed Russia would help them—as it did actually, sending weapons and in lots of other ways. Now the country isn't rich any longer, and the Serbs are furious. They don't like Milosevic, because they're poor. And for me? Life isn't the same. The men that were killed—they were destroyed quickly. We women . . . we were also destroyed, but left to die slowly. Life without joy isn't life.* In fact, Kada spends her time mostly with other women who are mourning dead or missing men and boys. Sometimes, she confesses, she finds their company boring. On a recent excursion, she shared a room with two other women who kept telling her their stories. She left and joined the men in the restaurant, to play cards.

Kada may tire of hearing others' tales, but she's ready to talk to me about her husband and son, as a way of holding on to rich relationships now reduced to memories. *My husband and I knew everything about each other. We had no secrets—*

at work, or at home. We got to where we liked almost exactly the same things. Srebrenica has woods all around. I love nature—gathering mushrooms. He took to going out and picking mushrooms with me. I loved swimming in a small brook near there. He used to hold my dress while I was in the water. He'd spend the whole day with me out in the woods. [She pulls out of her purse a picture, sent her by her husband's cousin, of a dashing young man.] *I grieve more for my pictures than for my flat. Every detail is precious. He was medium tall, not fat, with Asian features, more like an Arab—dark skin with a lovely moustache and beautiful teeth . . . deep black eyes, wavy hair that eventually turned gray. He wrote beautiful poetry. I loved reading his poems. I tried to make him have them published somewhere, but he was writing only for his soul. Sometimes he taught sociology. He was a leader, always head or director or some important position. Whenever he wanted to change his job, he'd ask if I thought it was good for him, or if he could do it. I always said he'd do it better than anyone else, and it was always true. So we had a lot in common. Thirty years. We spent all our free time together. At parties, we'd sing then laugh and break our glasses. We both loved music. We loved dancing and playing. I loved romantic French songs . . . traditional folk tunes . . . Serbian, Croat, and Bosnian singers of the '60s . . . Greek . . . oriental music. Now I seldom listen to music. I just don't want to do those things. Sometimes I try to hum a song, but the beauty's gone. Then I start crying.*

In addition to the murder of her husband, Kada grieves for her son. *He was born in 1966. He grew tall. His hair was thin, like mine, but he had a beautifully shaped head, with full lips, a long face, and a thin nose like an eagle.* Kada sounds like mothers across the Western world. *I asked my son why he was listening to foreign music, because he didn't understand the words. He said he loved the rhythm. He'd put speakers in every corner and turn the volume way up. We weren't like a mother and son. We were friends, pals. He used to confide in me, telling me a girl had left him, and he was hurt. Once he was just sitting there, and I asked, "What's the matter, son?" "She got married,"* he said. *I told him, "It will pass. I've been through the same thing. When you're young and in love, there are ups and downs. That's just life." He didn't get married, just because of that girl. And then came the war, and he said, "It'd be stupid to get married during the war,"* which was true.

I wake up in the night and remember everything. I think of my son and don't get back to sleep for hours. When sleep finally closes my eyes, it's only for a short time. In the morning, I sit in my small room. I have my coffee and drink it alone. I have a cigarette. Then I remember how my son made smoke rings. I cry. And I wipe my tears in my loneliness.

Divisions, Devastation, and Donors

GRETA: *Someone recently offered to take me into Serb territory, to Banja Luka. I instantly felt a knot in my stomach — a vague, undefined threat — and I said, "No, thank you." That feeling is new, and I don't like it. Who is the enemy? It is our own citizens.*

SABIHA: *The only good thing about Dayton is that it stopped the war and accepted Bosnia as a sovereign state. But Dayton needs to grow with the times.*

TANJA: *I was against the division agreed on at Dayton. I told Mr. Clinton in person that we have many cultures, traditions, ethnic groups. Any division would be artificial.*

SUZANA: *Dayton was a success because it stopped the war . . . and a failure because it divided our country.*

MEDIHA: *We hoped the international community would somehow come in and make everything right. However, as you can see, after years a civil structure has still not been created.*

Concessions to the war makers in the Dayton Agreement, signed in Paris in December 1995, have compounded the emotional trauma of the war. On the one hand, the peace agreement was a success. As ALMA says: *With the cease-fire and Dayton, thank God, the guns stopped talking and the people started talking.*[7] But the peace treaty's constructive ideas were only partially enforced, thus deepening the divisions desired by the nationalists who led the war.[8]

The agreement was the result of a quick-moving series of events: The July massacre at Srebrenica had gruesomely highlighted the consequences of inaction by the international community. At roughly this time, President Clinton in-structed his advisors to solve the Bosnian problem, and the United States, led by Richard Holbrooke, began diplomatic negotiations. The Europeans and Ameri-cans were finally acting in unison: NATO was spring-loaded for action. Tudjman launched a blitzkrieg on August 4, with arms he'd been collecting in defiance of the UN embargo. The Bosnian army joined the push. After a mortar shell ex-ploded in the Sarajevo downtown market on August 28, 1995, killing thirty-seven people, NATO bombing commenced. The two-week bombing campaign struck Bosnian Serb army targets around Sarajevo, crippling their communications system. The fortunes of war had turned, and the Serb army—at last facing meaningful opposition—was on the run.

Some 150,000 lives had been lost, in part due to American foot-dragging out of fear of another Vietnam. This time, President Clinton declared, the United States would keep bombing until the Serbs lifted the siege of the capital and agreed to a cease-fire and negotiations to end the war. In the last three days of the bombing campaign, U.S. Ambassador Menzies in Sarajevo sent numerous telegrams to the secretary of state, urging him not to stop before the Serbs had retreated far enough so that Bosnia would not be divided.[9] Instead, the United States stepped in to save Milosevic and to keep the Serbs from being driven out of Bosnia. Under intense American pressure, the Bosnian/Croat army stopped their successful counteroffensive short of Banja Luka, allowing the Serbs to keep much of their conquest as "Republika Srpska." That controversial decision likely kept hundreds of thousands of Serbs from being routed from their homes or simply fleeing in fear; but it also protected and rewarded the original aggressors. Now rebel nationalist Croats wondered why they shouldn't have a separate chunk they could call "Herzeg Bosna."[10]

The U.S. diplomatic effort was a lifeline for Milosevic, who was facing a political disaster at home. Serbia, its economy already in ruins, was now burdened with Bosnian refugees who were both miserable and not welcome. In November, representatives from all sides met in Dayton, Ohio, to negotiate a new political system for the beleaguered land. Bosnian Serb President Karadzic had been indicted (although not apprehended) as a war criminal by the UN tribunal at The Hague. Milosevic took charge of the negotiations for the Serbs, pushing aside the Bosnian Serb delegation. He was a fitting substitute, since he had masterminded the start of the war from Belgrade.[11] The political world focused on the drama of a contest between the forceful and cunning Holbrooke, and the mendacious and wily Milosevic. No one was invited to formally or informally represent the women of Bosnia, who had been pushing for peace throughout the conflict. The goal was to get a deal as quickly as possible, to end the killing and stop the political hemorrhaging.

The Dayton Agreement, which established a governance structure for the postconflict period, required all sides to turn in those indicted for war crimes. That portion of the agreement failed for two reasons: It didn't provide an enforcement mechanism for recalcitrant local authorities who ignored or protected the alleged criminals, and under U.S. leadership the international military force made a conscious decision during the first years of its presence not to go after war criminals and turn them in to the international tribunal at The Hague. With many of those responsible for the depravity of the war left in place—some even as police chiefs and mayors—most refugees could not safely return to their communities. Thus the imbalance caused by ethnic cleansing in large part continued, and the large ethnic majorities strengthened the hands of nationalists. At the end of the day, despite whatever was written on paper about a unified country, Bosnia was divided between two "political entities": Republika Srpska (controlled by Bosnian Serbs) and the Federation of Bosnia and Herzegovina (controlled by Bosniaks and Bosnian Croats). The economy was in shambles. The population was grieving. Electricity was sporadic. Had Dayton been implemented, Bosnia would have been limping, but on the road to recovery. Instead, the military elements (separating of forces and turning in heavy weapons) were quickly enforced, while the civilian efforts were stymied.

In the spring of 1996, there was a general shuffle of populations in response to the maps drawn at Dayton. In some cases the shifts were voluntary; more often, they were sparked by death threats and other forms of harassment—by enemies, or extremist bullies within the person's own ethnic group. The most notable example is the exodus I witnessed of 100,000 Serbs from Sarajevo suburbs, after the neighborhood was defined as part of the Federation. They were both fearful of living under Bosniak rule and hounded by hysterical warnings of their own leaders that they would not be safe if they stayed. Thus DANICA, longing to go home, watched with enormous anticipation. But her hopes were dashed, as she was left to reconstruct life within lines on maps drawn by political leaders intent on keeping control of the territorial spoils of war. *In a way, a miracle happened at Dayton. But the Serbs didn't resist leaving towns given to the Federation. They had burnt everything they could, and no house was inhabitable. Refugees who had fled came over the weekends (if they were nearby) or once a month (if they were in Germany, Austria, Switzerland, or Croatia). Without water and electricity, they rebuilt their own homes. I know one town. I've no idea how they've managed. Some humanitarian aid, there are chicken farms . . . but people had to build a bakery and a post office. They're living an almost normal life—it's unbelievable—with the little money they earned in Germany or Austria. People came back despite everything, because it's still their home—and they had no other place to go.*

As Danica talked on about towns in her home region, I got the sense of a process that was almost capricious. *According to Dayton, one of the towns in my can-*

ton was returned to the Federation. Out of eight, just one. As if it were accidental. One morning, they said, "Odzak is back." None of us could believe it. I talked to a general from that area. "Have you heard?" he said. "Odzak has been returned to us by Dayton!" And I said, "My God, that's amazing! People will go back to my husband's village!" He told me, "My wife and my children called and said, 'Guess what! We're free! We can go back home!' Nobody can believe it!" Then he added, "But what good is it if we all return? What are we going to do with Odzak without other towns around it?" You see, those places are connected by the river. [She has been drawing a detailed map.] The entire populace used to work in a neighboring town. They need to go there — otherwise there's no industry. Dayton was signed, and that's that. This place is yours, but you can't do anything with it.

Danica wraps up, reflecting on the decade: During the war, every negotiation gave us hope. Even though little has been implemented, every person knows when the peace was signed. The greatest joy is, of course, that the war stopped. But if Dayton had been carried out, I'd be home. Instead, look at me. I'm here, just like the day it was signed, thinking the same things, wishing the same things. All these years since Dayton, so many people are waiting. I'll tell you what the agreement means: a little bit of luck, and a lot of sadness.

That failure resounds despite the international community's attempt to implement the agreement by setting up an office with a whopping seven hundred employees, larger and more expensive than the entire Bosnian government. Multiple nations lent personnel to the office, which meant short tenures (sometimes only a few months), constant turnover, and uneven talent. That inefficient force had an extremely difficult task, since the agreement provided for the country to be divided politically into two parts, essentially to satisfy the Serb aggressors. Assertions that refugees had the right to return with complete "freedom of movement" were undercut when half the country was allowed to be called "Republika Srpska" ("The Serb Republic"). The Serbs' unwritten expectation was clear: nationalist politicians would drag their feet on allowing non-Serb refugees to return until the international peacekeeping forces were pulled out. Then the Republika Srpska could secede from Bosnia and become part of Milosevic's "Greater Serbia." Croat nationalists would follow suit.

Squabbles inside the United States and with our partners undercut the goals of Dayton. The United States whittled down the mandate of the high commissioner, who, it was agreed, would be a European. But the American-led military refused to enforce critical civilian provisions of the agreement. These machinations have huge impact on the women determined to rebuild their country. Dayton *condoned everything that happened in this war by recognizing Republika Srpska,* says EMSUDA. On top of that outrage, she reels off other challenges, such as destroyed property, no jobs, and inept international aid organizations that run roughshod over cultural sensitivities and waste money, often doing harm while trying to do good. Despite her impressive organizational skills and fundraising know-how, she's frustrated with the parade of would-be helpers who move regularly from one world crisis to the next. *I can't stay in contact with the donors, because they keep changing.*

SABIHA chimes in. *In the past year, I've managed to get four women's projects financed by different international organizations. I was able to work without pay in the process, because of money I earned abroad, or I couldn't have helped them get started.*[12] *Most of the time, the donors give money to the organizations, but don't teach women how to use it. Or they give machines and money for production, but they don't help find a market.*

Many of the women—such as AMNA, in central Bosnia—point to the relationship between aid, economic hardship, and the inability of refugees to return. *The international community gives money to an international organization, and that international organization gives money to another international organization, then the other gives money to the local NGOs, then the NGOs give money to the construction companies, and the construction companies build houses. Every level takes a percentage. So if you have one million at the beginning, it could be half a million by the time it gets to the beneficiaries.*

Heavy middle-management cost is not the only problem with the delivery of aid. There's a gap between the plans of providers and the actual needs of the recipients trying to eke out an existence. *Returnees were promised their houses would be reconstructed. Not completely—just two rooms with electricity and water. They would've been completely happy with even that. But the international community gave them just the houses. And a house without electricity isn't useful during winter. And if you have a house but no employment, what can you do? You'll have nothing to eat. The houses were reconstructed by the end of the year. The next year they'll get electricity. The year after that we'll get to employment. It's too much to ask. Ultimately, the return of displaced people depends on the economy. But whenever we raise that, decision makers say something like: "Yes, but in central Bosnia there are thousands and thousands of returnees, and we have to feed them."* Amna distils her frustration into a policy formulation: *If you want aid to be sustainable, you can't dole it out in small pieces. If you're going to give help, then give help.*

Amna conjectures that even with a functioning economy, only half the displaced people will return to their homes from abroad. They've become relatively comfortable. They have new jobs, new neighbors, and the basics of a stable life. There's also a more pernicious reason people are still displaced: fear. After all, hostile acts—death threats, grenades tossed into houses in the middle of the night, intimidation by masked men—drove them from their homes. No one is guaranteeing them protection if they come back. *They know they'll be a minority when they return. And because of that they'll have problems with electricity, with telephone connections, with whatever. They'll have problems in a shop, when they want to buy something. Storekeepers will say, "There's nothing for you here."* That's all assuming they would have money with which to shop. As Amna explains: *Our economy is in deep trouble. Even many who weren't displaced are unemployed; and those with jobs, whether private or public sector, can't pay their electricity bills. They're not sure if next month they'll have the same income, or lower, or any at all.*

No situation represents a greater challenge than the restoration of the remnant of the community of Srebrenica, in eastern Bosnia. As a step toward eventual return, the international community has organized "confidence-building" visits, small steps toward normalization, such as an excursion so that expelled citizens can look at their former homes from a bus window. Widows from Srebrenica, including KADA, went back for an extremely emotional and politically charged visit to their hometown, now inhabited by Serbs who came from other areas, such as Sarajevo. The result of that population switch is a nonsensical mismatch of urban dwellers in a small town, and rural refugees living in the capital: *I don't know anyone who has an answer to our problem. The way things are now isn't good for Serbs or for us. I was in Srebrenica a while back for lunch with the Serb women who live there now. The spirit was tolerable. We were trying to understand each other. We didn't insult each other, but each of us talked about the hardships from her own point of view. Everybody blames somebody else. Nobody thinks she's guilty herself.*

The organizers were happy to keep this occasion as low-key as possible, but Kada isn't sympathetic with that careful approach. *Those of us who were kicked out of Srebrenica met the Serbs at the hotel. There was not a single journalist, no TV. I asked, "Are you hiding this meeting from your townspeople?" But I saw how in Srebrenica life is awful. It's a dying town. The streets have become narrower. Nobody cuts the weeds. All the mosques are destroyed. There was one called "the white mosque," with a graveyard around it. There were pigs running around—a desecration! When we lived there, not even chickens were allowed there, and the grass was always trimmed. We took a short walk, two or three of us. I asked the women living there: "Don't you believe in God? These are graves! Animals never walked around this place. Aren't you afraid of God's curse?"*

One of them said, "Hmph" and made a sign with her hands, like she was helpless. I don't know why they're not doing anything in Srebrenica.

Kada is appalled by the overgrown hedges, roses and grapevines running wild. *There are places you still can't walk, because they haven't been cleaned up. In such a short time it looks so awful. Just a few more cobwebs, and it would be a perfect setting for horror films. One street with the old, traditional houses that had craft shops was completely destroyed. They haven't cleared up the very center of the town. I cried when I was taking that walk. And when I looked at the building where my flat was, I wished I could go up there. Then I promised myself, "I'm coming back to live in Srebrenica."*

As homes have been reconstructed, they've been burned down again by Serb extremists. Mob violence, bomb attacks, beatings, and murder have increased as sporadic returns of refugees have occurred. Returnees have spent months in tents, waiting for construction materials from aid organizations.[13] In spite of the obstacles, Kada sees some movement. *I think they're now working toward return. The Serbs aren't using ethnic slurs anymore, but it seems to me it's because of money more than anything else. As it is now, in Srebrenica there's no life. It's impossible to live there until industry is restarted. They haven't even reconstructed the water supply or electricity. What was destroyed during the siege looks even worse now. They live in terrible misery.* In contrast, many of the homes deserted by the Serbs who fled the capital after Dayton now are inhabited by refugees from Srebrenica. The result has an ironic twist. *Even as refugees, we live much better than these Serbs who took over our town. We're living on their land here, near Sarajevo. We till that land. We work it. We trim the hedges, cut the grass, grow flowers. If they come back to their property, they'll find everything in order.*

It's difficult to figure out a good entry point to address such a convoluted situation. Donors who set up employment programs often taught women skills like knitting and sewing that would not enable them to be competitive in the modern labor market. In some cases, women with prior professional careers were offered courses that represented "de-skilling."[14] *I was a member of an NGO. At the beginning, it was like psychotherapy. Later we had some support from women from the States and from Canada that we were paired with. My "sister" in Canada sent me a bit of money—about $20 a month. Half went to the organization because they were supposedly training me. The idea was to train women in some skill so they could support themselves. But these were rough skills, like upholstering. A woman isn't fit for doing that. She could do it, but to be trained, she should have an upholstering workshop. Instead, they put up some old sewing machines, and they had an old retired man with trembling hands to teach us to thread that old machine. One day they brought a curtain* *to be made. That old man was teaching me, but I told him that I could do it myself. I made the curtain. They spread it out and took a picture of it—as advertising for the project, even though I already knew how to sew before. I left. It was useless. A lot of projects are complete failures. It's a misuse and an abuse. Four or five well-educated people running a program, earning big salaries. They aren't teaching anybody anything new. It's just a way for the humanitarian aid professionals to justify their salaries.* And then comes the obvious conclusion, an understated warning to would-be helpers. *The donors should be careful.*

The flaws of the aid delivery system pale next to the flagrant postwar corruption and abuse of power of Bosnians themselves, with estimates of up to a billion aid dollars having been stolen by government officials from all three ethnic groups. Millions were unaccounted for by Izetbegovic's party officials. Croat extremists siphoned funds to create parallel political structures in their proposed territory. And indicted Serb leader Radovan Karadzic purportedly has special police on his payroll.[15] Meanwhile, KRISTINA describes how she's trying to survive on a small stipend that doesn't cover her bills. She adds ruefully: *People who before had nothing are suddenly rich, while my family, who was stable, is barely surviving.* Despite these challenges, Kristina is optimistic about the difference she can make in the rebuilding of her hometown. A Bosnian Serb herself, she describes how a Muslim schoolteacher—her former colleague—came back to Sipovo for a meeting, after having fled to Sarajevo as a refugee during the ethnic cleansing of the war. *When the rest of us saw her come in, we all hugged her and cried. I think that says it all. Men would never have done that.*

Olympic Village on the outskirts of Sarajevo. December 1995.

6

Women Transforming

ALMA: *A Muslim woman — by religious rules — should be only a homemaker. But Bosnian women work. It's not like Algeria or some other place where they're fighting for basic rights. We should help the women of Kabul. Bosniak women are an inspiration for women all over the world.*

AMNA: *When I went into technical engineering, I was told, "That's for men, not women." They said I'd never finish, but I did — and graduate school too. Still, women hold themselves back — women themselves! We've got to be tough!* [She pounds the table, smiling.] *We girls have to be ten times better than boys to be recognized as equal. Fortunately, that's possible.*

MIRHUNISA: *Balkan men say my work is men's work. Well, if it's men's work, what does that make me? And how do I know how to do the job?*

EMSUDA: *At some point women just have to take over situations and make decisions. We've got to take responsibility.*

BILJANA: *Every woman will tell you: If women were ruling the country, there would never be a war.*

When over five hundred women gathered in June 1996 in the capital of Bosnia, they called their conference "Women Transforming Themselves and Society." At the request of Nurdzihana and other planners, I helped secure funding and keynoted the conference. This was the first such attempt at bringing citizens together across ethnic lines since the signing of the Dayton Peace Agreement in Paris six months earlier. I didn't tell the planners I found the name of the conference overreaching.

I was wrong. At a conceptual level, the women were correct in asserting how critical they were to the postwar transformation that lay ahead. Their importance was at least threefold: They held key jobs as professionals and academics, exerted great influence on their families at home, and one in five actually headed a household.

But the women were right in another sense as well. The grand optimism of their conference title was matched by their determination to turn rhetoric into reality.[1] They were successful in spreading the word of the gathering, even though telephone (and fax) service was unreliable for technical reasons and blocked for political reasons. Many delegates made their way across illegal military checkpoints from Republika Srpska, risking retribution against themselves and their already traumatized families. Clearly these were women with a mission, embracing the huge problems staring them in the face. In doing so, they were transforming themselves—from victims, into healers.

For all the frustration that comes along with mending of a war-wrecked society, in my dealings with hundreds of Bosnians I saw how those who felt themselves engaged and acting with purpose had the greatest opportunity for joy, however minute or grand.[2] In that sense, Bosnian women leaders were typical of hundreds of women across the new democracies of Eastern Europe who came together for another conference I organized in Vienna in July 1997, called "Vital Voices: Women in Democracy." Women across the region have coalesced in new alliances, leading the large majority of NGOs that have emerged as the building blocks of postcommunist civil society. This development makes sense to ALENKA, who comments, *Women have smaller, but more concrete agendas: everyday life, homes, children.* But she goes further to apply the principle to stabilizing a fragile post-conflict situation. *We have common ground with women across any divide. We don't fight in the army or think hierarchically, and we reconcile easily. We're not afraid to go to the other side. Maybe that's because everyone knows we weren't carrying guns; we weren't in the death squads.*

JELKA chimes in. *Women bring a positive, hopeful perspective into the family. That's important since now, after the war, there's still a fear among young people—especially boys. Long after the shooting stopped, my younger son still couldn't cross the bridge to the western part of Mostar. Young men were being murdered, because they had been soldiers. It took a long time before he dared cross, even to visit his grandparents. Since men were in the military, it's not easy for them to recreate relationships with their former enemies. That's why women are the solution!*

Jelka is suddenly energized by the thought of women moving into leadership.

I can't stand seeing only men in the parliament, deciding on maternity leave and how much freedom they want to give women. I'm not too old to start changing things. During the war, I frequently went to donate blood. Men fainted, and women propped them up.

It's not only a fascinating question but also an important one, whether women are better suited to deal with the delicate and dangerous situations of war. MAJA, a physician and administrator maneuvering life in the middle of the fighting in Mostar, believes so. *I knew how to handle the paramilitaries who got out of control. I'd have them sit down, offer them something to drink, and tell them everything was OK. Finally I'd see them off, and we'd all take a deep breath. It was a different way of resolving conflict. Men are more aggressive, but women are more courageous.*

Jelka's and Maja's strong views about women's abilities are widely held. Of the twenty-six women I interviewed, all but one insisted that Bosnian women were committed to values antithetical to the war, and that now that the war is over, they are a force for the restoration of their country. In the United States, religious institutions have been a primary training ground for women whose lay service has been a stepping stone to political and civic leadership. In contrast, Croatian women in Zagreb expressed to me their unease that Tudjman's nationalism had given the Roman Catholic Church greater influence in Croatian society, with a concomitant theme of bringing women back to the hearth. I heard the same concern addressed in Belgrade with reference to the Orthodox faith, which was being nourished by Milosevic's nationalism. In Bosnia, intelligence reports described Islamic extremists requiring that women receiving aid cover their heads, a step toward keeping them "in their place." Thus the circle was complete. War fueled the influence of traditional religions that demanded the withdrawal of women from decision-making positions where they might be a moderating influence on the war.

Pulling against those pressures, the women I met with are leading essential community-based initiatives — running for office, helping the traumatized, repairing houses, producing a radio program, directing a summer camp — despite daunting challenges. VESNA sounds at first like any energized activist. *Whatever I've been through, there are others who've endured much, much more. They somehow manage to keep on. So how can I think of giving up? I'd lose a lot — not society, but me.* But when she talks matter-of-factly about starting an NGO, she does so as a woman traumatized by being on the run for years: reunited with her husband, who was severely beaten, then in exile; caring for a father-in-law who lost part of his leg to a land mine; working in a society without a tradition of charitable organizations; dealing with a scandalously inflammatory press; depending on unreliable outside donors; and enduring discrimination in a culture where women are trivialized. In short, organizers like Vesna are overcoming obstacles that I, as an onlooker, could never fully appreciate.

Joining the Political Battle

NURDZIHANA: *"Can't." Politicians always "can't" do something. The truth is, this current situation suits many politicians. They have more wealth and power than ever, and they want to preserve that status.*

KAROLINA: *Women stop conflicts by negotiating. They negotiate with their husbands all the time. When a man wants war, his wife doesn't; so she'll try to stop him. Pity we don't have more women in politics. Problem is, men don't trust women. They think they're the stronger sex; but—except physically—we women are stronger in everything.*

JELKA: *In Mostar, any good effort can be destroyed in an instant by politics. But through organizations like mine—and the work of women—we can pressure our politicians from the grassroots. A politician can never identify himself as the leader of the whole population. There's an alternative to whatever he does—people like me, who don't agree with him.*

MEDIHA: *There's plenty women can do in politics, here and everywhere else. No country is so richly endowed that it needs only half its brainpower. But we need to fight not to be left out of the game. Imagine a country doubling its brains, by including women.*

After the war, Bosnian women choosing a political route to help stabilize their country were swimming against the strong current that swept away the strong gender representation prevalent in most socialist countries. Women were not integral to the inner sanctum of policymaking before the transition from communism to democracy. But as a new chapter of freedom was being written, ironically, Eastern European women found themselves even more poorly represented. Although communist parliaments were little more than rubber stamp bodies, women were at least visible, their presence ensured by state-imposed quotas. To some extent, that ruse was pernicious, since communist leaders could crow over gender parity when the reality was quite different. But women's stature decreased significantly as the pretense of political representation was replaced by a transparent reality of nonrepresentation after the fall of communism.[3]

In Tito's Yugoslavia, women tended to be well represented at the lower levels, such as urban councils, but their numbers decreased as the government body became more politically important. With the demise of Tito, the number of women in upper-level government across Yugoslavia plummeted.[4] But women continued to organize, for example, protesting the wars in Slovenia, Croatia, Bosnia, and Kosovo. In May 1999, women in southern Serbia took to the streets to demand that their sons and husbands not be sent back into Kosovo, sparking widespread mutinies that helped undermine Milosevic domestically.[5]

To further strengthen the voice of women in Bosnian politics, in 1998 I invited Nada and five other women to help organize a conference of women across Bosnia's political parties. The five women, representing the three largest nationalist groups, a women's party, and two multiethnic coalitions, came to Washington for a series of meetings at venues such as the State Department and the U.S. Institute of Peace. Their parties' leaders had caused incalculable dislocation, loss, and pain to the Bosnian people. Still, over the course of a several-day collaboration, the five put aside their reasons to hate and managed to find common ground. Returning to Bosnia, our organizing group invited every political party (dozens had sprung up) to send representatives to a conference I chaired in Sarajevo, titled "Women: A New Political Future." Two hundred women came from over two dozen political parties—a remarkable 40 percent from Republika Srpska, many visiting the capital for the first time since the beginning of the war six years earlier. This conference, cosponsored by the Organization for Security and Cooperation in Europe and my private foundation, helped create a momentum. One result was a rule requiring that women be one in three candidates distributed evenly throughout all party lists.

Similarly, in December 2000 I chaired a meeting in Belgrade to reunite more than ninety women from across the former Yugoslavia who had organized democratic election campaigns to oust the nationalists who'd brought ruin to their country. In all these gatherings, the women were filled with energy and ideas of what they could do to promote women's role in politics. Frankly speaking, engaging in electoral politics meant joining bad company. For example, after being a local leader in the prewar Communist Party, MAJA left the political scene when it turned nationalistic in the early 1990s. That decision led to the loss of her hospital management position. *When the rigid parties were formed, I dropped any political affiliation and put my white physician's coat back on. As a human being, I found it too constraining to belong to a party just out of nationalist sentiment. I completed my term of office, handed over my things to the HDZ, and went back to my professional work, which I'd never stopped anyway.*

Now Maja is free to say: *I want to speak frankly, with no political agenda—although all life is politics, and you can't avoid it completely.* Even more interesting is her commentary on the relationship between gender and politics. *When I was appointed to political office, I knew it wouldn't last forever, so leaving wasn't that difficult. It's easier for women to give up official positions without psychological complications. Maybe that's because I always believed I was first a mother, then everything else. That's basic to my framework somehow. Men are motivated more by careers, and belonging to a party is a precondition to advancing those careers. Women are probably less ambitious in that way. Their views are more refined.* Maja seems ambivalent about leaving politics, in part because she wants to stand up for women. *In Bosnia and Herzegovina it's always been hard for women. When I chaired meetings where I was one of just a couple of women, I'd say to my male colleagues, "I envy you. You don't have to be smart and elegant, and you can vent all you want." I could never behave like that. Still, today I'm the only woman doctor working with eight men.*

One of the scars of the war is the great increase in ethnic-based divisions. Damage in Bosnia extended beyond the official war years. During the conflict and immediately afterward, I frequently met Bosniak leaders of government and business who took pride in pointing out to me their closest colleagues who were Bosnian Croat, Bosnian Serb, or from a mixed marriage. But in the years following the Dayton Agreement, which reserved political positions for people who identified themselves by ethnicity, nationalists controlled the agenda and ethnic identity became much, much more important. The powerful SDA political party, for example, devolved into a group of Bosniaks led almost exclusively by men, many of whom were widely suspected of corruption and who demonstrated very little of the vision required to restore the multicultural society that existed before the war. Sitting next to me at the one-year memorial service in Tuzla for those massacred at Srebrenica, an SDA leader dismissed the extraordinary role of TANJA, who was calling the world's attention to the plight of the 30,000 Bosniak survivors. "But she's a Serb," he muttered, with disdain.

Tanja was a member of the seven-person Bosnian presidency, but after the war she rejected the nationalist Serb line and insisted on an independent affiliation. That decision cost her a public role in the postwar government, since the new regime was essentially the spoils of the nationalists on different sides. Tempted to abandon politics altogether, she observes: *If everybody who wants a better life did that, we'd get nowhere.* She remembers the war years. *I was the only woman in the highest rank of politics, although we have a lot of educated, multilingual women who could have filled those jobs. Women are much more flexible, and they bring charm into negotiations. They constantly think of life rooted in their concern for their families. But at high-level meetings, I don't see a single woman except Madeleine Albright. It's a disaster, a parade of one man after another after another.*

Given her stint in politics, Tanja has done considerable reflecting on the gender aspects of her experience. *Men can't stand having accomplished women around; but women, too, are reluctant. Many are oriented toward their husbands, and they don't easily accept a role outside. The problem doesn't stem from school. We have a lot of educated women. But in our tradition, a woman's place is at home. This view of women permeates society. Seldom can you find women executives, although before the war there were women managers of companies—more than now.* Tanja's words reminded me of a visit I made to the city bread factory a week after the war ended, at the suggestion of President Alija Izetbegovic. After a fascinating hour with the five managers, during which they pointed out to me their ethnic diversity, I pointed out, in turn, that they were all men. They seemed surprised that gender was raised as an issue, then gave me examples of women in positions of leadership before the war. The men, however, didn't see anything strange about a workplace with 70 percent of the general employees women, and all six of the highest decision makers men. Hence the importance of Tanja's final thought: *Unless it's legally mandated, men will never let them have their rights. Women need to speak out more.*

That same spirit of obligation is shared by MEDIHA, who represented a liberal multiethnic party as the only woman in the National Parliament immediately after the war ended. *We women are a force no one can stop, but we have to fight for our place, even in our own parties. We can't just wait around to be invited.* Meanwhile, NADA, representing Biljana Plavsic's party, was one of two women out of eighty-three members in the Republika Srpska parliament.[6] She's much less intentional than Mediha, describing herself as swept into public office just by not refusing to be on the party list. But she adds: *We women were merely decoration. During the war, all that mattered was that a politician was a nationalist. I thought I could change that, but I couldn't.* Nada didn't fight to maintain her place on the party list, and for the next election she was dropped down to number thirteen. Her party won twelve seats.

Nada's discouragement about whether women can make a difference is not uncommon. There's a camouflage effect as women who rise within male-constructed and dominated systems often assume characteristics of the men they depend on for success. In addition, the prevailing role expectations (based on male performance in those roles) demand compromises in content and style. Afraid they'll not be taken seriously if they "act like women," many try to blend in with the men around them. Their reluctance to express countervailing perspectives diminishes the mix of ideas brought to the table. The larger the number of women, the less they need to act like men. To build the numbers, VESNA, with Nurdzihana, helped organize a League of Women Voters of Bosnia and Herzegovina, to encourage women to run for office and to vote. The organization formed a partnership with the American mother organization, which conducted training sessions for Bosnian women.[7] The Bosnian League has taken on issues of particular concern to women, such as maternity leave, asking women in parliament to band together across party lines. Can such an unusual initiative succeed in a former communist country? *We can, we have to, and we will,* Vesna asserts.

Bosnian women have found ways to be politically active despite the extreme challenges of war, engaging inside and outside the official system to help restore their country — and restore themselves in the process. In addition to participating in humanitarian projects that aided people of all ethnicities, FAHRIJA organized a letter-writing campaign to President Clinton even while she was a refugee in Buffalo, New York. *I know he didn't open all those letters, but somebody had to, and so I was helping spread the truth about what was going on in my country.* Similarly, while living as a journalist in Moscow, in addition to gathering aid to send home, SABIHA gathered signatures from over a hundred Russian intellectuals to protest the war. Sixty showed up for her press conference to demand a lift of the siege of Sarajevo by the Serbs, even though they were political cousins to the Russians. Despite her own activity, Sabiha isn't optimistic about women in politics. *I've been working with women's organizations for twenty years. I was president of several, and I've thought a lot about the psychology of all this. There's a lot of hypocrisy. Women don't stand up for women political leaders. There's solidarity among male politicians, but not among women — even though women are the most vulnerable.*

Women may be more successful at political action from outside, directed at the system. MIRHUNISA worked with refugees from the Srebrenica massacre, to help them organize into a potent political force. *There were various groups, each identifying itself as representing the women of Srebrenica. Trust was a challenge. How could I convince a woman who'd lost her whole family, "Listen to me, I'm telling you the truth!" A group came to my office. I told them, "You can't accomplish anything piecemeal like this. You need an official association. You've got to organize, form a committee, create an initiative." That's how these associations of women started. Later they had some problems, but that scene in my office was the most important moment I ever witnessed.*

KADA has been one of the leaders of that grassroots political movement. She describes how tens of thousands of people waited in 1995 for help by the international community. While the Serb army forces tightened their noose, a natural leadership selection process was underway within the UN-designated "safe area." *We had to get organized — out of the clear blue sky. Simple people had to take charge to try to protect us. We created some diversions and stole a few weapons from the Chetniks, but we didn't have any way to defend ourselves. Forty guns among us, and we were surrounded by tanks.* As if the victims must answer for their victimization, she asks: *What could we have done? Is there some genius out there who can say?*

The Bosniaks who had gathered from the surrounding rural area had been left to their own devices as their men and boys were rounded up and executed. But now the women were in charge of their own survival. According to UN estimates, some thirty-five thousand women, elderly, and children flooded into Tuzla, where they waited in tents on the airport tarmac, anticipating the arrival of thousands of boys and men who had, unbeknown to them, been massacred. *We asked the government officials where the men were who had stayed behind in Srebrenica. We went to the International Committee of the Red Cross and the Red Crescent.*[8] *When they didn't want to listen to us, we took to the streets and protested.* Week after week passed. The women became desperate for word of their missing sons and husbands. Their protests became noisier.

For Kada and her wounded community, inaction is dangerously close to complicity with the aggressors. Years of fear and deprivation during the siege of Srebrenica, followed by a melee of widespread rape and killing, were capped off by an international community that mostly ignored the needs of victims. We can ensure that international troops have gymnasium equipment to keep morale high, while traumatized women and children are lucky if they have four walls and a roof to keep them dry. The survivors have formed several associations and launched dozens of initiatives — including street protests that paralyze the traffic in the capital — to pressure local and international governments to respond to their plight. Progress has not been in a straight line. Distrust among different groups of survivors has led to infighting. Local politicians have used the survivors for their own purposes. But Kada keeps at it. In a sense, political action has moved into the space left vacant by the destruction of Kada's family. *Now we have an organization to look for the missing, to demand an answer about the fate of 10,000 people. As an individual, I can't do anything, but as an association we're strong.*

Opting for change, not charity, Kada has learned that political action is not only about influencing others. It's also about preserving her last shred of self-

Mostar cafe life. July 1997.

respect. That sense of self is critical, for ultimately she has no one to turn to except herself. *If I hold myself back, I can't expect someone to come along and rescue me.* In fact, even comfort from others comes at an unacceptable price. *No one can feel the pain of my wound. They can only show compassion. Then I feel like I've become a beggar. I feel better when I protest.*

Easing the Anguish

IRMA: *In the war, women were calmer. They faced it: "Okay, we have to survive.*

We have to eat. We have to find water. We have to figure this out."

GALINA: *Talking to people touches my soul, and then I know what to do.*

Several women I met with are running programs addressing the physical and psychological anguish of war survivors. They understand that trauma is the enemy of trust, and that trust is a basic building block in the reconstruction of their society. For example, returning from her own concentration camp and exile experience, EMSUDA made a point of visiting other refugee camps. *I saw people I knew—intellectuals and entrepreneurs—now destroyed, just staring into the mud. They asked the same questions a hundred times, or wouldn't say a word. I thought to myself, they need me.* Emsuda trains community organizers who must work in a context of fear of indicted war criminals still on the loose. She includes among her trainees Bosnian Serbs, a difficult feat for a woman who endured a Serb concentration camp. In addition to her training workshops, Emsuda has founded two nongovernmental organizations and arranged educational opportunities outside the country for hundreds of Bosnian children.

Along the same lines, during the war, KAROLINA organized an art group, really to maintain her sanity, she says. As the siege stretched on, year after year, friends brought her paints and brushes through the tunnel under the Sarajevo airport, which teenaged Irma used for her escape. With about $600 from the Open Society Institute,[9] Karolina furnished a studio from a space with all the windows blown out. Now her group puts on exhibits and sells crafts. Even though she can't make ends meet, the profits from the sales go to support the mentally retarded. *I've gone through some hard times, but the colors I use are vivid and bright—which means I still have some life inside.*

In addition to her political work, VESNA has helped start a church-sponsored NGO called "Antonia," using sewing and knitting to raise funds to take care of vulnerable people, particularly elderly and women. Professionals among the volunteers offer various services and training. *The women we help arrive uncertain and timid, but they leave feeling like they've received the greatest gift in the world, just because someone took the time to teach them.* In Mostar, ALMA has organized women veterans of the war, like herself, to create jobs (in greenhouses, for example) and to support each other emotionally as they deal with problems such as posttraumatic stress disorder, from which she herself suffers. *We're the women who stayed in the country throughout the war instead of going somewhere and waiting for humanitarian aid. All those days and nights in the trenches, rained on, rescuing people, nursing them. We'll overcome our trauma now only if we have jobs. We don't yet have the laws and regulations we need. But then a wheel can't roll 200 miles an hour. Slowly but surely . . .*

In the heart of Republika Srpska is GALINA, caring for refugees in Banja Luka. The city was mixed ethnically before the war; during the war, it became a Serb stronghold. When I talked with Galina about the mosques and Roman Catholic churches that were razed,[10] she said she doesn't want her home city to be singled out as a symbol of Serb aggression. Instead, she insisted that the physical destruction and the flood of Croats and Muslims leaving the city was the unfortunate result of Serb refugees pouring into Banja Luka from other regions and forcing non-Serbs out of their homes in the city. She wanted to be sure I know that one million Serbs have left their homes. *Who knows how or why, including 90 percent of the Serbs in Mostar and Tuzla.* Galina seemed unaware that both cities she named were being shelled by Serbs during the war.[11] It wasn't fruitful to get into a back and forth with her about who started what, and who reacted to whom. Whatever the order of the expulsions, she says, *It was really hell.* In our conversation, she let wars become intertwined across decades, underscoring the cumulative psychological and physical effect of deprivation and violence. *Some people went from one war into another without being aware the first one ever stopped.* Galina echoed the sentiments swirling among ethnic Serbs throughout Yugoslavia, as the media and politicians revived memories of World War II concentration camps in Croatia, where hundreds of thousands of Serbs perished. *Half the local people I've talked with were in camps. They keep saying, "In that war, mothers and fathers were killed, just like now." There was a lot of mistrust. And when there's mistrust, it's easy to manipulate the citizenry.* Ultimately, however, it's not propaganda or politics but people Galina cares about. *I've seen so many tortured faces and held the hands of honest, hardworking peasants. Even under socialism, they always suffered most. Some of them never had enough to eat. And now they're hungry once more, and again there's war. They say, "First my father, now my grandson."*

By mid-1995, Franjo Tudjman had built up a strong fighting force to expel the Serbs occupying a large portion of Croatia. A ground offensive of combined Croat and Bosniak military, together with NATO bombing, drove the Serbs back. Now Serbs were fleeing the same areas from which Croats and Bosniaks had earlier been driven. As the fortunes of war reversed, streams of Serb civilians poured into Banja Luka ahead of advancing Croat and Bosniak troops. Galina's wartime and postwar work was sparked by scenes passing on the street beneath her. *I saw so much from only one window. The stories are almost endless. There was a vocational school near my house. Serb refugees from Croatia started coming there in late 1991. One cold and rainy night I looked out and saw some cars and tractors, with women and children soaking wet. It was dark — around 9 P.M. — when I went out to see who they were and where they came from. They were sitting in the bare school corridor, hungry. Everything was closed — shops, the Red Cross office. Nothing was being organized. My home was across the road. In my fridge I had a packet of margarine, some lettuce, a little bread. They needed much more, but with my half a loaf I fed some kids who were the hungriest. The next day I took them some cookies, and I started looking for their lost family members. They didn't know where their fathers and mothers were.*

That was the day I started this work, and every day since I've been with the refugees. In '93 and '94 they came from central Bosnia, around Sarajevo, and near Mostar. We filled the schools as makeshift shelters. In '95, ten thousand people arrived in one long stream. Twenty-four hours earlier all those people had been in their homes, frightened. Now they were homeless, and who knew for how long? If they had been vagabonds, maybe I'd have felt differently. But they were people like me: teachers, professors, doctors, landowners. Children who were well cared for, with their own beds, toys, TV sets. Suddenly they'd lost everything. They were hungry and afraid. The images were surreal. Tractors loaded down with furniture, people, and pigs. Lines strung up for drying clothes. Old women knitting in the middle of it all. A few of us women took some hot loaves of bread up to a truck. Someone said, "Hey, lady, bring us that bread! There's an old woman here who hasn't eaten for three days." But at another, a man said, "Forget the bread! There's a woman here we need to bury; and take this new mother to the hospital." The grandmother had died on the truck, and the granddaughter was lying there in blood from giving birth.

Galina created a system of emergency medical response, bringing doctors to the refugees' trucks or tractors, or to the "collective center" set up in the school. *The doctors examined hundreds of children; we'd take the sick ones in our car to the hospital. Then we began visiting the hospitals. The wounded men were soldiers and were taken care of by their families, one way or another. But the wounded women . . . In '92, women were injured either on the front line or by snipers and shells from across the river. Some had been imprisoned in their houses and in camps.*

In the face of this suffering, Galina created the NGO "Duga" ("Rainbow"), gathering some seventy women at a time to commit for one to three years of service to the most vulnerable among the refugees. The members operate with the guiding principle, she says, of do no harm — which seems rather rudimentary until one remembers that "Duga" is operating in a world in which violence has become, if not the norm, then commonplace. They provide everything from direct care to hand-knitted sweaters. Galina gave me one of their handmade dolls when I visited her in Banja Luka. With proceeds from sales, they managed to get an office. But this is a shoestring operation, with volunteer members compensated occasionally with the likes of an $8 bus ticket, or perhaps a meal.

It's clear, as she speaks, that Galina's focus is on the individuals she's helped. She's opened herself up to the pain that now permeates her city, and one story follows another: *A woman refugee had a baby in Banja Luka. While she was giving birth, they removed a tumor. She lost a huge amount of blood. We took care of her in the hospital for three months, and I brought her to my place to bathe her. The day after the operation she learned everybody from her region had had to evacuate. She didn't know if anyone had survived or if she'd ever see them again. Many of us made calls to help her look for family members. Through an NGO, we found her husband in a camp in Croatia. She was desperate to get a message to him.*

Galina's word portraits are painted with not only vulnerability but also human connection. *One young woman was so modest and miserable. We'd tell her, "No, we don't have clothes, but we do have some flour." But whatever we offered, she'd say, "No, I don't want that," or "I'll come back tomorrow." I finally realized — and explained to our psychologist — that what she needed most was to be with people, and if she was given the physical things she needed, she wouldn't have a reason to come again. Every time she came, I'd hug her. I think she was coming for that touch — that small touch of life. Once I took her into the kitchen and asked her, "Who are you? Where do you come from? Where's your husband?" She said her husband was on the front, and she had no word about him. She had a small baby. Her mother-in-law was calling her names. It was a general mess. She was so fragile; she actually just came to hear some kind words directed toward her. We worked with her about six months. I used to tell her, "You just sit here on this chair. I'll look after things. Don't worry about anything." If there'd been an earthquake, I would've stayed there with her. It felt good knowing I was helping someone who needed me.*

The first time I met her, in early 1996, Galina introduced me to half a dozen Serb women who related to me terrible experiences they'd experienced during the counteroffensive. One of those women was Radmila, from a nearby village. Galina told me more of her story. *She was with about twenty other people, mostly women and children, in a house. The Muslim "Green Berets"[12] threw a grenade in, and then massacred them. She fell first, and the other bodies fell on top of her. After the voices of the soldiers stopped, she crawled out. She was the only one who wasn't killed, but she was severely wounded. The night of the attack, she'd sent two of her children to her mother's place in a Serb village, so they survived.*

For two months, she was in shock — couldn't speak. We learned she was five months pregnant, and her husband had been killed. Father-in-law, mother-in-law, uncle, sister-in-law, three brothers-in-law — they were all killed. I used to bring soup to her, or trim her nails and hair, with other women from Duga. We asked her if she wanted to see her children. She didn't react. But the nurse noticed that at 3 o'clock she'd start looking toward the clock, probably expecting someone. That was the first sort of communication — visual more than anything else. Some emotions were awakening. Eventually she said to me, "I want to see my children." So we brought them to her. [Galina begins to cry.] *She said that for months she'd been afraid they wouldn't recognize her, because they were small, and she was so scarred and in a cast. In fact, the girls didn't recognize her at first. They said she wasn't their mother.*

When it came time for her delivery, Radmila was still in bad shape. She practically gave birth between the orthopedic ward and the delivery room. For two more years, she was on the orthopedic ward, trying to heal her legs and arms. She grew psychologically stronger alongside her baby. Galina maneuvered through the war-choked bureaucracy for Radmila, helping her to secure a place to live and open a small shop. *Now she and her sister-in-law are raising their six children. The other day, she passed her driving test. We've supported her for over three years.* It's precisely this sort of extreme vulnerability that Galina is devoting her life to address. *We identify the hardest cases, because we can't help everyone. We organize into two groups: one for logistics, clothes, food, etc. The other works on psychological rehabilitation, which takes longer. These seven years, we've helped five hundred women, spending a full year, on average, with each woman. We select cases where many members of the family have been killed, including a lot of war orphans. We've also worked with raped women. That's profound trauma. A group of thirty-six women from Posavina needed much more care than we were able to offer them; they were shuttled from one shelter to another. And I'm especially sorry for elderly people. These have been hard times.*

To be sure I understand that she doesn't buy into the idea of ethnic-based separation, Galina says: *Duga has helped Muslim families too. We brought them a Muslim doctor, took them coffee, clothes, and food. We notified the International Red Cross, who visited them and tried to get them back home. We didn't have the authority to give them back their houses, which are now full of refugees; but as the Muslims were leaving Banja Luka, I felt it deeply and personally. My uncle, a Muslim married to a Serb woman, went to Denmark and my family feels terrible about that. They were rich and lost what they had. We didn't have enough food, and there was mistrust. But they weren't kicked out of their house. They left because they couldn't handle not having enough to feed their grandchildren. Their son is in a mixed marriage; they couldn't go to Muslim cities, because the wife wouldn't be accepted.*

Listening to Galina's account, I wondered how closely her uncle's version of his story would match hers. In the moral confusion of war, Galina's stout effort may have to be couched in myth so that it can bear to exist at all. That doesn't mean her work isn't essential, and, indeed, laudable. Though she fails to acknowledge the ethnic cleansing that drastically changed the composition of her city, she tells me: *We worked with women of other ethnic groups — Muslims and Croats — who remained in Banja Luka when their families had fled. They've trusted us, and we've visited them in their homes. We thought it best to go to them. Usually those women are alone. Women stay in their homes till the last minute, after their sons and husbands leave. It's important that they know—and their neighbors know—there's someone behind them, supporting them.*

Galina's analysis of the place of NGOs is sophisticated, given that no such organizations existed prior to the war. *An individual can't give the same support as an organization. From '92 onward, we've offered all kinds of help. Duga was the only women's NGO. We applied to foreign sources for funding for lots of projects. In '97, seventy-four outside organizations visited Duga. The next year we had twenty-five more than that. We applied to about thirty of them, but we only got help from five.* Galina is in a particularly tough position, because U.S. aid was conditioned on Republika Srpska's compliance with the Dayton Agreement—for example, letting refugees return to their homes. Harassment and intimidation occurred on all sides, but in the first two years after Dayton, 8,551 Serbs returned to the Federation, compared to 1,125 Croats and Bosniaks to Republika Srpska.[13] That meant a large disproportion of postconflict aid to the Bosniak/Croat–led Federation. *We've conducted seminars in how to develop businesses. And we've met with organizations in the Federation, because they were way ahead of us in that type of training.* One of the groups with which she met was the feminist collaborative that produced the magazine *Zena 21* in Sarajevo, started by Nurdzihana, with help from Rada. *I was really sorry the international humanitarian organizations didn't come into Republika Srpska until the end of '95, when the peace agreement was signed. By then the Federation already had a lot of projects; but we were alone, fighting for recognition.*

During its first year, Duga gave temporary assistance to more than a thousand people, while about eighty women who had suffered severe war trauma received long-term aid. Galina describes her motivation: *Knowing that people are in need, that there are helpless people who are suffering. I do only what little I can and never promise more than that, because then I'd be traumatized myself. Just to give a hot meal, a cup of soup, some warm words, or schoolbooks makes me feel better. That's a gift from the women I help. I write a lot of funding proposals, but working directly with people is best. In all the turmoil, there may be fifty women asking for food or clothes. At least I can talk to them, give them warm socks or a sweater, or write a letter to look for somebody's son. I was the first person from here to join the International Red Cross, and I was thrilled when we reunited some families. That's kept me going.*

Bringing Them Home

GALINA: *Everyone wants a little piece of earth under the sun.*

SABIHA: *What's the meaning of human rights or of multiculturalism without the return of refugees? To speak of justice is to speak of bringing people home.*

At the heart of the most gripping hardship in postconflict Bosnia is the right of refugees to return to their homes. Viewed from opposite sides of the war lines, the struggle is the same. As these women described to me their work they spoke in one voice, insisting on the right of every person to go home. Slain children, parents, or lovers can't be brought back to life. Severed limbs don't reappear. Physical and mental trauma will not be erased. But the survivors can be allowed back into the precious familiar—the homes from which they were driven. More than regaining property, this is an issue of psychological restoration.

Upon her graduation from the university, AMNA set to work on projects to reintegrate minorities into her home area of Mostar, dominated by Croat nationalists. *A house has a completely different meaning here. If you destroy a man's house, you destroy his possibility of returning to that place.* She ignored the common wisdom that the war-shocked populace would never return. *I found homes that were in good shape—I mean with a door that opened.* Amna searched until she located the original, displaced owners, then claimed their homes, arranging for security as well as construction materials. *You should have seen their faces! A destroyed village—no electricity, just one well—but they were singing, they were so happy to be home.*

DANICA, still living in exile (since her home is now part of Republika Srpska), has poured her energy into supporting refugees to keep the Croat diaspora connected and hopeful as they wait for the day they can return. *When a needy person arrived, I wanted others to automatically say, "I know someone who will help you."* She contrasts her years of waiting with Kosovar refugees, who ignored UN workers warning them not to return. *We were punished because we played nice, waiting for years and years for someone to figure out a way around our problems.* Meanwhile, Danica has gathered refugees like herself in Croatia, helping them think through how they'll organize their communities upon their return. Her eyes fill as she concludes, *When we gathered for the dinner I put together, it seemed to them like they were no longer refugees, because they were among their own. You see how a few unimportant people can create an evening that means so much to others.*

ALENKA, a practical civil engineer, works for Mercy Corps, providing shelter to returnees. But ultimately, she understands, refugee return is a matter of tolerance and compassion as much as bricks and mortar. *Look, if you wanted, you could pick a fight with your own mother, but that's not the point. As for the women in our program, I know their opinions, so why ask? We'd just argue and get nowhere. It's much better to have indirect influence. So we bring women from both sides together. They have a good time, form new friendships, then change their attitude much more than if we'd argued with them.* Alenka can speak from firsthand experience. *When trauma's fresh, arguments are useless.*

Having fled from her home ahead of advancing Croat troops, KRISTINA returned to find 50 percent of her town and 80 percent of the surrounding rural area uninhabitable. Her home was in ashes, but that didn't keep her from reaching out to others. Since 1992, she's been part of the Association of Serb Sisters,[14] distributing clothing and food to refugees. As a provider, she's distributed international aid to thirteen refugee centers. Having also been a beneficiary of help, she has incorporated into her work in Sipovo the lessons she learned on the receiving end of charity. After school hours (she's an elementary school teacher), she works with needy and handicapped people—mostly children—pulling in help from the British troops stationed in that area to guard the peace. *Whatever I ask for, they try to give.* In fact, Kristina says the soldiers are more helpful than the international humanitarian groups. In a pointed contrast, she notes that her organization is made up of volunteers, a fact not lost on the troops who provide Kristina and her friends transport. *They bring us out to the farthest villages. They give us secondhand clothes and go with us to make deliveries to the most vulnerable.*

Vulnerability is a concept Kristina understands firsthand as she directs her work toward children, who, she says, suffered most in the war. Her second priority is women. Kristina has looked beyond food and shelter to help women like herself, whose dignity has been destroyed along with their homes and families. *Women need to return to normal life, so I asked the British troops to help me organize a fitness club. They said it was too expensive, so I asked them to help me with an aerobic center for women. They were so surprised! One of their soldiers was trained in "step aerobics," and they suggested we start with twenty women. It was unbelievable. When we announced our aerobics class, eighty women crowded into our gym. The soldiers said they hadn't agreed on so many, but I said I couldn't turn them away. Every Monday and Friday we have an hour of exercise. I can't thank* SFOR *enough.* When the unit rotated out, the military hospital physiotherapist agreed to double as the aerobics teacher. *The therapist has also come with us to visit very old or disabled people, including children with cerebral palsy. She's helped ease their suffering—a little, at least. She even promised to try to provide a chair to support the children, since they can't sit or stand or even hold their heads up.* Kristina goes on to describe her difficulty, first begging for help from humanitarian agencies, then deciding who of the most needy will be the recipients.

Against that backdrop of intimate involvement in the community, Kristina discusses the return of those who left because of the war. At first she sounds optimistic: *In Sipovo, we were 18 percent Muslims and maybe 1 percent Croats. Muslims are coming back and having no problems. Sipovo is an "open city."*[15] As a Serb, she's proud: *It's a stark contrast to most places I've heard of.* But she also knows the problems she faces: *A lot of humanitarian organizations supported this work at the beginning, but now they've all gone. Of course others want their help, but we need it to establish some sort of a life for returnees. The problem isn't finding people who want to return, or a community wanting them to come back. There's the physical reality. What are people going to do? They need to earn money to support themselves. So what if you're in your home? If there's no economy, you're not going to make it.*

The international community shouldn't be surprised that returning people to their homes isn't easy. It's been years, and they've built another life. For them to return would be another displacement. Maybe they just want to forget. Most of the returnees are older people, who couldn't start again after the war, or the poor, who didn't earn anything in their time abroad. Her reasoning is accurate but incomplete. She doesn't mention the difficulty of those who've survived terror or torture returning to a region now bearing the name of the perpetrators. Leaving past politics aside, Kristina focuses like a laser on the here and now. *Do you understand what this is doing to the structure of the community and how much the war devastated us? We've lost the people we need to rebuild this country. Our most educated people have left and created another life. Now we hear that they're trying to exchange or sell the damaged houses they left behind. It's like cement on top of our future.* She adds: *That's true for all three ethnic groups.*

Kristina's words are personal and emotional as she describes not only the damage to her community but that within her closest sphere. *All the members of my family were refugees, and nobody else has returned.* She doesn't blame her brothers for not coming back. *This problem has so many levels — and no simple answer. They don't have a place to return to because their apartments are destroyed. It's so hard to re-create a normal life. Look at me. Everything I had was burned. But there are worse cases and more vulnerable people. The economy is dead; people have no way to earn any money. Everything they had is destroyed, and even if they do manage to make a few pennies somewhere, where do they buy a pot, a bed, or a blanket?*

She says some of her Muslim and Croat friends are not coming back. *But it's not because relations are strained. You know, some people don't want to live in a place torn apart by war.* Kristina wants to be clear: She doesn't believe the problems in her hometown are because of discrimination. *I was raised not to hate anyone. As much as I can, I try to assist any vulnerable person in any moment . . . no matter the ethnic background. When we received a donation of clothing from* sfor, *we distributed it to the Muslims as well as the Serbs who returned.* Ultimately, for Kristina, the key is personal: *I'm thoroughly content, and I don't envy people who have more than I do. In fact, I'd love to see as many wealthy people as possible, so they don't need to ask anything from anyone.*

Meanwhile, given the scarcity of resources, refugees returning to a home that is inhabitable must expel other refugees who've taken shelter there. But Kristina can't stay too long on the debit side of the ledger. Her mind invariably drifts to solutions. *The international community could play a big role in this process—through credit, micro or macro, through revitalization of businesses and factories. When people earn some money, they'll know how to allocate it. They'll buy what their families need most. If that weren't so* [she adds sardonically], *we'd really be in trouble!*

Kristina pulls a piece of paper out of her purse. She had time on the bus trip to our appointment to ruminate on what's needed to support the returnees; and she wants to make sure I, as a potential source of help, have this practical list: *English instruction, computer courses, sewing and knitting lessons, handcrafts, and the production of traditional costumes for folk dancing.* Before I can ask if the folk dancing revival is a response to new ethnic-based identities, Kristina has moved on with her rush of ideas: *A women's information technology course, psychosocial assistance, legal help, preventive health care, and agriculture projects such as gathering medicinal herbs.* She's soliciting me, just as she has the sfor troops.

mirhunisa is approaching the same problem from the opposite side of the war divide. *Here's the scenario: I come to your apartment, grab you and your family, and say, "Get out! Everyone outside!" "Where are we going to go?" you ask. And I shout, "I don't care! Just get out!" And you're happy I didn't kill you.* This scene has been described to Mirhunisa over and over as she's worked to get refugees back into their homes. As an accounting professor she's well suited for the job, but the task is huge. During the time of our interviews, Mirhunisa reported that there were 530,000 Bosnians without roofs over their heads. She's driven by the challenge of such statistics. *I must get them back to their original house. I feel personally responsible for them. I'll be successful, because I'll never give up! I was named a "human rights hero," but my response was, "Thank you, but that will be true only when I've got everyone back home."*

Her work to help thousands who want to come home is set against enormous structural challenges. *Our people have been driven from one place to another. In addition to what they endured during the war, they still can't go home. The 2,500,000 who left their houses—they're lucky to be alive, since many who tried to preserve their property died.* Mirhunisa sees those who stayed behind not as foolish or blind but as martyrs. *They died for all of us who survived.* That attitude, glorifying those who perished trying to hold onto their homes, is typical of Mirhunisa, who champions those shunted aside by others. Still, the political divisions drawn in Dayton make her work much, much harder. *Someone sits in my office, returning with just his suitcase. He asks, "Can you put me up anywhere?" We have agreements with local authorities that everything is fine and people can return. But when a person shows up, everything has been destroyed, and we haven't even got an address to which we can send him for assistance.*

I asked Mirhunisa how and why she keeps going. She reflected on a scene described earlier by Nurdzihana: the massacre of civilians by radical Serb forces on June 17, 1992, near the Sarajevo airport. *That day will go down in history as the greatest shame this town has ever known. People were slaughtered in their bedrooms. Before the war, the neighborhood was part of the Olympic village. It represented the future, infusing Sarajevo with new life.* But Mirhunisa adds: *That horrible event moved me; it gave me strength.*

Horrific experiences from which others retreat pull Mirhunisa forward into engagement. *In the early years of the war, June to October '92, when I was collecting statements from raped women, I learned that many of them were pregnant, and they obviously didn't want to keep the pregnancies. They had no place to go. Sarajevo was packed with refugees. I tried to find them shelter. Every hotel in town that was left was damaged, but we tried to house people in one of them. Then imagine, in 1993, when Sarajevo was under heavy shelling, we organized the founding assembly of our Association of Displaced Persons and Refugees of Bosnia and Herzegovina.*

Experiences with women from the rape camps fortified Mirhunisa for her work with the survivors of Srebrenica. *In July 1995, we were informed by eyewitnesses that there were 50,000 people living in "safe havens" in eastern Bosnia. They were from towns there but also from other places, fleeing ethnic cleansing, moving to any place that was safe.* The country was in chaos. Communications were extremely difficult. Mirhunisa was working in a city under siege. But she persevered: *We kept searching till we found them shelter. We fought for those women. I mobilized my friends—anyone I could find.*

Instead of resting as the war drew to a close, Mirhunisa geared up, taking on the task of registering 2,500,000 people displaced from their homes. She formed regional associations for refugees in four towns, helping them organize, advocate, and work through one obstacle after another in a determined, systematic way. *I had a lot of assistance from the media, as well as from international groups and from NGOs throughout Europe. We had to deal with legal, social, psychological, and housing issues. When we organized an association, there were people from all three ethnic groups leading it. We started working as if we were living in peacetime, with meetings, a presidency group, and committees for gathering data on refugees. More than forty-five people canvassed house-to-house, writing down the information. I still have their lists — pages and pages.*

With 60 percent of the housing stock destroyed during the war, the return of refugees has been an evolving nightmare. Exercising one's right to return has meant evicting not only other refugees but also people who've put their time and savings into restoring the damaged structure. Mirhunisa has been in the middle of this quagmire, in which already difficult situations are further complicated. *Also, some people face reprisals from hardliners if they say they want to return.*

Rather than focusing on the problems, Mirhunisa keeps bringing our conversation back to what can be done. Because she works across the country, she can arrange exchanges. *Bosniaks, Serbs, Croats — they all want their houses back. Recently I visited twenty towns. I was with Croats who resisted the HDZ nationalist police forces. They were offered villas if they'd stay, but they said, "No. We're going back to our homes in Republika Srpska," even though their houses there were completely destroyed. That gathering of Croats seemed to me like any gathering of Bosniaks who want to return to their homes.* Mirhunisa's efforts include Bosnians like Nada, who fled or were driven from the Bosniak-Croat Federation and settled in the Republika Srpska. *I've been working a lot on the return of the Serbs and the Croats who are in Republika Srpska; that way the return of Bosniaks will be possible.*

Her role on both sides of the conflict has not endeared Mirhunisa to political leaders. When she met with the minister for refugees in the Republika Srpska, she was criticized by officials from the Federation. *They said I should blunt my efforts. It was a sort of threat, but they didn't frighten me. Ninety-nine percent of my time I've worked with men, so I don't get frightened. I talk to them only when I need them, not when they need me. From seven years' experience I can say our politicians don't really bother you unless you want power. And they know I don't want any power whatsoever. I was asked if I wanted to be a government minister. When they learned I didn't, they were pleased. I'm not in their way. They don't have the least idea what I'm working on. They learn it from newspapers. So I'm not pulled by powerful people from political parties.*

I returned to the question of Mirhunisa's source of strength. *The power of living comes from helping. Through my organization, I've located 1,600,000 people. When I think about all that's happened . . . the number who tell me they're happy, the letters I receive from abroad from various associations. . . . Can what I lost be compared to what I've gained?* She means more than abstractly gaining meaning from contributing to society. The strength of others becomes her own. In particular, there's a survivor of the Srebrenica massacre who, like so many other women, is now alone. *She lost all the men in her immediate family, but she lives full of energy, always ready to face the next day. When I need a break, I visit her hut in the woods. She shows me photographs of her two sons, who were eighteen and twenty, and says, "I don't have a television. If my sons come back, they won't have anything to watch . . . but they can look at these pictures."* She's a pitiable figure, a simple farmer, with no clear future. But Mirhunisa says: *I gain strength from her. And when I think of her, I'm ashamed I ever complain.*

Getting the Message Out

BILJANA: *During the war the TV kept showing Bosnian women wearing black, with scarves on their heads, calling them "the Muslims." Sure, if you looked on U.S. farms you could find some poor, depressed people and call them "the Americans."*

GALINA: *I read dailies from Zagreb, Sarajevo, all over. Sometimes they make you laugh, the way the same news is treated so differently. Journalists have damaged this country a lot. We need new ones now, with more training.*

ALENKA: *The more TV, radio, and papers, the better, so you can read them all, then create your own picture. Nothing's black or white; it's somewhere in the middle.*

With a multiparty system emerging several years after the war, Bosnian media vastly improved, although the situation has a long way to go before the necessary legal reforms are in place and implemented. Judges must be trained to crack down on political harassment of media professionals such as SUZANA, who's been fearless as an investigative journalist. With a Serb name, she was able to go into the field with the Yugoslav National Army. She collected over a hundred interviews with key political and military players, some of whom are now indicted or convicted war criminals. Suzana used a wartime pseudonym to protect her parents. Since the war, leaders of different political parties have tried to discredit her as she's investigated the secret intelligence system, political corruption, and state terrorism. Bosnian President Izetbegovic alluded to her as a journalistic whore. *That was his exact wording. In an open letter, we asked him to back up his statement with facts, as we had in our article. He never did. After that we felt burned out—not depressed by his statement so much as by the fact that for months after our exposé, the minister didn't take any action and parliament didn't discuss it. Our accusations weren't followed up, so dust fell on the whole case.*

Meanwhile, working within the political system, TANJA observed: *Media shapes people, telling them over and over that if they return home they'll be killed. But media can also be calming, softening antagonisms among political parties by looking at issues globally and urging agreement on essential points.* Tanja was relieved when the UN finally insisted on a media code of conduct. Until then, state-controlled journalists felt free to spread scandalous rumors for political purposes. Those reforms haven't come a day too soon for AMNA, in Mostar. *The media started the war, and only the media can finish it.* She describes her radio station, which broadcasts balanced news coverage in her divided city—a much-needed refutation of the nationalists who still dominate the region. *If the radio broadcasters say, "Croats are no good," "Bosniaks are no good," "Serbs are no good," people on the street won't think, "Well, I have a Serb who's a good friend, and he's the same today as he was yesterday. Why should I hate him now?"* Amna lives in a community rife with harassment, by not only criminals but also police. Her work at the radio station is completely voluntary, and she's spent her salary, and part of her mother's salary, to cover the costs of her ten-minute broadcast every hour. She beams as she tells me about her talk show profiling a successful woman, with a discussion of how to balance home life and work.

Given the history of a controlled press under Tito and the powerful misuse of media thereafter, Bosnians rebuilding their country have a great appreciation for accurate news. Although hate-filled broadcasts began before the war and continued well into the implementation of the Dayton Agreement, the accord curiously contains only one narrowly defined reference to protecting independent media. Abuses of freedom of expression by Milosevic, Tudjman, and Izetbegovic, who signed the 1995 agreement, were well documented.[16] Lack of media standards made the fragile peace even more difficult to sustain, as the earliest elections, under the influence of unscrupulous journalists, legitimized nationalist leaders. After almost four years of noncompliance, the UN Office of the High Representative began to insist on open, independent media fundamental to democracy.

A seasoned journalist, NURDZIHANA has scathing words for the Dayton Agreement, which requires political collaboration among nationalists, creating a deadlock that prevented the country from moving forward during the immediate postwar years. She's quick to point out that central to that difficulty were the media. Each faction had its own cheering section, reinforcing misinformation that deepened the lines of division drawn by the politicians.

In contrast, in her professional work, Nurdzihana has committed herself to alleviating discrimination and suffering. She spends hours over cigarettes and espresso telling me about her life before the war—filled with new places, new people, and new ideas. Nurdzihana's vision was expansive. *My spirit was like a leaf carried by the wind.* She drafted a proposal to create a women's magazine for *Oslobodjenje,* Sarajevo's leading nonnationalist newspaper. The newspaper's name means "Liberation," and it was started in 1943 as an underground publication of Tito's Partisans. In the late 1980s *Oslobodjenje*'s staff abandoned communism for a more democratic approach. Leading up to the 1990 elections, the newspaper rejected the nationalistic rhetoric coming from all the parties. *Despite great popular interest, the manager just put my proposal in a drawer. Later, an older, male colleague of mine wrote up the same idea on just a half page. His project was immediately approved.*

I started working on something even more interesting. Weekends, I'd lower the curtains, unplug the phone, and close myself off with my papers for two or three days. I started a newspaper column called "She and He," taking real-life situations and commenting on them from a woman's and a man's perspective. Readers talked about them on the streets, and some journalist friends used to go down to the printing room to read them before they were published. The psychological base from which she writes underlies Nurdzihana's account of her father's death in 1991. *That was a huge loss for me. I felt completely alone, just my voice echoing, "My father's died. What will I do now?" I'd lost part of myself, but part of me became stronger in that wretchedness. I was deeply sad, but I didn't cry. My father didn't accept hopelessness.*

Nurdzihana turned her grief into action. *After his death, I organized a counseling center for women and families. We needed a place where people could talk with some expert about what worried them. From more than a thousand readers' letters, I saw how many people have problems—and no time for each other. Psychologists spoke of society's increasing alienation. I wrote an article about a man who'd been dead four days without anyone knowing.* Two receptionists linked the callers with the 150 professionals who rotated through the center. The professionals didn't wear white coats. They were there as listeners and problem solvers. *The two people sat and talked as trusted equals. Clients—I don't like calling them clients—could be honest. They found something they could find nowhere else.* Nurdzihana occasionally sat in the reception room, which was filled with flowers. *A woman came out of a room assigned to psychiatrists, crying and smiling at the same time. As she walked by, she hugged me and said, "I'm the happiest person in the world today."* Launching the center was unusual work for a journalist and editor. Why did she do it? *I thought it was needed, and it nourished me.*

In a similar way, Nurdzihana's wartime journalism drew from examination of human nature, particularly the battlefield version of good and evil. After seven months with her mother and nephew in a cellar in Dobrinja, which she calls "The Hell of Sarajevo," her words could paint pictures of dramatically compelling scenes. In June 1994 she published the first edition of the monthly *Zena 21* (invoking "Women of the 21st Century"), including many first-hand accounts she'd recorded. In the turmoil and deprivation of war, a publication for women coming off the presses had immense meaning. To buy refreshments for the launching event, Nurdzihana had only about $20—in an inflated war economy. Braving heavy shelling, nearly 200 people crammed into the reception.

The ongoing production group assembled spontaneously. Some had no publishing experience; they were engineers, psychiatrists, saleswomen. When electricity was cut off, the staff worked by candlelight in a cellar café across the street. The readership was devoted, as well. Without public (or, of course, private) transportation, distribution throughout the city was on foot, at risk of sniper fire. Members hand-carried fifty or a hundred copies to different parts of town. Readers would walk up to two hours from the suburbs into the city on the day they thought *Zena 21* would be published. One person would make the trek to pick up a copy, which might be read by up to fifty people holed up together, as they waited for the war to end.

Five thousand copies were printed—and distributed for free. The first financial supporter was a German women's group, which funded the magazine for a year and a half. After that, the UN High Commission on Refugees and some other donors pitched in. The UNHCR distributed around 2,000 copies to refugees in their emergency shelter projects. In postwar Sarajevo, *Zena 21* became much more than a magazine. I knew it as a convener, a clubhouse, and the sponsor of conferences and contests promoting women's full participation in rebuilding Bosnia. I originally met Rada Sesar there, as she helped out, although she was a radio journalist.

As our meeting draws to a close, Nurdzihana pauses. She's been telling me her life story ever since we met in Sarajevo in July 1994, the middle of the war. What shall she say now, to condense into paragraphs these postconflict years that drag on like millennia? She describes a recent two-hour radio interview in which she was the guest, not the journalist. *I talked simply, openly. When the first listeners started calling, the topic of war spontaneously intruded. I mentioned some names of ordinary people I'd met, whom I'll always remember, given the experiences we shared. I talked about their readiness to help others.* [Nurdzihana leans forward, crossing and recrossing her hands.] *As listeners called in, emotions swelled. Some called to say they remembered me. They were crying because I hadn't forgotten them. I couldn't hold back my tears either—I get goose bumps now even talking about this. We were connected in some way. Mostly they didn't know me or what I'm doing. I reexperienced the whole war in those two hours.*

I've been thinking a lot about this broadcast. It's still in my heart. Listeners jammed the lines, and the next day, they looked me up in my editorial office. They weren't calling because we'd talked about such important and sophisticated issues. We talked about everyday things—small but great people, who are anonymous. Those listeners Nurdzihana touched through her interview are the citizens who must ultimately knit their society back together. As she was with *Zena 21*, Nurdzihana is their guide, balancing the need for emotional catharsis even as she insists on no-excuses social activism.

Grooming the Next Generation

ANA: *My first-grade daughter is the only Croat in her school, but she's happy. An older girl is the only Serb, and she's happy too. The children are not the problem.*

AMNA: *The next generation . . . they basically believe everything will be okay, because they weren't soldiers during the war; they didn't kill. But Bosnia is too small for them; they consider themselves part of Europe. They won't accept these ghettos in which local authorities want them to grow up.*

SABIHA: *The problems come when our schools focus on Bosnia's invasion by the Turks, instead of thinking of the future: space exploration, computers.*

GALINA: *In Bosnia, we can count on the young people. Kids can accept anything.*

Some of the women I interviewed are devoting themselves to grooming the next generation, convinced that the future of Bosnia is inextricably tied to the opportunities—and perplexing difficulties—faced by young people. During the conflict, a mass exodus swept many of the most able youth to other shores. Who could blame them for leaving? In July 1994 I asked a University of Sarajevo professor of architecture if I should send her, perhaps through the U.S. diplomatic pouch, some recent magazines for her classroom instruction. She smiled weakly, then responded patiently, "Sure, but what we really need are pencils."

The young people who left created a talent vacuum, resulting in a substantial weakening of the fragile new political system. During and following the war, as sympathetic Western universities have created places for Bosnians, the brain drain has been dramatic. Homegrown proposals to launch local entrepreneurial ventures for Bosnian young people have languished due to the lack of outside support.

Several mothers have already described the drama of parenting in wartime, and how their choices impinged on their sons and daughters. In Sarajevo alone, over 1,800 children were killed.[17] As Bosnian parents were distracted by issues of survival, they frequently described to me being torn between needing to protect their children and wanting to provide opportunities for their children to become independent.

A different kind of danger has come in the form of separate educational curricula, created by nationalists, with "specialized" accounts of Bosnian history and culture. ALENKA, in Tuzla, recalls schoolbooks during the war: *They were filled with propaganda, saying things like "our poor people were massacred by Chetniks, by Ustashas, by these, by those. . . ." The books in different areas had the same stories, just with different names. They had a lot of horrible details about killing. I read some analyses of schoolbooks sponsored by different political groups. It was terrible! This is a huge complication for the return of refugees. How can parents send their kids to a school that's teaching that their ethnic group is the enemy?*[18] History is being rewritten in Bosnian schools, SABIHA concurs. As an outrageous example, she tells me how in Prijedor, where Emsuda was imprisoned in a concentration camp, Serb children are being taught that Bosniaks committed those atrocities against Serbs. As a journalist, she sees communication as the answer. *If we can teach the next generation that our diversity is actually a big advantage, our country will stay united.* With a grant from the Bosnian Women's Initiative, Sabiha has started a business producing dolls of all four different ethnic backgrounds, each with stories and songs about landmarks, folklore, and traditions. Her dolls don't talk about war. She'll eventually have a product for boys, but she's started with girls. *We're strong, so we should be first.*

It wasn't easy for Sabiha to get funding for her doll enterprise. Donors often come at a steep price, especially if they're trying to proselytize. For example, very conservative Islamic states have sent in humanitarian aid for children, with the requirement that the recipients' mothers wear headscarves. Children in these situations become pawns in a political game, while their parents are often distressed by the teachings of a new religious conservatism foreign to Bosnian tradition.

Such challenges are a somber backdrop for youth programs, such as the summer camp organized by KRISTINA, who lives in an area from which all non-Serbs were expelled. As if I were one of her students, she insists: *Now look at this picture. Here are the tents and beds the international troops gave us.* Beginning with just an open field, Kristina went from one business to another, begging for supplies to create the camp for children, many of whom are orphans or are Bosniaks returning home. *Look, here are the children arriving. At the end, they said, "We hope the bus breaks down, so we can stay longer."* Kristina has dozens of ideas of programs for the children: from musical training, to an ecology course, to sports uniforms. She wants her kids in Republika Srpska to compete with teams in the half of Bosnia controlled by Bosniaks and Croats, known as the Federation.

JELKA's organizing has been in the Federation, in Mostar. Even that small city was further split into two parts after Bosnian Croat nationalists proposed it as the capital of a breakaway region to be annexed to neighboring Croatia. Children huddled with their mothers in basements as the neighborhood that was predominantly Muslim was shelled relentlessly by the Croats. Jelka lives in the part of town shelled by nationalists of her own ethnic group. She organized school lessons near the front line that cut through the center of her town. *That was my first effort helping kids. When there was shelling, teachers went from basement to basement. We had no electricity, water, or paper.* Organizing a school is a challenge. Organizing a school with no supplies, with terrified students and exhausted adults, in a town in which ten people are being killed each day, is a near miracle.

Jelka's social activism was cemented the day fifteen people died a few meters from her home. After the war, her spontaneous organizing of cellar schools evolved into a Center for Culture and Youth on the line of separation. *First, we wanted to help kids overcome the years of education they missed. But our second goal was to reanimate our culture, because I believe a spiritual revival would lift the quality of life in our town. The third, but not least, goal was to connect youth from the west and east parts of town. I knew it would be possible, since the young people kept sending letters to each other throughout the war by the Red Cross system. Romantic relationships were sustained with those letters.*[19] *Several weddings followed the end of the war—ethnically mixed marriages.*

Jelka isn't surprised that love crossed battle lines in Mostar. Her confidence has an authenticity born out of her internal experience, as she's redefined her identity, erasing lines of separation. *I felt so guilty, because all this destruction was being done in the name of my own ethnic group. Now I don't like to think of myself as Croat. I'm a Bosnian Catholic.* Likewise, she speaks of her hometown with almost palpable pride, refusing to give in to the nationalist politics keeping the city divided and dangerous.[20] *Now some people even in the Croat-controlled part think we must be reunited. The west part has modern housing units, but the soul of our town is the old section in the east part. One needs the other. Even the people who aren't from Mostar are fighting for unity. It's not natural to divide such a small town and name half Croat and half Bosniak. That can't be sustained.*

Despite the political recalcitrance in her community, Jelka's eyes shine as she describes her new center: *A place for kids to meet, make their own rules, reestablish cultural ties, get to know and respect each other again. A place where they don't think about politics.* I had the privilege of visiting Jelka's center in July 1997, when she mounted an exhibit of my photographs of children from around the world. Posters advertising the exhibit hung around town on walls reduced to rubble, and a throng turned out for the occasion. Jelka invited people from both sides of town and set up appointments for me with the two dueling mayors, but the more memorable hour was in the center meeting with the young people, who crossed the lines that stopped the adults. The kids asked me what I thought about the future of Mostar. "You are the future," I responded, inspired by the gleam in their eyes.

Jelka's youth center is more than an activity spot for young people. It's a hotbed of fresh ideas. She tells me about the extensive networking she's undertaken. *I've made contact with alternative movements. Everything the political opposition hadn't been able to do, we did in our center. I started organizing in 1995, when delegates from across the country declared their commitment to staying in touch culturally and spiritually. These were people from Belgrade, coming to Mostar for the first time since the war started.* It was an amazing feat in a community that had been under relentless bombardment. Her efforts attracted media and political attention. The mayor hosted a cocktail reception for the group and presented her a certificate of appreciation. These early ventures had lasting impact, not only on the people at the conference but also on Jelka, who's convinced that the arts can pull people together. *Given our difficult political situation, people slip into apathy.* To fight the depression, Jelka is organizing an arts festival. *We had a drama performance the first night with an audience of 600, including civic leaders from west Mostar.*

In all this activity, children are never far from Jelka's mind. Cultural revival and the youth of Mostar share not only the physical space of the center but also a space in the founder's vision and soul. Jelka's energy is fed by her great hurt. When she learned, a few days before the end of the war, that her twenty-two-year-old son had been killed in a car accident, her grief might have caused her to close up, to withdraw. But Jelka was galvanized. *With help from my husband, I've actually managed to transform this grief into a positive force. The only way for me to deal with my loss is to help others who are also trying to return to normal life, despite their pain.*

Of all the women I interviewed, Jelka lives closest to her feelings, whether of love or loss. Rather than being debilitated, she's committed herself to giving to others the care she would have given her son. In that sense, her son is always present. *The only time I didn't obey my husband was after our son died, when he asked me not to have so many of our boy's pictures around, because people who visited us felt uncomfortable. I couldn't agree. I've had lots of pictures of him enlarged. They fill my living room. Every morning, the first thing I do is say, "Good morning." It's difficult for me to speak about it; this is the first time I've told anyone.* [Jelka is weeping.] *He was such a wonderful young man, with a great sense of humor. When I tell about his life, I always start laughing. They're all lovely stories, his stories. I go, very often, to his grave. I make sure there are always flowers. Those are my intimate moments.* Jelka is keenly aware of how in those gestures of mourning she's holding onto a life. She exerts an inner discipline, as she carefully apportions her care. First comes the relationship she maintains with her deceased son. *The rest I've given to everyone who wants to work with me.* And the rest is enough.

Sarajevo bread factory, which operated throughout the siege. December 1995.

7

The Road to Reconciliation

FAHRIJA: *I lost many things in this war . . . and learned even more: what it means to be afraid, to be betrayed, to have those you thought were friends turn their backs because of your name. But the kindness showed me in America helped me teach my children to believe in humanity and not see the world through cynical eyes.*

MAJA: *Men justified their caution, saying it wasn't safe. Women have ventured out more across the lines.*

ALENKA: *If we could live together for fifty years, why can't we now?*

KRISTINA: *Why shouldn't we live together again? I know it's extremely difficult for people who've lost their own family members, and it will probably take them longer than others. But we simply must reconcile.*

Kristina's statement isn't naïve. She's a realist in a small country where, in 2000 alone, over four hundred incidents against minorities were reported to the International Police Task Force.[1] She understands the lowest scheming and the highest aspirations of her community. Her voice, however, can be almost drowned out by a chorus of international cynics quick to pronounce the futility of reconciliation. Among the most vocal has been Henry Kissinger, former secretary of state for presidents Nixon and Ford. He criticized Clinton's intervention in Kosovo, citing how "we are forcing three reluctant nationalities to live together in Bosnia."[2] Arguing that American security was not threatened by the conflict in Kosovo, he told U.S. senators on February 23, 1999, "Ethnic conflict has been endemic in the Balkans for centuries. Waves of conquest have congealed divisions between ethnic groups and religions. Through the centuries, these conflicts have been fought with unparalleled ferocity because none of the populations has any experience with, and essentially no belief in, Western concepts of toleration." Such experts in Realpolitik seem oblivious to the steady restorative process that rebuilds, block by block, destroyed homes, or heals, gesture by gesture, damaged trust. To hold up another lens, the same foreign policy experts who called for a division of Bosnians into ethnically designated regions would surely not have proposed that solution in America, splitting post-riot Watts or Cincinnati into racially separated administrations.

Kristina doesn't have time to waste with such analyses; she, like thousands of other Bosnian women, is too busy doing the work the cynics say can't be done. But what qualifies her to claim, so insistently, that reconciliation is possible? Given their social roles, women often are particularly suited to the sensitive work of helping not only their families, but also their societies, recover from trauma. Sadly, in a mismatch of expertise and authority, their assessments and recommendations usually go unnoted. Instead, professionals hang out shingles declaring themselves experts in "conflict resolution"; from their comfortable offices they describe, prescribe, and proscribe. Clear rules and discrete stages of recovery are laid out. Indeed, "reconciliation" has become a sort of hybrid subfield crossing psychology and international affairs. Ironically, this sphere of reconciliation is marked by considerable contention. Some delineate between forces external to a society imposing justice versus forces within the society bringing about reconciliation.[3] Others insist that the very notion of reconciliation is an inappropriate attempt to resolve what cannot be resolved, to forgive what is, and should remain, unforgivable.[4]

Breathing life into such abstract analyses, Biljana, Karolina, Maja, and Vesna discuss the difficulty of postwar reconciliation. Each is imagining how she would have reacted had she been the person affected — if her husband or son had been killed, or if she had been beaten and her face slit with a knife. Perhaps it's MAJA's medical training that helps her remember the suffering she's been spared. *People say, "I can forgive, but I can't forget." They have a right to their memories, but we don't have to emphasize the negative.* Then, as if she hears a judgmental tone in her comment, she adds: *I can say these things today because nobody in my family was killed. Maybe I can be tolerant now, because I haven't lost anyone. People who lost their closest family . . . Things can be reconstructed — factories, bridges — but lost lives can't. When I think about mothers and fathers who lost their children . . .*

Just as Maja has empathy for others' suffering, BILJANA identifies with the Bosniak refugee nursing her dying mother. The woman's husband had been murdered, and she feared her two teenage sons would be sent to the front lines by the Croat army. *So after my mother died, my brother saved the two boys, helping them get out of the country. Just think, they were about seventeen and nineteen. Now they live in Germany. But what's going to happen with those boys? What kind of feelings are they going to have? Do we really think they're going to say, "Let's forgive and forget"? The perpetrators: What are they thinking as people? The lives of these two young men were destroyed overnight. Their mother was an educated person, an engineer. Now they're probably all three working in some factory.* Biljana, a convert to Judaism, has seen the scars of victimization. *It's only natural to feel vengeful. I certainly would.* [Her Jewish husband, Al, who's in the room, seems uncomfortable with her statement and attempts to soften it, but she's adamant.] *If someone came into my house and killed my husband, all I can say is, "God help them."* [She pounds the table.] *For me there would be no life other than to get them. Those people in Bosnia lost everything. Why shouldn't they become vengeful?*

Biljana's reaction is not unusual for those in the diaspora, who live isolated from the perpetrators. She has no practical need for reconciliation; and even if she did desire it, she'd have little occasion to venture forward in small interactions with the Serbs and Croats who launched the genocide.[5] Reconciliation, after all, requires forgiveness, one of the most problematic of human interactions.

In fact, none of the women I interviewed describes herself as a forgiving soul. VESNA, for example, joins Biljana in asserting just the opposite, although she speaks of forgiveness as a virtue, even if it's out of reach for her. *When the war started, my daughter and I went to Zagreb, in Croatia. We just wanted to get away, maybe for a couple of weeks. I never thought it would last.* Her husband and his father, Bosnian Serbs, stayed home. Vesna asked her brother, a Bosnian Croat, to stay with them, just in case. After an anonymous call, Croat paramilitaries broke into the apartment, saying the brother of one of them had been captured by Serbs, and they wanted revenge. *They asked my brother why he was staying in a Chetnik's home. He said they weren't Chetniks, but loyal citizens, with no relation whatsoever with the Serb paramilitary. The gang didn't care. They beat my husband so severely that he had a hernia. One of the thugs grabbed my father-in-law's head and cut his face with a big knife, down the side, from his temple to his cheekbone. He barely escaped with his life. Then with a white flag, my husband crossed the minefields to the Serb positions. They interrogated him for three days. How had he managed to get there? Why? He finally was able to get in touch with some old school friends and got some document allowing him to go further, to Belgrade.* Vesna's father-in-law stepped on a mine, and his leg had to be amputated below the knee. Ultimately, he was exchanged by the Red Cross in a prisoner swap.

Those thugs who destroyed my family . . . [her voice becomes more energized]. *I'm glad two of them were later murdered. But one is still alive. He was actually my husband's friend—the goalie of the soccer team my husband covered as a sports journalist. They stole whatever they wanted from my place, but that's not important; as we say, "As long as you have your life, you have everything."* Vesna would like to live beyond a craving for retribution, but thinking of the lone gang survivor, she declares, with spite: *Surely God's punishment is on him. Just to let you know how good my husband is, here's what he says: "Vesna, don't curse them; I forgave them. If you can't, please try to forget." I'm a believer; he's an atheist. But every time I think of evil, I see that man, holding the knife, slicing my father-in-law's face. I can't forgive them . . . and that's okay.*

Like Vesna, KAROLINA's passion is in defense of others who've suffered more than she. *My son, eighteen, was given the job of standing guard, with a rifle that didn't work. It was actually bent; it couldn't fool anyone. Can you believe it?* [She brings her hands to her face.] *But there is a God, and He saved some of our children. I thank God my son survived.* Then a moment for self-reflection: *I'm probably not as forgiving as others. If I'd lost him, I'd probably have taken revenge.*

The vengefulness of Maja, Biljana, Vesna, and Karolina is intense—and hypothetical. They were the only women of the twenty-six I interviewed who spoke of revenge, and they did so only when empathizing with those who had suffered more than they. Speaking about the hardship they actually experienced, they were not bitter. For example, KAROLINA was not only a mother fearful of her son being killed, she was also a Croat living in the old Muslim part of town, while the ragtag Bosnian militia was trying to defend towns from attacks by not only Serbs, but also Croats. *I was someone other Sarajevans could target for their anger.* But she excuses those who harassed her: *People were suffering, and they were influenced by extremists.* She bears no grudge.

Similarly, MAJA, after saying she might not be able to forgive, talks about her friendships on both sides of the conflict. In the crucible of war, those relationships were tested, and postwar, they've emerged galvanized. *Life is empty without friends.* It's a simple statement, but spoken by a woman who's mastered the art of nuance. *Bridges were destroyed, but true friendships couldn't be.* The troubled terrain of her city becomes the symbol of her attitude toward life. *There's only one Mostar; I walk on both sides, visiting my friends—not only today, but also when it was much more dangerous. I never divided them in my mind into one group or another. I didn't forget them, and they didn't forget me. We need to nurture friendships like flowers. You can find many more ties in a real friend than you can find in your family. Maybe I was lucky in choosing friends, or maybe I've been a good friend to them. Many people say how they distinguish between friends from before the war and friends from after the war, but all my friendships survived. Sure, there are always small disappointments, but they're not so important that they destroy the relationship.*

The women tried to tell me what it was like to live in fear of being raped, to clutch their ears for hours against the bombing, to embrace the inconsolable father grieving his dead child. They've sifted through ashes, looking for precious remains of a photo album. They've lain awake at night, worrying how they will feed hungry children. They've walked home from the train depot weeping, after seeing their oldest child off to build a future in a more promising society. But they've been able to transform their suffering into motivation for rebuilding shattered communities. Their work for their country has informed their personal understanding; conversely, their personal understanding informs their work.

Part of their expertise is their ability to judge the cost of reconciliation not attempted. They've studied their situation and concluded, obstinately: *We simply must reconcile.* With that decided, the women offer three fundamental imperatives: Tell the truth. Impose justice. But remember that the perpetrators are human. The three principles are not only linked but also interactive: All three must be at work in a community to effect reconciliation. Without truthfulness, justice is impossible; and without truthfulness, the enemy remains a two-dimensional demon. In turn, the possibility of justice emboldens those pursuing the truth. Truth, in turn, is most often discovered in the wide, gray zone between good and evil, where perpetrators share space with the rest of humanity. And humanizing the enemy is required of those seeking justice in place of revenge. The three imperatives function as a network, supporting the mysterious internal transformation known as reconciliation.

The Truth Must Come Out

SABIHA: *We have to find out what happened. All of us — children and adults — need to know. History is the teacher of life. We've got to learn the truth so this horror won't be repeated.*

KADA: *It would be much easier if I knew my Samir was dead.*

There are several models for a new democracy dealing with a sordid past: amnesia (Churchill's "blessed act of oblivion"); a purge of collaborators from public office (Czech Republic and East Germany); Nuremberg-type trials (the trade-mark of victors); and truth commissions (more prone toward reconciliation than the pure imposition of justice).[6] In Bosnia, the formal setting for exposing the truth hasn't been local and regional media, discredited by rampant abuse under communism and manipulation by nationalists. Instead, truth telling has been organized around the UN war crimes tribunal and a new truth commission as the primary means of sorting through allegations of atrocities.[7]

Having a place and a process for getting to the truth serves many functions: it points to the guilty and absolves the innocent; it asserts the value of the vic-tims; it distinguishes history from propaganda; it allows the survivors to move on to the future; and it lays the groundwork for reconciliation.[8] But finding ade-quate words to describe atrocities is futile. What adjectives exist for a father's anguish watching his young daughter raped by a dozen men, then killed? For me to even write these words seems maudlin, too dramatic, over-the-top. Yet they are the reality. Silence in the face of the unspeakable is understandable, but it col-ludes with those who don't want to hear what has happened.[9] Thus enormous internal strength is required of victims who voice the truth. Their drive comes from a desire for answers, but also their understanding that reawakened memo-ries—while painful—may be essential for healing not only themselves but also the entire cast of the tragedy.[10]

Outside forces ripped apart the world—families, communities, and coun-try—of the women I interviewed. Postwar, they look back on a multicultural homeland that was a model of tolerance, and they long for restoration. Here, two women ask for the truth about the crime that leaders of the international community, ashamed of their bungling or complicity, attempted to cover up: the massacre at Srebrenica. Theories abound as to why UN officials refused to inter-vene to stop the massacre. Was a deal struck with the Serbs to save the lightly armed UN Protection Forces harm or humiliation, after troops had been shown on CNN, handcuffed to telephone poles? Did the international community need a jolt to free itself from policy paralysis? Or was it, most benignly, simple incom-petence? Kada was inside, Mirhunisa outside the scene of the worst atrocity in Europe since the dark days of the Third Reich.

KADA speaks with the gut-level understanding of a survivor: *Many Bosnians are missing, but Srebrenica is unique, because so many people disappeared in just one day. They were sacrificed for some ridiculous goal: some kind of negotiation with Chet-niks—or it might have been the price to end the war. We were disarmed and "protected by the UN."* The pretense of protection was a disaster. The Dutch battalion charged with ensuring the security in the safe haven was not equipped to intervene when the Serbs launched their assault. When the refugees packed into the Dutch compound, sanitation and health facilities were so overwhelmed that the battalion agreed to monitor the Serbs' "evacuation" of the refugees, in effect participating in the process of ethnic cleansing. Serb troops expelled over twenty-three thousand women and children, and captured and executed the fighting-age boys and men.

Beyond her grief, Kada describes another emotion—a primal, furious worry like that of a lioness searching for her cubs. *Those who know the truth about the missing of Srebrenica are silent. I don't know why.* Her words spiral. *The* UN *troops that protected us must know what happened. The Dutch battalion stayed there ten days after the fall of Srebrenica. How long does it take a bulldozer to bury 10,700 bodies?*[11] *There's not one mass grave with thousands of people. It doesn't add up.*[12] *Our women went to Holland, begging them to say what was done to our men who were taken away. Nobody would say anything except, "I don't know." The Chetniks are silent, too. Who gave the orders? Not the soldiers who pulled the trigger; they're not the guilty ones. The commanders should be indicted and taken to court.*[13]

Kada's insistence that the tribunal should not be prosecuting ordinary soldiers acting under orders but rather the commanders and political leaders who gave those orders is not uncommon. In fact, the tribunal has met arduous evidentiary standards in indicting (in both sealed and public indictments) a number of military and political commanders, including Ratko Mladic, Radovan Karadzic, and Slobodan Milosevic. The bottleneck was not in indicting these leaders but rather in arresting them, a task the international political and military leaders were very reluctant to take up. But until the war criminals are apprehended, the survivors will continue to "fill in the blanks," trying to piece together just what happened.

General Mladic was the direct commander of the Serb troops. He's a high officer of the former Yugoslav army. He knows the price of killing all those people. That's why I think there must be survivors hidden somewhere—probably in the coal mines of Serbia. Lots of men can be hidden in underground tunnels—after all, President Milosevic is a clever man. Her words flow, as if she is negotiating with a terrorist: *I don't ask to have our men returned, if they were killed. I just want to know if they're no longer alive.*[14] *We have religious rituals. We mothers would rest easier if someone would just come on out and admit it—would tell the truth so others can learn from our tragedy.*

Like Jelka surrounded by enlarged photographs of her dead child, Kada's energy is fueled by the memory of her son. *Now, in the night, when I think of him, that's when I hurt most. That's the greatest pain of my life. I picture him. Where is he?*

Who shot him? How did they shoot him? Was he killed by the bullet? Maybe only in-jured . . . then buried by a bulldozer. Maybe he's still alive somewhere, in a prison. Maybe he's hungry and eating rotten bread. I don't know. Uncertainty is the worst part — be-lieve me. The kindest thing someone could do is to tell me the truth. Everything else is bearable. If I knew he was dead, I wouldn't suffer. It would be over. We must know the truth. The world wants to hear us. I'll give interviews to anyone who'll listen. I don't care who they are and what their interest is, as long as they report exactly what I tell them — report the truth. Only truth will heal.

The campaign for truth has been waged not only by the survivors and some in the international community,[15] but also by Kada's countrywoman MIRHUNISA, who was trying to organize help for people flooding into Sarajevo from eastern Bosnia in the middle of the war: *I sent a fax to Madeleine Albright and the presi-dents of Bosnia and Herzegovina just before Srebrenica fell: "Please protect the 30–40,000 people crammed into the 'UN safe havens.' We've been informed that something terrible is going to happen; fighting has started up in the surrounding area." The people were unarmed; they couldn't defend themselves.* Tragically, Mirhunisa's information was correct. *When the first refugees arrived in Tuzla, I contacted the Ministry for Refugees, saying, "We're missing people!" They answered, "Your information is wrong. People are coming out." But we were right. We were missing ten thousand people.* [Mirhunisa is in tears.] *Ten thousand . . .*

Different truths need to be told: Kada's informational truth about what hap-pened to her husband, son, and brothers, as well as the confessional truth of per-petrators. But there are also those like RADA, a Serb for whom "truth" includes acknowledging her identification with those who committed the crimes, and ask-ing the victims for forgiveness. Without that step, Rada won't be able to move beyond the collapse of history caused by "her people." *How to justify the Serbian aggression?* It can't be done; but at the same time, Rada will not deny her roots: *I'm a Serb woman, and I wouldn't renounce my identity, ever. Never. I don't think it's a handicap or an advantage.* Rada offers advice to innocent Serbs: *Those who didn't commit crimes must face the fact that others who belong to their ethnic group really did those things. It's difficult to accept that one part of the people I belong to did what they did.* [Her hands, usually moving constantly, are strangely still.] *No matter how I've tried to rid myself of that feeling of guilt . . . it's still there.*

Justice, Not Revenge

GALINA: *A mother shouldn't differentiate, saying, "These children are good and these are bad"—even though she may be right—because she'll create a problem among her children.*

ALENKA: *I don't like to judge others, because, what if the same happened to me? I can't tell you now what I'd think. Maybe one day I'll be in that situation. Who knows how I'll behave?*

SUZANA: *We tend to blame only the Serbs and Croats, but we have to know what every side did . . . and that's for the tribunal to decide.*

FAHRIJA: *This war taught me that people may be good or bad, but that's independent of race and religion.*

TANJA: *People who say, "There are no good guys or bad guys in this fight," don't know Bosnia.*

Even in the aftermath of extreme vulnerability, not one of the twenty-six women I interviewed called for greater military power. Revenge wasn't on their minds. That includes ALMA, who spent years with the fighting forces trying to lift the siege around Sarajevo. *I'd be the happiest person in the world to hear there was no army anywhere. An army is an evil necessity.*

Instead of greater militarization, the women put their faith in justice. As an American, I took for granted a robust system of accountability that divides criminals from victims. But in a postwar society, the lines are not so clearly drawn. Justice necessitates judgment, and judgment comes at a price—for laying blame is at the same time beneficial and disturbing to a postconflict society. Even the concept of blind fairness loses its luster when outsiders try to judge citizens who've lived under a bombardment by outrageous political propaganda, or who are trying to preserve a shred of respect for the group into which they were born.

In extremes, practicalities easily override principles. For example, when Slobodan Milosevic was indicted for war crimes,[16] even Western policymakers convinced of his guilt debated the political advisability of that step.[17] Some felt he was necessary to maintain as a leader to broker peace in the region. Others felt that to let him go free would not only be wrong at an individual level but also undermine the entire effort to hold perpetrators responsible. Serbian society, in turn, was split in their response to Milosevic's imprisonment. Some felt they were once more victims of a worldwide conspiracy against the Serbs; others saw his being brought to trial as an opportunity for justice to speed the process of healing from the war.

The very process of judgment of war crimes can be — at its worst — an autistic, self-absorbed concern. It can consume tens of millions of dollars when victims lack a roof over their heads. But it can also be a rigorous exercise, sharpening thinking, and fueling a person's motivation to get involved in shaping the future. A woman like Kada, jobless and homeless, with the five closest men in her family murdered, hardly has the psychological energy to turn her attention to the larger world and future generations. She needs an external social process that allows her to see beyond her own misery, and an internal psychological process to let her move through her grief. The two processes are related. A solid justice system encourages the victim to eschew revenge.

In postconflict situations around the world, as the interaction of wrongdoing, memory, confession, forgiveness, justice, and reconciliation is probed, variations of imperfect retributive and restorative measures have been crafted: war crimes tribunals, community-based transitional courts, truth and reconciliation commissions. The creation of a court system to deliver justice is complicated by delays in funding, political morasses, logistical snafus, and personnel inadequacies. The international court must conform to the bureaucratic formulae of a dozen other institutions. Thus months, then years go by with no action. Victims are pushed into the background as questions of jurisdiction, or the definition of war crimes, or military mandates are debated. By the time the court opens, concern for the victims has been subordinated to the UN administrative schedule, the UN member states' fiscal years, the judges' personal holidays. Given these limitations, one might question whether such grand attempts at justice are worth the expense and effort. A hundred years of trials won't bring back the dead; the money spent on lawyers and cells is sorely needed to rebuild homes across war-ravaged landscapes and jump-start economic activity; and true accountability lies far beyond the reach of a courthouse. The system becomes hopelessly clogged, overwhelmed by numbers far beyond what it was designed to handle.[18]

Despite these problems, the Bosnian women have been at the forefront of the call for justice. At the end of the 1998 Sarajevo meeting I chaired with two hundred women from the most nationalist to moderate political parties, the women voted unanimously to support implementation of the Dayton Peace Agreement, which included the apprehension of all indicted war criminals. What common principle trumped their political differences? A million women suffered the Bosnian war in a million ways, but the women at that conference shared the sense that those who had suffered were owed a public reckoning.

There's a gendered aspect to their concern, as well: Women have less social power, and without an external system to defend them, they're all the more vulnerable. Subtle and blatant layers of discrimination allow women to be targeted, for example with rape, which is a form of torture often treated by officials as nothing more than an incidental by-product of warring boys being boys. Bands of males may assert their manhood as warriors, but war affords women no corresponding empowering role; instead, they become victims, not only displaced and damaged, mourning the loss of family members, but also prey for men on the enemy side.

The Bosnian war is associated with rape, since it was in relation to this conflict that sexual violence was finally given the status of a war crime, rather than simply the unfortunate but inevitable behavior of marauding paramilitaries scouring the countryside. Although the Red Cross and UN purportedly ignored early reports of systemic rape,[19] as the 1995 UN Fourth World Conference on Women in Beijing approached, the rapes of Balkan women received attention from advocates all over the world. Strong pronouncements such as Hillary Clinton's that "women's rights are human rights" became a rallying cry for a movement that insisted that the newly formed UN war crimes tribunal include violence against women in their scope. But the ideal imagined in Beijing is far from reality. For example, Bosnian law considers rape only penile penetration. So the woman a UN official described to me who had an AK-47 shoved up her vagina was not legally raped. Instead, the perpetrator committed an indecent act. The crime itself is defined, in Bosnian law, in terms of the perpetrator's experience.[20]

The justice process not only can provide women relief; it also wounds. By coming forward to testify, Bosnian women and girls bring social shame on themselves and their families. Whatever good may come of the ordeal of testifying is offset by the risks of being met with incredulity, being targeted as the cause of the rape, being trivialized, or being deemed unmarriageable. Men rape women because they're ordered to by commanders intent on humiliating the enemy, or because they're caught up in a spree of violence. In either situation, rape in wartime is a dramatic act of male dominance over women. The prosecution of such crimes is, therefore, highly symbolic, not only at a personal level but for women as a group. The recognition of rape as a form of torture acknowledges that sexuality is not only personal but also political; and the appointment of women as judges and prosecutors, and the inclusion of rape in the list of war crimes at the tribunal, sent an unmistakable signal to women not only in Bosnia but around the world.

When the universe is out of joint; when the solid foundation has evaporated; when life is no longer work laced with joy, but suffering occasionally ameliorated by humanitarian relief—in such a time, the longing for what's right becomes an all-consuming passion. Justice stubbornly insists on some sort of order in the wake of chaos, a rebalancing of what is off kilter, an expression that there is yet a core around which to build a new life.

KADA, a survivor of relentless depravity in Srebrenica, carefully separates justice from revenge, in self-examination with profound social implication: *I don't curse anyone. I couldn't torture anyone—not even those who caused me this pain. But I'd like to see those people singled out and have them admit they're guilty. Their lives can be spared, but I want them put away so they can't do any more wrong . . . so they can't lure anyone else into evil. If they were taken to court, maybe we'd be able to talk about living together.*[21] *We don't have to love each other, just respect each other's rights. I hate General Mladic, because he was there when my husband was taken away. I'd love to see him pay. But I couldn't do anything to hurt him. After I did, I wouldn't be me anymore. Why would I burden myself with that? I've never consciously harmed anyone in my life.* Kada has one area left in her control—her conscience. *That's why I'm at peace. I'm reconciled with myself.*

What is the mechanism by which that reconciliation occurs? The question is not rhetorical for MEDIHA, a sophisticated professor who endured Sarajevo under siege. As a member of parliament, she must now consider justice for a country in which the majority of the population has been violated: killed, tortured, or robbed. She moves the issue to a higher level. *Reconciliation is possible, but certain conditions must be met: the unification of our country, including freedom of movement and allowing people to return home; and the punishment of war criminals who committed the genocide of the Bosniak people.*[22] Neither Mediha nor any other woman I interviewed is demanding retribution or compensation from one people on behalf of another. She draws a clear line between collective and individual guilt: *A finger needs to point to the ethnic group, but we can't charge an ethnic group. Within that group, as in every group, the names of the criminals are known. In fact, the whole world knows who they are.*

Like many mothers across cultures, Mediha turns to homespun wisdom, in a penetratingly apt assessment of the wartime fiasco of international players who turned their back on the slaughter. *I've often wondered what my son, Bojan, would look like if I had raised him without any principles, like the international community during the war. When a child tells a lie once, if you pretend you don't notice, he'll lie to you again. If you ignore it again, the child will stop respecting you, because both of you know about the lie. In the same way, the countries with the ability to intervene when we called should have acted more honestly.*

On the other side of this war story is GALINA, who, for all I know, could have nursed the mother of the soldier who executed Kada's Samir or offered solace to the family of a sniper picking off civilians like Mediha's Bojan. Galina is tired of hearing her leaders being blamed for the war. She represents thousands of Bosnian Serbs who live in communities in which mosques were razed and Catholics expelled, but who've been inundated with warnings about impending persecution of Serbs. She's in a difficult position. An empathetic, tireless advocate for those near her who are hurting, she feels that the Serb people are misunderstood, misjudged, and maligned. Confronted with human rights reports of ethnic cleansing, she notes simply that hundreds of thousands of people left her home city of Banja Luka and Serbs moved into their homes — as if the non-Serbs preferred a different climate or were following a new job opportunity.

Galina has great sympathy, however, for the Serbs streaming into Banja Luka as refugees from other fronts, fleeing the dangers of war, or the reverse ethnic cleansing perpetrated by Croat and Bosniak troops pushing back against the Belgrade-backed onslaught. She's frustrated that, for political leverage, distribution of aid after the war was linked to compliance with the Dayton Agreement. This policy was highly criticized by humanitarian workers (including Americans) I met in Republika Srpska. Those supporting the aid-ban decision noted that short-term hardship was balanced by the possibilities of long-term gain for refugees ultimately returning to their homes, a provision of Dayton being stymied by the hard-liners elected by Serbs in that area. But Galina wants to keep politics out of the aid question. *People in war are vulnerable. We were caring for the hungry, the sick. We didn't even get ten kilos of flour in aid. A single foreigner could have come to help us. Then you listen to* CNN *or the* BBC *talking about us as aggressors. I don't feel like an aggressor.* If aggression means trying to take what is not rightfully yours, by Galina's logic, the Serbs were not aggressors but liberators of their own land. *My people have been here for centuries. I can't be aggressive in my own home.*

Her unease at hearing her people blamed extends to a distrust of the tribunal. Still she recognizes the essential need for justice, not only to expose the perpetrators but to preclude collective guilt and prejudice: *If someone is taken to court, there are proceedings and witnesses. Once it's proved that this or that was done by this or that person, nobody can deny it.*[23] *It's finished through normal procedures. But if it's just hearsay or rumors . . . ("These crimes were committed . . ." "They weren't committed . . ." "We did . . ." "They did . . .") then it's a problem.* As a Serb, Galina feels maligned. *Anyone who's guilty should pay; but many things haven't been officially proved, and now anyone who's against the Serbs is OK. I hate that. Our side suffered too. There are people responsible for massacres in Serb villages.* She pulls herself up short with a noncontroversial generality: *Everybody should be judged fairly.*

Galina is wary of the UN international criminal tribunal, which she sees as politicized. *The Croats say, "We're all in prison in The Hague." And then the Serbs say all the Serbs are in The Hague.* Galina doesn't adopt the nationalist line that the court is simply a tool of NATO. But she is skeptical about fairness. *People are biased, especially given their emotional trauma and fear; plus, the international community doesn't treat all sides the same.* That last complaint is ironic. A great obstacle to justice was the attitude of U.S. commanders who were sent in to maintain the peace immediately after the Dayton Peace Agreement was signed. Preoccupied with their own "force protection," the military leaders refused to apprehend indicted war criminals, saying first that this action wasn't in their mandate, and second that it would not be "even-handed." Their concept of even-handedness was Galina's: the same number of Croats, Muslims, and Serbs. Indictments issued according to who did what to whom were irrelevant in this logic-defying reckoning.[24]

Galina points out that Bosniak leader Alija Izetbegovic had not been indicted as a war criminal when he died in 2003; yet, she asserts, if he didn't know about the atrocities his soldiers committed, he was guilty for not knowing. Likewise, Croatian leader Tudjman was not taken to The Hague. *But he started ethnic cleansing — the rest was just a reaction.* Had he not died of cancer, Tudjman might well have been indicted like Milosevic, but Galina's last statement reflects a remarkable revision of history. Although human rights groups have documented that the overwhelming majority of the atrocities committed in the war were by Serbs, Galina says that her people are convinced that the call to justice is one-sided. *It's fine if you think badly of Milosevic; but everyone must be taken to court at the same time, and then the guilt will be decided.*

Such denial of Serb responsibility for the war is hard to take for NURDZIHANA, who witnessed and documented tragedy at the hands of Belgrade-backed paramilitaries. She focuses not on the importance of formal justice but on finding an even larger framework that allows her to resist revenge. During the siege, she used her journalistic training to record tales of carnage and courage. Reflecting on all she heard, she moves the notion of justice beyond earthly courts to a spiritual reckoning in which people receive their due rewards: *Why did the Bosnian Serb leader Karadzic bring such destruction to his own people — not just to us Bosniaks (who suffered the most), but to his own people. Now justice prevails — although sometimes very slowly. I'm not sure if I believed in God before the war, but I believe there is Something, and everything we do and whatever happens is in relation to that Something. A person can't do whatever he or she pleases without having it come back in some way — not just as a sanction by a court. There is a God, and sooner or later everyone gets what he or she deserves.*

Nurdzihana had ample moments for theological reflection during the long days and nights of Sarajevo's bombardment. She watched her community divide among those who fled as refugees to escape danger and deprivation (creating a serious talent drain), those who left due to political pressure because they were ethnic Serbs or Croats (and thus at war with the Bosniaks), and those who remained, regardless of ethnic heritage. She tried to explain to me how the postconflict psychological divisions among those groups have been as difficult to overcome as any notion of ethnicity. *The people who stayed in Bosnia were the real victims. The ones who left — I'm not sure they really knew why they were leaving.* Yet despite the atrocities she witnessed at the hands of "Chetniks," Nurdzihana can empathize with her Serb neighbors who left. They were, after all, hearing constant propaganda about their saintly people being persecuted by heathen Muslims. *When somebody keeps telling you you're a saint, you start believing it.* Then the sentiment that grabbed my attention, as I heard it from one woman after another: *Maybe I'd like to be told that too; I don't know.*

How can she speak so matter-of-factly, and even empathically, about people who were part of a group who robbed her and those around her of friends, lovers, security, beauty? Even outside a formal justice system, Nurdzihana's belief in an ultimate reckoning allows her to escape revenge, to leave behind a wretched past and move into the future. Rather than becoming mired in her victim status, she's willing to excuse those around her with a blanket statement: *People I knew didn't start this war.*

Humanizing the Enemy

MAJA: *Whatever I wish to have happen to others, let it happen to me and my family.*

SABIHA: *During the war, when I collected food to send to my country from abroad, I never thought about whether it would go to Croat, Bosniaks, or*

Serbs—just hungry Bosnians.

GRETA: *The snipers. Who were they? What are they like inside?*

AMNA: *The soldiers were ordinary Serbs, Croats, and Muslims. It's sad but true.*

They were normal people, trusting their leaders, in a simple, rural region

where people believe what they hear.

Women like Greta and Amna seem to know intuitively the trap of demonizing the enemy. One was deported to Auschwitz because she was a Jew; the other was tossed out of the university because she was a Muslim. Both have been victims of distortions over politicized airwaves that transformed cultural heritage into a ticket to hell. But neither they nor the other women described themselves to me as having progressed from martyrs to saints. In fact, given the complexity of morals, values, and loyalties, our conversations were far from simple as the women I met with struggled with questions of others' motivation and the extent to which the perpetrators were acting with free will. Many wanted to give the boys and men who wreaked havoc in their lives the benefit of the doubt. *Perhaps they were misled. . . . Surely they were duped. . . . In the same situation, maybe I would have done the same. . . .* They were reluctant to judge, even as they recognized the importance of assigning responsibility for the raging aggression let loose on innocents.

As they spoke of what they'd experienced, several of the women found themselves beyond the continuum that runs between good and bad. They'd witnessed evil, and they were haunted by questions: When Milosevic reached into the bowels of Serbia's prisons to find criminals who would take pleasure in terrorizing the Bosnian people,[25] what well of psychopathology did he plumb? Is sadism a sickness or—worse—a choice? And who ultimately bears the responsibility, the drunken soldiers laughing as they mutilate an old woman,[26] or the political architect of the war, lounging in a leather chair, sipping slivovitz with visiting diplomats?

"Humanizing the enemy" is a complicated process, as my conversations with the women demonstrate. For one, the most important element is an acceptance that "the enemy" are really normal, everyday people. Another deals with the issue by saying "the system" is accountable for leading individuals into temptation. Another describes victims forgiving perpetrators. Another recounts acts of kindness toward those on the other side. Each reaches into a psychological space closed to those who demonize others as a way of coping with overwhelming evil. Each represents a voice calling for a reconciled community.

SABIHA, from the eastern enclave of Gorazde, watched the war brewing while living abroad: *The Bosnian Serb political party was strong. They brainwashed their party members in Sarajevo: "Pack a few things and go away for the weekend. We'll take the capital in three days." Once those Sarajevan Serbs were caught up in the game, it was difficult to get out of it.* For a Sarajevo Serb who had left, to reconnect to her former neighbors after the shooting started, she'd have to cross a psychological distance littered with corpses. But Sabiha's analysis invites reconciliation: *Maybe even those who didn't want to be part of Milosevic's game didn't have the inner strength to return and say, "I made a mistake. Will you take me back?" The war in Sarajevo was horrible; everyone wanted to escape. But among some of the bravest people who stayed to defend the city were Serbs.*

In a cellar of the Sarajevo suburbs, NURDZIHANA learned a lesson of recon-ciliation from her mother, whom she describes as the soul of the community. *She was an unusual woman, full of optimism and energy. People in Dobrinja were panicked: packing, trying to escape, running back in, shouting, insisting they had to get out. She said, "Excuse me, may I ask where you're going?" Nobody had an answer. Then when we moved into the cellar, we took down a telephone. People would make calls, going on and on about how horrible it was. And she'd say, "I'd like to ask something of you. When you talk to people by phone, don't say it's so bad for us here. Don't you see how good it is?" We had a mini-TV, a transistor radio, and some mattresses piled up high on the floor. "Look, this is like a café! It's not as awful as you're saying."* The elderly woman was more than a naïve optimist; her whole attitude was rooted in reconciliation as a stubborn possibility. *And then there was something I didn't expect: When people would talk against the Serbs as if they all were the same, my mother would say, "Please don't talk like that around me. They are not all the same." She kept saying that throughout the war. She spoke with authority . . . and people respected what she said.*

That same generosity is woven throughout DANICA's description of the man who was the final impetus for her fleeing her community in northern Bosnia. As tensions mounted, she'd been holding out, not wanting to leave her home and business to cross the river to Croatia. One day, there was a pounding on her door. There was nothing obviously different about the man standing there. *He was completely average: between forty and fifty years old, average height and build. Just a normal man.* But he had a wild look in his eyes. In his panic, this normal man was her signal of danger. *My daughter had been resisting leaving, but after she saw him, she packed her kids up so I could take them to safety. He looked just like any of us, but when I realized his mental state, I knew there was going to be a war, and I had to leave.* Danica converts the threat into a gift: *So he's the one, in a way, who saved our lives, because the next day, the war started.* I asked her more about the man, but Danica let me know that wasn't her point. *I have no idea what he did when he left, if he became a war criminal, if he killed people . . .* Her message is broader. *That's how war is. We're all similar. We all look alike.*

ALENKA knows how it is to live under the burden of stereotypes: *My mother is Slovene; my father is Serbian. I don't feel like any one identity. I'm a zero, and that's perfect for me. No one can insult me. I'm above that. I did my own silly experiments working in a shelter project in '94. The shelling was terrible, and a lot of people were killed.* Interviewing people about their homes that needed repair, Alenka slipped in another question: *"What do you think of me? Because . . . well, I'm not, uh . . . You know . . . I'm Serb . . . and I'm here. So what do you think?"* And the people would always say, *"No problem. You're with us. You're helping us. Don't worry. It's fine."* Even in refugee centers, she received the same answer. And so she concludes: *The problems are political. There's not that much ethnic trouble between ordinary people. Or if there is, it's because of political manipulation. It's easy to break through prejudice if you have the right attitude.* For five years, she's been working across ethnic lines. *Never, ever, did I have any trouble, because I don't have an ethnic agenda. If you just behave normally, you don't have those problems.*

But such social optimism doesn't explain the carnage she witnessed. *I ask myself, how could people divide into these herds? These are good people. So what happened? They're simply easy to manipulate. It's probably because we had no democratic traditions. Before, someone else was thinking instead of you. You didn't have to have your own opinion. You weren't taught to think independently. So when some idiots came along, they could easily manipulate the population.* Alenka repeatedly distances "ordinary people" from the evil that was perpetrated. *People think they have their own opinion, but they just believe the media and politicians. Today they say, "Ooh, ah, I hate this. I hate that." But tomorrow they change their minds quicker than you can imagine. A different politician . . . different propaganda . . . and your mind-set changes.*

To the extent that "the enemy" was everyday citizens, Alenka is ready to excuse their actions, including killing. *There were criminal gangs, but there were also just ordinary people. How many of them honestly accepted the idea of killing and war? How many were forced to pick up a gun, put on a uniform and fight?* Her excuses for those soldiers range from the practical to the psychological. *Many had no choice. What could they do? Some couldn't find work. Call it stupid. Call it crazy. Call it . . .*

You don't know yourself until you're in a situation. She moves to the broader question: *How could this war start, and then go on so long? A massive spiral was spinning out of control, and you had no choice but to become part of the army. Of course, there was no reason to become more criminal and massacre people, but those are two different categories. You can stay human in any situation. You had ordinary soldiers firing rifles and tanks, and then you had criminals. That's the choice. But to take up a gun or not, people had less choice.*[27]

Those who insist on seeing Bosnia in terms of ethnic groups might point out that since Alenka's father and husband were Serb, her excusing the soldiers may be one more example of Serbs not being willing to come to grips with their complicity in the aggression. But not so KADA, who lost every man in her world to a massacre perpetrated by Serbs. She speaks with legitimacy as she puts aside her grief to enter the reality of the aggressors. *How can people like that live with themselves? They must have flashbacks all the time—cutting people's throats . . .* Her words are much more like a care provider than a victim. But she goes further, allowing the soldiers complete freedom from responsibility. *There must be something inside making them do that. When they come to their senses, I wonder how they feel. It must be so hard for them. We all can get upset and break down, but after that we're sorry. I can't understand what happened in the war. It's as if the people didn't want to have a good life any more, as if they wanted some spectacle, even if it was evil. It's unbelievable.*

She moves to the larger questions: *Why did God create us if we do evil to others? It's better not to be alive. They were awarding medals to whoever committed the worst crime, to the one who killed the most people in the fiercest way, or raped the most women. He was a hero by their standards. And the worst part is, that soldier believed he was doing good for his people and for his religion. I'm sure they're not aware even now that they were committing crimes, and that they did evil to other people.*

Ultimately, some of the women are able to go even further, actually mustering some modicum of kindness toward the enemy. EMSUDA, who saw her neighbors turn into monsters who murdered, tortured, maimed, and raped, still wants to remember the old times when they were just neighbors. She puts herself through mental gymnastics to escape the trap of hatred: *When I see those people, I try to think of the pleasant times before. It works . . . as long as they don't start talking about what happened. I haven't felt any anger or hatred toward them—just pity.* Emsuda's sense of justice is cosmic. *The evil they did, even when they really believed they were doing the right thing, will remain for them and for their descendants a curse—not only personally, but for the whole nation.*

But is her sense of ultimate justice enough? How does Emsuda control her natural feelings of revulsion or revenge? *No matter how depraved a person is, I try to find in the depth of his soul at least a little positive spark that could be a nucleus for change. If I find there's no possibility, I give up—but with great sadness. Even the most horrendous criminal in the world has a bit of positive energy and can change. The soldier who saved me from being taken to the Omarska death camp had no doubt killed hundreds of people; but after we met, I bet he didn't kill again, but saved hundreds. He changed, and friends who were with him also were turned around. That's when I realized we need to work with people and look for what can help them become better. They have to create those changes inside themselves, instead of having me tell them what's good or bad.* I asked Emsuda about the contact she had with the soldier afterward. She didn't have any, she told me; she was just certain that he must have changed.

RADA was the recipient of such a benevolent spirit, during the war. *I was doing a documentary story. It was 1993—a spring of hunger. I went to a neighborhood at the edge of Sarajevo where all the houses had been destroyed. The people were mainly Muslims; now they were living underground—in holes they had dug only two hundred meters away from the front line. It was a dangerous place, with bitter people who didn't want to set eyes on a Serb. We were a symbol of evil, of crime, and all the horrible things that had happened.*

I understand people—especially country folk—so I was ready for what lay ahead. The first five minutes were always crucial. Often, people didn't want to shake hands when they heard my Serb name, "Radmila." They'd keep silent or just walk away. I was met by a group of people in the street. Among them, a seventy-year-old man, wearing an old, shabby but clean suit. He stared at me. Then he shook my hand and said, "When you've finished, please come visit me. They call me 'Hadjija.' Where do you come from?" I should have said "Sarajevo." I wanted to. But then I thought twice and imagined someone might tell him otherwise, so I said, "I am from Pale" [the town of the Bosnian Serb headquarters]. *He said "No problem! You're mine."*

The cameraman and I completed our assignment then went to see him. He was highly respected; despite his age he had joined the army with his son to try to defend their community. Now he was living in a space he had dug out under his burnt house. He had even managed to run a phone line into that hole! When we arrived, he had a fire going. It was Ramadan, when no Muslim eats during the day, but his wife had made big plates of pita and sauerkraut. Sauerkraut! It was unimaginable at that time! My God, that aroma! And the beauty of the place! It has stayed in my soul. It was difficult; I was the only one eating. He asked me, "How do you manage? Do you have a family?" I told him, "I have two children and a husband. Nobody is earning money." I was being honest; we didn't have any money for five years. Then he said, "Why didn't you say so? I have plenty of flour!" I told Hadjija, "I can't take anything." The old man worked in his garden every night, with his wife. They had managed to grow onions and potatoes. They wanted to pack something for me to bring home. There was nothing in town . . . not even salt . . . not even bread . . . only hunger; but I left empty-handed. I didn't want to take anything from him.

I broadcast this story on the radio. I polished it, as a work of art, with all my love. He heard it, and then he called me, saying we had to meet the next day. He told me to wait outside the studio. He had no transportation, of course, and it was a long way. He got up at five that morning to walk two-and-a-half hours. I was waiting for him outside the building. He was carrying a rucksack on his back. He was a small man, and the heavy load dug into his shoulders. He told me to take the rucksack. When I opened it at home, it was full of potatoes, beets, onions, sauerkraut, and smoked plums. Then I found, in a pocket, something more: a box of cigarettes! Cigarettes were only a dream during that time. That was unimaginable! And in the packet of cigarettes was a piece of paper, wrapped around some money. A few Deutschmarks. The note read: "Radmila, this is from Allah. Don't be offended."

I didn't cry even when my father died. But at that moment, I cried from happiness. We're still friends. I visit his home as if I'm his own child. I'm part of his family. That feeling has kept me going.

Keeping going is, after all, the first task of each of the women in this book as they walk the long road to reconciliation. And so KRISTINA sums up the lessons of these twenty-six women in a final benediction and call to action. *It's time for us to return to our normal flow of life, for our children to play outside without fear, without having to dread the next shelling, or snipers, or any other danger. Like all other children in the world, they want to live free—not only our children, but all of us.* All, including journalists, NGO leaders, farmers, politicians, greenhouse managers, stay-at-home mothers, retired entrepreneurs, artists, publishers, dress designers, school teachers, massacre survivors, students, physicians, engineers . . . all the women of Bosnia and Herzegovina, and with their help, all the people of that country. For, as Kristina insists: *The war has ended . . . and it's time to put a full stop on that story.*

Epilogue

Commerce shattered under siege. December 1995.

The Courage to Hope

GRETA: *Why should I be afraid? I never went to the cellar when there was shelling. Even in Auschwitz I was confident. I don't know why. I'd lost everybody. But even when my strength was gone, when I was nothing but bones, I still didn't want to die.*

ALENKA: *This is a country you have to love and hate at the same time. . . . On one side such hope, and on the other side so much hopelessness.*

NADA: *Things will get better. After all, they can't be worse. Do you know what my name means in English? "Hope."*

KADA: *If nothing else, we can at least try to be sure that all we experienced in Srebrenica isn't forgotten.*

SWANEE: *Well, Amna, thank you for telling me all this.*

AMNA: *I hope you make something happen with it.*

I have two confessions. First, I'm one of those Americans who paid attention sporadically to the Balkan people over the past years. When I had the time or the inclination, I focused on their plight and gave them support. But most of the time I was an observer, a spectator, a voyeur even, curled up with a book, coffee, and cushions as I watched war correspondents on TV or read through political reports of the unfolding horror these twenty-six women were encountering. I didn't do all I could have done, and what bit I did isn't nearly enough to assuage my sense of responsibility. The truth is, I was close enough to them and to world leaders to know how to help. I should have done more.

The second confession is about real limitations I'm not able to overcome. Writing to give voice to women whose paths have crossed mine, to share their wisdom with the wider world, I can relay only a sliver of their experience. I edit or shape their words with no illusion that I do them justice. This simple book cannot embrace such complicated women. They aren't pacifists, but they hate war. They aren't sentimentalists, but they passionately love their families, their homes, their country. Their views are as thoughtful and complex as their experiences are dense. I'm daunted by the notion of speaking for them. Still, to let my inadequacy block me from trying to do what Amna asks seems a worse choice. So it's with apologies all around that I offer this insufficient rendition of the wealth of spirit I've witnessed in the vibrant lives of Bosnian women.

This book is more than a collection of their stories. It's a calling to account that grabs hold of our excuses and refuses to let go. What are the lessons for people like me, sitting behind a grand mahogany desk in Vienna, or a less-than-grand metal desk at Harvard? The Bosnian war made mush of the hopes that heralded the collapse of communism. Ronald Reagan was wrong. Empires, it turns out, are not evil. Actions are. We'd do well to weave relationships within the webs of empires around the world, especially relationships with the women, who could play a powerful role in averting violent conflict.

In the decade since the start of the war, the United States has spent more than $24 billion to secure peace in the Balkans.[1] After I began working on this book, the United States intervened to quell the conflict in Kosovo. Macedonia heated up. Milosevic ended up at The Hague—of this development the last U.S. ambassador to Yugoslavia says, "I could not have imagined [it], even in my wildest dreams."[2] As cargo planes load up for relief missions to the next Iraq, Liberia, or Afghanistan, will policymakers strapping themselves between giant bags of flour wonder about the women on the ground who've been organizing, with heart and soul, to try to avert war? Will they spend time on that plane planning ways to funnel support to the women's activities traditionally outside the power mainstream? Will they send embassy political officers to report on the women's work across conflict lines, or make sure government aid programs send the women a "request for proposals" precisely because, as second-class citizens, the women aren't considered so threatening that their initiatives must be suppressed by the warmongers?[3] Will the embassy public affairs officers suggest to news reporters that they talk with a Jelka, Rada, or Alenka—women who know the nuanced inner workings of their communities?

Our work and our world would be different if we saw it through the eyes of women who haven't stared at reality through the sights of rifles. We need a new vision. Bosnia, at the time of this writing, hasn't returned to the solid multicultural society some envisioned at the Dayton peace talks.[4] Although that much-heralded agreement silenced the guns, it has largely failed in many of its other objectives, succeeding instead in dividing the country geographically along nationalist lines, all the while declaring an end to nationalist ideals. The impunity with which indicted war criminals still roam free has prohibited many refugees from returning home. Local political leaders have thwarted the multicultural goals expressed not only at Dayton but also by the women who speak here.

In light of those failures, what to make of the assertion by Haris Silajdzic (former Bosnian foreign minister and prime minister) that "if women had been in charge, there would never have been a war"?[5] The international community hasn't grappled with his statement. World leaders and global funders have done little to support women's voices for reconciliation in Bosnian society, and Balkan political leaders haven't stepped forward to share power voluntarily with women.[6] On their part, Bosnian women's declaration that this was not their war has cut both ways: distancing them from the root causes but also from the power center.

Two questions present themselves to policymakers. First, if women are particularly effective in conflict situations, what obstacles keep their work from being supported? And second, after decades in a highly restricted political system followed by years of war, what sort of external support do women need as they step forward to help mold a new Bosnia out of the postconflict mud and morass?

The answers remain for policymakers to codify. Meanwhile, as prototypes of new possibility, the characters in this book are chock full of ideas, energy, and a determination to restore their country. They're smart and savvy — a remarkably good bet for outsiders looking for inside partners to move an agenda for stabilization. The women's expertise spans multiple spheres. Their aptitude is matched by attitude. Irma insists on a first kiss in the cellar, defiant innocence in a perverse reality. Likewise, Greta, sixty years Irma's senior, insists on changing into pajamas and sleeping in her own bed, popping a sedative to block out the exploding mortars, and declaring that she will not be moved.

Such women are the bearers of a hope that endures on a personal level — and therefore on political levels as well; for we can take heart as long as individuals like Mediha continue to insist: *In the end, good will prevail.* Balkan demagogues may lead their people into disaster, pilfering precious resources, sacrificing lives, and squandering opportunities. We outsiders may compound the madness with our multiple conflicting agendas, our dawdling foreign policy, our broken promises. But at the ground level, where hope meets history, Mediha understands, and she reminds us: *Life goes on, and life wins.*

Profiles

I'm just a small stone in the mosaic of Bosnian women. — EMSUDA

Descriptions of the twenty-six main characters follow.[1] Despite the richness of these women's stories, it was difficult to determine the criteria by which to select protagonists, reflecting a wide range of life circumstances and backgrounds. The most obvious differentiating category was ethnic background—until one woman after another insisted that identifying Bosnians by ethnicity was either a fabrication of war or a concept imposed by the outside. Thus there was a great irony in my seeking out "three more Croats" or "two more Serbs." Even in my attempts at balance, I was buying into a politicized cultural myth.

The task of finding my subjects was aided tremendously by Sunita Samarah, a well-connected Bosnian activist who introduced me to women with a wide range of characteristics.[2] These women were not chosen randomly or because they were somehow "typical" of all Bosnian women; for the most part they were actively engaged in rebuilding their country, with creative ideas and the spirit to implement them. In many cases, they were identified leaders in their communities, known among their neighbors to have a vision they could persuasively articulate. But that is where the similarities ended; the women did not share political views, life experiences, family situations, or religious traditions.

I was guided by many questions. What was it like to experience the war from outside the country? How was the perspective of an adolescent different from that of a grown woman? How did wealth make a difference? Clearly, I could have interviewed 26,000 women and still not constructed a complete picture. No one woman speaks for the women of Bosnia and Herzegovina. Nor do twenty-six. But there are generalities at least to be pondered, if not accepted, as these individuals create a collective voice. Those women who survived the war have emerged not only with profiles that are riveting but with personalities powerful in the breadth of their perceptiveness and depth of their inner strength.

ALENKA SAVIC

It's not easy to hate. It takes too much energy.

ALENKA SAVIC is a no-nonsense woman in her early forties. Her husband died in a car accident in 1989, but she says single motherhood isn't so difficult, given her training as a civil engineer. She was born in Slovenia (her mother's homeland), and her father was a Serb from northeastern Bosnia. She speaks often about the value of "staying normal," which included not leaving Tuzla when it was shelled by Serbs. Though laid off from a construction company when the war started, Alenka recounts the school achievements of her son and daughter as evidence that there was no prejudice against her family, despite their last name. Friends urged her to join her sister in Slovenia; but she refused, saying first, she didn't want to abandon her parents; second, she felt there'd be no real danger in Tuzla; and, third, *I wasn't about to pick up a plastic bag and become another "displaced person."* In 1994, she went to Llubljana for a few days' respite but returned to live out the war in Tuzla. *When everyone's in the same trouble, you feel like a member of a group. You've shared experiences, good or bad, and you're part of the team.* For four years, she and her children often felt imprisoned in their house, with sporadic electricity and water. Despite the hardships, the war provided an opportunity to prove herself: *I could survive, overcome, and remain a human being, not an animal.* Alenka offered herself as "an engineer who speaks terrible English" to the NGO Mercy Corps, where she worked with shelters. She manages the northeast quadrant of the Bosnian Women's Initiative, helping women start businesses. Working with Muslim women returning to Srebrenica and their former Serb neighbors, she says: *Given the slaughter, this is almost unbelievable. It's easy for women to work on reconciliation. We're not afraid to go to the other side — maybe because everyone knows we weren't carrying guns; we weren't in the death squads.*

ALMA KECO

Men feared being killed . . .

We women were afraid of being caught alive.

ALMA KECO, twenty-five, found herself trapped as she traveled home from a holiday with her parents in Sarajevo. An athlete, she joined the fighting on Mount
Igman as a paramedic for Bosniak troops trying to lift the siege of the capital, where she was born. She received the "Golden Lily" medal. An engineer in
Mostar, she's straightforward: She doesn't smile much, and when saying something difficult, she bites her lip, blows air out, lifts her eyebrows, and scans the
ceiling, searching for words. Battling post-traumatic stress disorder, Alma seems
older than she is; after she was wounded a third time, gangrene led to the loss of
several teeth. One brother was killed in Mostar, another permanently disabled;
her father was heavily injured, and her mother became very ill. Alma has head,
stomach, and hand injuries for which she still receives regular treatment. After
years in the trenches, surrounded by death, Alma organized women throughout
her area in a veterans group. She insists that society give back to those who made
such a sacrifice: *Women had a far more difficult time during the war—in part because
we feel more, and we're more sensitive. In the army, I saw how a woman gives much
more weight than a man does to the decision to kill. Maybe that's nature. You know,
every woman is a potential mother, and mothers are the core not only of our families, but
the whole society—whether we want to admit it or not.* That vision inspires Alma,
for whom strength is intertwined with the capacity to suffer, while remaining
connected with humanity. *When my brother was killed, my mother told me, "Every
mother sheds the same tears." Croat, Serb, and Muslim mothers feel the same pain. But
only women have that feeling. We're more moderate. If it had been up to women, this
war wouldn't have broken out at all.*

AMNA POPOVAC

Now they say, "Oh, I wasn't in the army; I wasn't so terrible."
But no gun shoots without a person. No shell explodes on its own.

AMNA POPOVAC was born in Mostar in 1970. A staunch, energetic idealist, in the early days of the negotiated peace she traveled through checkpoints to Republika Srpska, seeking out Serbs willing to return to their Mostar homes then coordinating with aid agencies to help ensure their safe return. She started a radio station with other youth to provide unbiased reporting. At the university in Split, she studied electrical engineering, specializing in computers. Amna and her family were frequently on the move because of the war: She fled the university to escape Serb aggression in Croatia; and twice—when Serbs shelled Mostar and when Bosnian Croats attacked the predominantly Muslim part of town—her family fled to Croatia. When Muslims were expelled from university housing, friends took Amna in so she could complete her schooling. Overall, she appears to be a well-put-together young woman, dressing with sophisticated professionalism, lipstick, and manicured nails to match her clothes. Her voice is low, her English is fluent, and her eyes crinkle in the corners when she smiles—which is often. Amna admires her father's stoicism: *When the fighting started, he gathered us around the table where we always sat if there was a family talk. We knew he wanted to say something important. "This is a war," he said. We all four sat there, in silence. I was thinking, "But it'll last only a few days." He said, "Some of us will survive, and some won't."* Wisely (but sadly), Amna's father's words didn't anticipate outside intervention. He advised his family to hunker down: *"Stay here, and just try to survive."* That blunt message is emblazoned in Amna's memory. She, in turn, was resolute in sticking out the war years, in part because she found the reasons given for the conflict to be ludicrous. *I kept speaking the same language; of course I don't know if it's Croatian, Bosnian, or Serbian!*

ANA PRANIC

If you'd met me when I was younger,

I'd have said I love men more than women.

[She throws her head back, laughing; then grows somber.]

Now I just want to be left alone.

I just want the shooting to be over.

An ethnic Croat in her early sixties, ANA PRANIC is one of eight children. She was raised in Visoko, a Muslim-majority merchant town. Her playmates were mostly Muslim, but also from other backgrounds. Her low, husky voice is punctuated with waving hands as she explains how the Catholic Church is important to her, but all religions must be respected. Ana's sister and brother married Muslims. When Ana married, she moved to nearby Podlugovi, a village with a Serb majority. Her husband worked in a steel factory until it was destroyed during the war. Ana first worked as a seamstress and with leather goods, although she left her job to raise her daughters, Vesna and Valentina. *I didn't mind their mini-skirts, as long as they were good students and didn't smoke.* When the girls were older, Ana worked ten years in a bakery. With the war, she was afraid to leave her home of thirty-six years. She has no idea who fired a shell that damaged not only her home but three others where, she notes wryly, people from all ethnic groups live. Ana survived off humanitarian aid; her husband worked in a bakery as part of his war service. She's now raising her niece after her widowed sister was killed by a shell on her way to work. Her divorced daughter and nephew live with her as well. After the war, her husband suffered a stroke. He can walk but has only a very small pension. In 1998 Ana received a ten-month loan from the Bosnian Women's Initiative. She bought sheep, from which she generated enough to repay her loan. With a second loan she bought a cow, which she slaughtered to sell dried meat. The project, while a success, does not make Ana financially secure.

BILJANA CHENGICH FEINSTEIN

We Jews haven't been able to convince the world.

It just keeps happening, again and again:

greedy people using religion as their excuse for war.

From Colorado Springs, BILJANA CHENGICH FEINSTEIN returned each summer with her children to the former Yugoslavia. In 1994 she went to be with her dying mother in Croatia, not knowing when the shooting and shelling might start around her. Despite her Serb surname, she grew up Muslim in Sarajevo, the youngest of four, and a descendant of royalty on her mother's side. Although her father died before she was born, she describes a happy childhood, with ballet lessons and children's choir. *I had it even better than my own children, and they were very, very privileged.* At nineteen, she sought greener pastures in Sweden and then went on to the United States, where she fell in love with "the open, welcoming American personality." She married and converted to Judaism, making a new life with her husband, a talented architect in Colorado Springs. There she opened a store as a cosmetician, creating her own makeup line. During the war, which she followed primarily through the media, she contacted the Red Cross but felt powerless to help and disconnected from her people, watching from a distance as her country was torn apart. Everything about Biljana is bold—from her raucous laugh, to the pizzazz of her art, to the political views she tosses into conversations at the drop of a hat: *With communism, women became more independent thinkers, more open, better able to express themselves. Yugoslav women had strong opinions, and everyone in the neighborhood heard them; still, they weren't allowed by the communists to exercise leadership. . . . Tito was a control freak, but he didn't plan his succession; that's why Yugoslavia as a country failed.* Biljana, with her thick Slavic accent, explains to anyone who'll listen that the war Americans observed from their living rooms was not about deep, ancient hatreds.

DANICA PETRIC

Men have had power not because they shoved women to the back,

but because we didn't fight for our positions.

We have ourselves to blame.

When DANICA PETRIC fled Serb paramilitaries, she left behind not only her home but also her flower shop, which provided coffins crafted for different religious traditions. Danica is dignified but nurturing. She smiles easily, cries frequently, and clouds over when concentrating. Danica knows the cruelties of World War II: Her father's health broke in a concentration camp, and she has flashbacks of Nazi and Partisan battles, with death all around. Danica's father was a Bosnian Croat policeman, a quiet, unhappy man; her mother grew up in Slovenia. *The family moved to a Bosnian village, bringing new vegetables and fruits and seeds — two or three wagons full. We were like a freak show. When our thermometer was loaned from house to house, it was a tossup whose temperature they were going to take — the pig's or the kid's.* Danica raised two daughters. In 1992 her family barely escaped across the river into Croatia, where various family members reunited as refugees, although one daughter preferred to find menial jobs in Austria. Danica isn't shy in her formula for a better world: *Women should change the rules so men take on more home responsibility. They'd have less time for violence, and women would have time to create peace initiatives.* Given her traditional view of the role of mothers, her insistence on gender equality may be because her life has been so hard. *I've lost my smile over the years.* However, subsequent to our final book interview, Danica was ecstatic, back home in what is now Republika Srpska. *People ask when I'll reopen my shop. I say, "I'm a grandmother, not a businesswoman!" Regardless of how our houses look, our faces are happy.*

EMSUDA MUJAGIC

Some people, even if they lived three hundred years,

might not have as many experiences as I've had.

EMSUDA MUJAGIC lived near Prijedor, where fertile fields and thick woods are now dotted with dozens of mass graves. The population was evenly Muslim and Serb, with a smattering of Croats. In April 1992, Belgrade-backed "reliable Serbs" took over the important posts, ousting Muslims and Croats, who were unarmed and unable to form a resistance.[3] Before the war, Emsuda convinced her husband to devote their life savings to training five hundred women from half a dozen towns to knit high-fashion clothes, so they could afford to educate themselves and their children. In the war, the business was destroyed, and some of those children were targeted. Emsuda's house was blown up. She and her son were separated from her husband and daughter but found them three days later in the Trepoljna concentration camp, where rape, torture, and mutilation were common. Her husband is psychologically scarred. Given her reputation as a leader, Emsuda was fingered as a potential troublemaker and slated for the Omarska death camp. A Serb soldier helped her escape to Zagreb, where she started an NGO. Post-Dayton, she returned to Sanski Most, opposite Prijedor, which was now in Republika Srpska. The 60,000 in Sanski Most are mostly Bosniaks expelled from other towns. Industry is functioning at about 20 percent capacity, and the return of displaced people to their homes is moving at a snail's pace. Emsuda has started another NGO serving women and schoolchildren and building bridges across ideological divides. Her husband teases callers that he's her secretary. When Emsuda hears bellicose talk from others, she asserts, *If there's going to be more war, I'll go — not my son and daughter.* She's impatient with women who don't push through obstacles: *Women withdraw and leave decisions to men, so we have to teach them to be independent and self-reliant. We can't just blame the men.*

FAHRIJA GANIC

I still consider all the republics as my country.

Whenever I cross a border of the former Yugoslavia, my heart starts pounding.

I'm coming home.

A dermatologist trained at Chicago's Cook County Hospital, FAHRIJA GANIC and her husband Ejup, a gregarious political figure, both come from Sandzak, a 95 percent Muslim region of about 700,000 in western Serbia. After eleven years in the United States, where Ejup taught engineering at the Massachusetts Institute of Technology, they moved back to Sarajevo. As war became imminent, Fahrija gathered the family jewels and fled to Turkey with her two young children. She made her way to Buffalo, New York, where, in lonely political asylum, she tried to convince American acquaintances that the conflict wasn't about neighbors who couldn't live together. Fahrija organized humanitarian aid to send back to Bosnia and a letter-writing campaign to President Clinton. She finished the war years sheltering her children in Vienna, with her husband in Sarajevo as one of the seven-member Bosnian presidency. After peace was secure, she opened a skin clinic in Sarajevo despite the war-ravaged economy. Fahrija's great-grandfather was Albania's King George Kastrioti; her grandmother Queen Dorothea Bashira. Although her grandfather was a wealthy merchant, her father was thrown out on the street by Partisans. Her mother, who had given birth that same night, went to Belgrade and took off her veil, interceding with Tito to win her husband's release from prison. Fahrija lives in a spacious Sarajevo home, her walls hung with art by Bosnia's most renowned painters. Her children speak English as their mother tongue: Emina, her sophisticated daughter, is a graduate of Oxford University; Emir, her son, is part of the set crowding Sarajevo cafes. *I taught my children: The friends they made, languages they've learned, and cultures they've come to understand are all costly gifts they received from the war.*

GALINA MARJANOVIC

*Despite our organizing, for a long time the government didn't
let us register as an NGO. They said, "Who cares what
these women are doing? We're at war!"*

GALINA MARJANOVIC is an ethnic Serb from Banja Luka, the capital of Republika Srpska. Despite problems she tackles every day, she smiles often when she speaks, drawing circles in the air when making a point. She describes her childhood in Banja Luka as living in a *mini-Europe*: her Muslim, Czech, and Austrian playmates were constantly in each other's homes, with families trading the foods of their respective traditions. Galina studied special education and worked for almost twenty-five years with deaf children. *We weren't members of the Communist Party, so we could preserve our open-mindedness.* Wartime economic sanctions cut into her husband's business—a small factory producing orthopedic appliances. When the tides of war shifted against the Serbs, the same compassion and patience she extended to disabled children moved Galina to action as she watched a stream of refugees pouring down her street, hungry, cold, weak, sick, and missing family members. Galina and her husband opened their large house as a shelter. After giving groceries from her cupboard, she pulled together women friends to create "Duga" (Rainbow), caring, among many others, for severely traumatized women. Nearly eighty co-workers (essentially volunteers) work with Galina to help these women and their children slowly piece their lives back together. In media interviews, she appeals for help for the suffering without naming an ethnic group. In fact, after the war, she was one of the first Bosnian Serb women to meet with other women's organizations outside the Serb region, including the Vital Voices conference in Vienna. She says mistakes were made and crimes committed by all sides. *But often people couldn't see the mistakes of their side, focusing on the mistakes of others. That's changing now.* Galina is Orthodox, and she lives by the Golden Rule: *Religions are like cultures, shaped by people. If we didn't do things we wouldn't want done to us, life would be perfect, despite religious differences.*

GRETA FERUSIC-WEINFELD

I survived Auschwitz, and I stayed in Sarajevo.

Maybe my spirit is inherited, or innate.

I don't know. I never was different.

GRETA FERUSIC-WEINFELD was born in 1924, in Novi Sad, in the Kingdom of Yugoslavia, now part of Serbia. Her hometown had citizens from many national origins, including many Germans who sympathized with Hitler. A Jew deported in April 1944 and shipped by rail to Auschwitz, she was a slave laborer until the camp was liberated by Soviets. Back in Belgrade she pursued her education in construction design. *There was no money, but it was more positive than today, where everyone is an individual with money. We're no longer united.* As for gender equity: *Women play a very, very, very diminished role in our society now; the situation was much more balanced before—never equal,*[4] *but women and men were equally paid.* Greta's career included a professorship in architecture and service as a government minister (1976–82), dealing with environmental concerns. She bridges cultures with fluent Hungarian, German, French, Italian, and English. Since her retirement in 1983, she's worked with La Benevolencija, a Jewish humanitarian and cultural association. She tells how, when Sarajevo Jews saw history beginning to repeat itself, they organized bus convoys out of the capital. She and her husband insisted they were too old to live out of a suitcase as refugees, only to return to a stripped apartment. Instead, she popped sedatives to endure nights of shelling and defiantly refused to go to shelters. *I slept in my own bed, in my pajamas. The next day, everybody'd say, "Did you hear such and such last night?" I'd say, "No, I was asleep."* She's a woman of enormous optimism. *I don't see the black. If I can't think of good things, I don't think.* As for her future: *If it's the end, it's the end.*

IRMA SAJE

None of us chose war; none of us girls wanted to fight.

IRMA SAJE could be a teen model. Her smile conveys a charming forthright-
ness. But like so many young people raised in war, Irma seems like a wise old
woman in the body of a child. Her father describes her as very independent, and
he takes some credit for not forcing her to follow any particular path. Although
her mother is Muslim and her father Catholic, ethnicity was not an issue in her
family. Typical of most Sarajevan teenagers, Irma's English is excellent. She revels
in American pop culture but is clearly proud of her Bosnian identity. Before the
war, Irma's parents were architects and worked in Iraq from time to time. From
age six to ten, she spent half of each year in Baghdad and the other half living with
her grandmother in Bosnia. Her adolescence was surviving the war in Sarajevo.
She shakes her head over small details of war life she's almost forgotten. After
three years of shelling and siege, she escaped to distant relatives in Austria, but a
year and a half later returned to pick up the pieces of her life. Like Anne Frank,
another girl coming of age in the exigency of war, Irma's reflections on the devastation of her external world are laced with personal accounts of the nuanced
inner workings of her family: the strength of her mother, the protective anxiety
of her father, and her sense of herself changing from girl into woman. She weeps
describing the injury and death of friends. There's a philosophical bent in her reflections on the intimacy among those who endured the terrors of war together,
and the regrettable return to normal emotional distance that accompanied the
peace. She's clear about her views of the gender differences that became apparent
under the stress of the conflict and asserts, boldly, *Women won the war in Bosnia.*

JELKA KEBO

Three of us four children married a person from a different ethnic group.

I'd say we were raised in the spirit of Bosnia and Herzegovina.

JELKA KEBO's life is about bridges. A historic stone bridge, built in 1556, connected the two sides of Mostar across the Neretva River. The community is half ethnic Croat (and Catholic, like Jelka) and half Bosniak (Muslim). *There were no divisions; we all swam in the same river and walked down the same alleys.* Jelka's husband is a painter. They had a gallery and traveled to exhibitions. She worked with developmentally disabled children for twenty-five years. During the war, her husband, older son, and brother fought in the army; her younger son had military training. The war in Mostar had two phases. First, Serbs attacked from the surrounding hills and were driven back. Then Croat nationalists, attempting to make Mostar their capital in a divided Bosnia, expelled Bosniaks to the older side of the city and relentlessly shelled it. *My parents were thrown out of their apartment on the west side because their grandson fought on the east side.* Jelka's older son died in a car accident, right after the fighting stopped. In a setting in which distrust runs rampant, Jelka has transformed her grief into action, creating connections between the two sides of town. She's won national recognition for her Center for Culture and Youth, which brings young people together and reminds all citizens of the social richness of prewar Mostar. Her eyes turn fiery when she talks about harnessing the strength of women in her country. *Before the war, my highest achievement was when my kids did well in school, when I saw an interesting exhibit with my husband or we went on a vacation abroad. I did some handcrafts, and I was proud when dinner guests admired my table. All women thought that way; it seemed natural. But now, only now in my mid-forties, I realize I was a victim.* Jelka has started traveling without her husband—a big step, she says. *I've rebelled!*

KADA HOTIC

After the evil we endured,

the world must develop enough of a conscience

so that this never, ever happens again.

KADA HOTIC's life in Srebrenica was typical of rural Bosnia: *We had a comfortable flat. We weren't rich like people in Western countries. I went for a summer holiday. I had nice clothes. We'd fish, go boating, swim, and have picnics and parties, drinking and singing.* Kada worked in a textile factory. Her husband had a degree in sociology and held white-collar jobs. The town, swelled with refugees, was surrounded by Serbs and shelled. Kada risked her life traversing woods and fields, search-ing for food. The three-year siege ended with a massacre in which an estimated 8,000 unarmed Muslim boys and men were executed, including Kada's son, hus-band, two brothers, and brother-in-law. *It gets more difficult with every passing day. Nights are harder too. I had more hope in the beginning. I believed in people. I thought they'd tell us the truth. Now my strength is gone. I've lost faith.* Kada and her daughter Lejla were separated by the war but have reunited in Sarajevo. A pharmaceuti-cal assistant, Lejla married a construction engineer. They have a young son—Kada's "only joy"—but currently are unemployed. The family of four is living on government pensions—about $237 a month. Kada distinguishes between simple people and those who created the war for their own ends. In spite of her isolating trauma, she feels connected to the larger world as she tells and retells what hap-pened. She hopes those who listen will repeat her story to others. *Evil can happen everywhere . . . and to anyone.* Asked if women see things differently then men, she's noncommittal: *I don't know. Where I live, we're mostly women—mothers . . . sisters . . . wives. I don't speak much to men.* [Kada pauses.] *You know . . . there aren't any men left.*

KAROLINA ATAGIC

You've got to understand people.

There were so many mothers who lost sons and husbands.

If my son had died, I wouldn't find as much understanding

within myself as they did.

When KAROLINA ATAGIC's eighteen-year-old took up arms, her husband couldn't bear the prospect of harm to his son. Tormented by his worry, he died of a heart attack. Karolina, a Catholic who married into a Muslim family, lives in the historically Muslim section of Sarajevo. She was born May 9, 1943, in the German concentration camp Reutligen, to a Polish Catholic mother and Croat Catholic father. When Karolina was six months old, her mother had to leave the women's barracks to work as slave labor in the fields. Next to the women's barracks were American prisoners of war, who became her first caretakers, giving her food through the barbed wire that separated them. At two she was speaking English, which her mother couldn't understand. After the liberation of the camp, she returned with her mother to Sarajevo, where she remained. Her parents divorced after the war; both had suffered enormous trauma. Her father lost his teeth and hair and died soon after. Karolina is a university graduate in business and economics. She works in the finance department of a large trading company. During the Bosnian war, she brought into her home two orphaned friends of her children. To calm her own fears and frustrations, she took up painting a few hours a week. Art had always been an interest, and for those hours at her canvas, the war would disappear. Together with other women, Karolina formed a painting club. In 1994, in the middle of the war, the group presented an exhibition of their work for International Women's Day; it was an island of normalcy in a sea of chaos. She is a founding member of a women's collective that produces ceramics and souvenirs. Proceeds fund the women's art initiatives, as well as care for mentally disabled children.

KRISTINA KOVAC

If you surveyed all the people, regardless of religion, and ask

how much they won or lost, and if they wanted this war in the first place,

you'd get exactly the same answers.

KRISTINA KOVAC is an ethnic Serb from Sipovo, a small town in Republika Srpska. She has the vivacious personality of a primary school teacher, her profession before the war and after. When violence broke out, the Muslim families in Sipovo asked to be transported to an area controlled by Bosniaks (about 17 percent of the population). Her husband, a forty-eight-year-old physical education teacher, like the majority of men, was mobilized by the Serb army. Kristina speaks fondly of him as a wonderful father and husband and a good friend. He's a bit grayer since the war. Kristina's two daughters were fifteen and twenty-two when the war started. During the conflict, she struggled to find clothing or food, much less schoolbooks, for her daughters. In September 1995, the eve of the Dayton Peace Agreement, Croat forces took the territory where Kristina lived; in a panicked exodus the Bosnian Serb population fled. After taking refuge in Banja Luka, Kristina returned to find 50 percent of the town rendered uninhabitable and 80 percent of rural housing destroyed. After the war, Kristina and her husband could no longer afford their older daughter's university studies. Despite these setbacks, Kristina maintains a can-do attitude. She's returned to Sipovo, where she and her husband are again teaching. She's recruited help from humanitarian agencies and international troops to refurnish the school and to set up a summer camp for children who lost parents during the war. *We can't live in isolation. There's always someone who needs someone else*, she explains, describing her work organizing the care of handicapped and vulnerable people. *Those who've had someone killed will need a lot of time for their wounds to heal.* Still, Kristina believes concern for children may reunify her society. *Women are mothers first—no matter the ethnic group. Why war? There's nothing holier than her child.*

MAJA JERKOVIC

Nationalism is junk, and things that aren't good quality can't last long.

Born in 1942, MAJA JERKOVIC has risen to positions of significant leadership since training as an orthodontic surgeon: She managed the Mostar regional hospital with over 3,500 employees. She was an official of the Communist Party but when the war was brewing didn't join the new nationalist Croat party, and thus lost her administrative position. Maja is committed to preserving the diversity she enjoyed in her family and workplace. *In the hospital we had Croats, Serbs, and Muslims working. Throughout the conflict we remained friends. We were just doctors. Working in the hospital in the ear, nose, and throat department, I was never interested in names and surnames, only disease and how to help. My happiest moments were when I could shake hands with healthy patients and wish them well.* It was devastating, watching her city be torn apart, but she persevered. *During the whole war I never missed one single day—or hour—of work. The hospital was almost on the front line. So was my home.* Surely a physician could have found a way out of the bedlam. *I stayed because I love my town and my profession.* Mother of two adolescent boys, during the war she protected her sons by sending them out of the country. *I lived to see my children saved. That was what drove me; and I wouldn't give up that drive for anything.* Her older son went to Cyprus and married an African; the couple has a boy. Maja's husband is an electrical engineer. Today she does what she can to reunite her community at a person-to-person level. Looking back on the emotional strain she endured as she calmed paramilitary thugs on a rampage, she's steady and strong. *No matter what happens, I remain the same as I've always been. Wartime is behind me.*

MEDIHA FILIPOVIC

I had no right to disregard my natural gifts;

I was obligated to humanity.

Maybe it sounds pretentious, but I felt I owed it

to the world around me.

MEDIHA FILIPOVIC was the only female member of parliament in the first Bosnian national assembly. Born in December 1944, she describes her heritage of sociopolitical shifts as a metaphor for Bosnian history: Her great-grandfather, an Ottoman nobleman, was in his later years a citizen of the Austro-Hungarian Empire. Her grandfather, born during those Hapsburg years, lived as an adult within the Kingdom of Yugoslavia. Her father's life began in the kingdom years, but he grew into manhood under communism. *I was born during communism, but now I must adjust to a new system. I wonder in what political structure my son's children will be raised.* In spite of the repression of communism, Mediha remembers her childhood as happy. Education was highly valued, as was sacrifice. Today, noblesse oblige is her theme: *I decided to have a child* and *a career, because I'm ambitious . . . a hard worker . . . and I was a good student. I object to people who are talented and capable wasting those gifts and taking them to their graves.* Mediha's mother inspired her to study medicine, and she trained as an orthodontist, including a year in Kentucky, then developed a low-cost alternative to braces. From Sarajevo, she moved with her husband to Belgrade, but her marriage dissolved when their son was one year old. Back in Sarajevo, she worked hard to maintain her son's relationship with his father, who was later killed in a car accident. When the war started, her husband's Belgrade relatives offered to take in her son. *Bojan decided to stay with me in Sarajevo. Of course, we didn't have any idea what was awaiting us.* She has been a voice for political moderation, insisting on a multiethnic society even as nationalist parties flex their muscles. She currently serves as ambassador to Sweden.

MIRHUNISA ZUCIC

Politicians who've known me for years just ignore me.

They never pick up the phone.

But I don't mind, because I know what I'm doing —

and I know what they're doing.

An accounting professor may be apt at keeping track of people who want to return to their homes, but MIRHUNISA ZUCIC (Komarica when these interviews began) doesn't talk easily about her own journey. She's watched life from different perspectives, having fled with her family from an affluent suburban Sarajevo apartment complex to a one-room existence. Although she believes she's never been taken seriously by the men in power, she has an air of confidence when she speaks of her accomplishments as co-owner of a successful ski equipment business and professor at the School of Economics for more than twenty years. (She revised her textbook by candlelight during the war.) Her teenage boy and girl survived the war, but her nineteen-year-old marriage didn't survive the peace. In a digression from her academic life, Mirhunisa began working with hundreds of rape victims, helping find shelter when they arrived as refugees in Sarajevo. She talks almost matter-of-factly, but with compassion, about the hundreds of atrocities she heard described as she interviewed victims. Her stories are relentlessly painful and poignant. Since the war, her work with refugees has demanded her focus and attention; she sleeps less than five hours a night. *When I spend time with women from the massacre of Srebrenica, I feel stronger. The loss of my marriage was my doing; but these women, their loved ones were taken from them. Still, they keep going.* In her work, she's acted with courage — some might say recklessness: During the war, she gathered fellow-organizers in the streets, in defiance of snipers. *I was sure nothing would happen to them — or to me.* That spirit has led Mirhunisa into invigorated work others would find impossible, as she helps people of all ethnic traditions return home.

NADA RAKOVIC

Some sick minds caused this war.

Not my patients. Not my colleagues.

Not me.

NADA RAKOVIC grew up fifty kilometers from Sarajevo. She describes her family's religious practice as like that of everyone else in the neighborhood: holidays, but little more. Hers was a working-class family. Her mother did domestic work, her father was alcoholic; they divorced. Her brother was deaf and mute from birth. As a girl, Nada was a straight-A student and fulfilled her mother's dream by breaking out of the cycle of hardship. In 1990 she returned to her hometown as a pediatrician, so she could live with her mother, to whom she says she's "joined at the hip." Late in the war, Nada was caught between fighting Bosniaks and Croats. She escaped with her family but had to abandon her home and belongings. In 1998 she joined five other Bosnian women from different political parties to plan a highly successful conference in Sarajevo, encouraging women to run for office. Nada herself served briefly in the parliament of Republika Srpska in the party led by Biljana Plavsic, who was later convicted as a war criminal. She lives now in northern Bosnia, near the Croatian border. I drove several hours to visit her home five years after the war. The road leading into her town looked like a movie scene: lined with stubs of trees between houses with roofs blown off, their red bricks pouring out like confetti spilling from giant boxes. Long, bare chimneys stretched awkwardly up from the foundations; on the remaining walls was scrawled in blue paint, "We keep our word," and, "Brought to you by . . ." Nada backs off discussion about gender disparity. *What do I know? I've never had a sense of less worth because I'm a woman. Maybe uneducated women in villages had less rights, but I was always independent. I don't think we're different from American or European women.*

NURDZIHANA DZOZIC

When we saw barricades, it was clear something was happening;

and from the Serb media, we knew something was brewing.

But I still could not imagine — not in my wildest dreams —

anything like this war.

Perhaps because of her long career as a journalist and editor, NURDZIHANA
DZOZIC speaks — in her low, flat voice — with remarkable candor about her personal and professional life. Smiles are few; more often her mouth is grimly set,
but she doesn't completely hide tender feelings. Born in Bratunac, a few miles
from Srebrenica, and educated in Tuzla, Sarajevo, then Belgrade, she worked for
a newspaper for young people. Moving to Sarajevo, she missed the lively arts and
culture of Belgrade, but she was innovative in her journalistic work, interweav-
ing her interests in psychology, sociology, and social needs. She's an organizer
as much as journalist, putting together walk-in clinics and hot lines for people in
dire straits. During the war, she managed to publish the magazine *Zena 21*, addressing concerns of Bosnian women ("zena") in the twenty-first century. Family
is extremely important to her. Although she has no children, Nurdzihana is devoted to several siblings and eleven nieces and nephews. As Serb forces terrorized
her neighborhood, she lived for months with her elderly mother in the cellar
of her apartment building. She reflects on the war: *Some things about it I'll never
understand. I've thought a lot about this war, written about it, tried to explain it, but it's
a great puzzle to me. I interviewed 2,000 people in my neighborhood, Dobrinja. What
moved me most was the readiness of people to help each other, risking their own lives to
save the injured. People who didn't know each other before would share the last thing
they had. . . . On the other hand, I've seen the flats in which snipers hid, and I've found
bombs made from jars for canning fruit. It was horrible . . . unbelievable.*

RADA SESAR

I'm a Serb, so I can say this:

only when we're able to face the fact that the aggression was intentional

—and condemn it—

will we be able to wash all Serbs of the crime.

RADA SESAR's hands hardly stop moving as she speaks—fists to describe her convictions, fingers playing with her necklace as she talks abstractly, hands flitting about to lay out a neighborhood scene. Ironically, with such expressive gestures, she's spent twenty-five years in the radio business. She links her sensitivity for human-interest stories with her upbringing in a village near Pale (just outside Sarajevo), one of four siblings. Her father was a railway man, her mother a housewife. Rada's eyes light up as she describes her village: *It was full of meadows, waterfalls. . . . I learned freedom there. All my life* [she makes fists with both hands], *I've carried my home village with me. I draw strength from it. But I wouldn't live there. People have romantic pictures of life in the country, but it's hard.* Rada didn't have the physical stamina for country life. *My dream was to be a professional.* She went to school in Sarajevo, graduating at the top of her class in Yugoslav literature. Jobs in academia were difficult to find, and by chance she fell into a position at Radio Sarajevo, quickly establishing herself in the world of journalism. She married a Bosnian Croat and had a son and daughter. When the war began, the Yugoslav National Army started shooting out the windows of their apartment complex in the suburbs, until Rada and her neighbors' apartments were completely destroyed. She and her husband and two children fled to his sister's in the center of town. Focusing on terrified and traumatized people pouring into Sarajevo from other parts of Bosnia, she broadcast intimate testimonies of their experience.

SABIHA HADZIMORATOVIC

This war was imported to my country.

Women didn't start it, but they're the ones who suffer from it.

Raised in Gorazde, where she managed the radio station, SABIHA HADZIMORA-
TOVIC moved with her husband to work in Iraq as a journalist in 1984. She witnessed the devastation of the Iran-Iraq war but never envisioned a similar situation in her own country. Sabiha was in Saudi Arabia during the Gulf War as a
radio and television correspondent and watched, astounded, as conflict grew in
her homeland. *Bosnia had a great education system. Our villages had schools; we had
culture, clubs; big, nice houses; everyone had a car and TV. My heart ached when people
compared Bosnia and Somalia. OK, we had a war, and there was war in Africa, and we're
all people. But four religions meet in Sarajevo. They were destroying mosques, destroying
churches, synagogues. . . . Civilization!* Gorazde was particularly hard hit, with supplies and power cut off; but the people ate roots from the forest and generated
electricity from the river. Sabiha wonders how her Serb and Croat media colleagues could have abandoned their community, leaving it an enclave of Bosniaks
who streamed in for refuge. From abroad, Sabiha arranged for relief. *In Oman,
children came to me with their two dollars for the children of Bosnia so they wouldn't be
hungry.* In Moscow, she organized similar humanitarian efforts while working as
a correspondent. Trained in psychology, Sabiha imagines an integrated Bosnia,
with women educating the next generation. She has organized her own news
agency, produced dolls representing diverse Bosnian ethnic traditions, and participated in a women's business coalition across Balkan states. Her vision is wider
still: *We're citizens of the world. I've been privileged to learn about different cultures, but
I've no right to hate the differences.*

SUZANA ANDJELIC

The truth is, we lost the war, because we lost our country—

and we lost it at Dayton.

Journalist SUZANA ANDJELIC's last name is pronounced like "angelic." It fits. She's remarkably winsome when she speaks, her eyes locking on her listener. Suzana was born in 1968 in Teslic, a town now in Republika Srpska. Both parents were atheists and her father a member of the Communist Party. An excellent student, Suzana joined the party at sixteen; she grew up without celebrating any specifically Serb traditions or embracing the nationalism that later swept across the area. Her studies in journalism took her to nearby Sarajevo. Upon graduation, she and several other young journalists started the progressive *Slobodna Bosna* ("Free Bosnia"), which—unlike most other magazines—took a strong position against the war and argued against its inevitability. Although former neighbors from Teslic criticized her work at what they considered a "Muslim" publication, her parents supported her fully. As a Serb, Suzana had better access to the Yugoslav National Army and covered their activities before the war, using an assumed name. During the siege of Sarajevo, the magazine ran out of money. Suzana visited Teslic to get some food from her parents; but her father asked her to leave for her own safety. In Novi Sad, Serbia, she met and married an artist from a Croat/Serb marriage, though she kept in touch with her colleagues from *Slobodna Bosna*. In 1995, when the magazine resumed, she rejoined as a correspondent from Serbia. In 1996 Suzana and her husband moved to Sarajevo. As a non-Muslim, he was unable to find work in his field. He went to England for two years, which created a strain on the marriage. They divorced. Suzana is currently working as a freelance journalist and writing a book with a Bosniak colleague about key players in the war.

TANJA LJUJIC-MIJATOVIC

Never did the presidency, of which I was a member,

approve the decision to divide Bosnia.

A "loyal Serb," TANJA LJUJIC-MIJATOVIC grew up in Sarajevo. Her father, a high-ranking commander in Tito's military, was a well-known figure in the Second World War. She attended elementary school, high school, and university in Sarajevo. She divorced when her daughters were ten and fourteen. Tanja's family name is widely recognized, which may be one reason she could leave her position as professor of landscape architecture to become a member of parliament before the war. There, and subsequently as a member of the seven-member presidency, Tanja watched political squabbles grow into deep rifts. But even as the conflict escalated, she could not imagine a war. Like others in Sarajevo, her life soon disintegrated into turmoil. *When we were shot at, we were more protective of our plastic water jugs than our own bodies, because water was so hard to get.* Tanja gave an interview with Vienna television about life under siege. She spoke so movingly that the Austrian foreign minister requested that she be named to the diplomatic corps. In 1993 she became the Bosnian ambassador to the UN in Vienna, allowing her to promote the cause of her people. She's tough and determined, although urbane. Tanja adamantly and consistently opposed the de facto division of Bosnia that occurred over the negotiating tables at Dayton. After the war, she continued her affiliation with the Social Democratic Party and was slotted to serve as vice-mayor of Sarajevo. She has an in-depth perspective on the challenges women face in politics — *In my own life, I've seen how tough it is for women to move ahead* — and insists that changes must be made legislatively to bring lasting and equitable peace. She has engaged in dozens of initiatives to bridge divides and proposed international support for the one-year commemoration of the massacre at Srebrenica, even though the perpetrators were Serbs, like herself.

VALENTINA PRANIC

The people who were waging the war . . . we didn't know those people.

We only knew we were scared.

There's a tiredness in VALENTINA PRANIC's eyes, typical of mothers of energetic toddler sons. She was born in 1974 and raised with her older sister near Sarajevo. *Pudlugovi is a bit larger than a village.* Pop culture was her passion, and she still has an Abba T-shirt. Valentina is an ethnic Croat married to a Bosnian Serb, a long-time family friend. She says their difference in backgrounds doesn't create difficulties. As far as gender goes: *Today, women aren't given the same chances as men, but at some point in the future we'll be treated as equal. After all, men or women can practice law or have some other kind of education.* [She smiles.] *We're all smart.* Still, Valentina's spoken paragraphs often begin with "What to say?"—after which she launches into important reflections on what caused the war or on her hopes for reconciliation. As the conflict encroached on her village, she escaped with her sister to Serbia, where she was kindly treated. She's grateful to the Serbian doctor who took care to see that she and her developing baby were healthy. Since the war, Valentina has lived with her husband, their child, and in-laws. Even as her mother, Ana, left the shoe factory while she raised two preschool daughters, Valentina tends her little son at home while her husband works as a driver. *These are difficult times in terms of money, but we love life.* Loans from the Bosnian Women's Initiative (through the NGO Women for Women) have helped her start a pig business, to provide her family with additional food and income. The war dominated most of her early life, she says ruefully; she hopes for better for her little Nadan. *All women are alike, no matter their ethnic tradition. In this war, we went through the same things: We suffered in the same way, and we were brave in the same way.*

VESNA KISIC

Ethnic backgrounds aren't important to us in our work.

We understand each other very well. Why wouldn't we?

We're all women.

VESNA KISIC was born in 1956 in "the most beautiful part of the former Yugoslavia, the flats of Slavonia," in eastern Croatia. She was brought up by a loving grandmother until she moved to Bosnia for primary school, followed by vocational school in economics. It was a good move; she describes Bosnian people as being "so warm and so nice." She found a job as an accountant immediately after graduation. Her expression is friendly and her voice soothing, even when she discusses distressing matters. Vesna's husband, a Bosnian Serb, was a sports journalist. They both lost their jobs as a result of their ethnicity. Their flat was on the front line. Vesna struggled with what to say to her adolescent daughter about her mixed parentage, and how that related to the reasons given for the violence raging around them. Her husband was beaten and expelled to Serbia; he missed five years of their daughter's life and was unable to protect her and his wife from privation and harm. Her father-in-law lost half his leg to a land mine. Vesna has sought solace in Catholicism. Before the war, she considered herself an atheist; but as the chaos increased, she renewed her faith. She runs "Antonia," an organization named after her hometown church, the biggest in Bosnia. The women of that organization donate their time to caring for the elderly, educating other women, and meeting community health needs. They've set up a tailoring enterprise to generate funds for their many projects. In addition, Vesna is a key player in the postwar League of Women Voters of Bosnia and Herzegovina, encouraging women's active participation in the political process.

SWANEE HUNT

Closing Thoughts

Over the years, these women have become an important part of my life, and I theirs. I've sat among them, stood before them, and shared a podium with them. We've exchanged e-mails, holiday cards, jewelry, journals, parenting tips, scarves, perfume, homebrew, jams, and strategies for changing the world. One week I might be calling Washington to bring attention to their proposed strategies. The next week we might be sharing grief over losses in each other's lives. These notes help explain how we fared as fellow travelers.

My Path

RADA: *Good luck to you. I hope your book is a success.*

SWANEE: *Actually, I haven't thought of this project in professional terms. I just couldn't walk away from Bosnia with so many hundreds of hours of conversations with women like you, without preserving them for others.*

NADA: *Do you see?* [pointing to her kitchen wall] *It's the calendar you sent me with scenes of Colorado. I think of you every day.*

AMNA: *It was almost worth living through this war to learn who my friends really were, and the real meaning of friendship.*

Twenty-seven paths converge on these pages: those of twenty-six Bosnian women and mine. Never, in my wildest dreams, had I imagined myself a spokesperson for women of another country; but the progression that led me into the lives of Bosnian women is logical, even if the end point was unexpected.

I came to this study of a former communist country having grown up in the household of an ardent anticommunist father, who devoted the last twenty years of his life to "saving the Republic USA from the mistaken enemies of freedom." As a young child, I looked with great alarm on the communist menace, but by adolescence my attention had moved beyond our country's borders. At church camp, I declared my intention to become a Southern Baptist missionary.

If my adult career in human services, diplomacy, and education turned out to be an unorthodox form of ministry, it was still driven by a sense of mission. That drive was reinforced when, long before I conceived this book, I immersed myself in the work of the Harvard child psychiatrist Robert Coles — sixty volumes and hundreds of articles — for my doctoral dissertation in pastoral care and counseling. I laid out the method by which Dr. Coles gleaned insights from "observer/participant" relationships, the basis of his vivid social critique, as he plunged into what I called "the socioethical dimensions of empathy." He insists on pushing past too-easy categories, recognizes the unexpected in human experience, and honors everyday heroism. Those principles shaped my relationships with Bosnian women a decade later.

While finishing my dissertation in the early 1980s, I helped launch the Women's Foundation of Colorado, which promoted economic self-sufficiency for women. The foundation proved the possibility, and value, of women reaching across lines of class, race, and experience to create solid alliances. I was inspired by the ingenuity of these women, often in extremely difficult circumstances, as they built their grassroots organizations. Additionally, for sixteen years in Colorado, I was involved in scores of initiatives tackling problems such as mental illness, teen pregnancy, illiteracy, poverty, violence, and racial discrimination.[1] I also witnessed the ordeal of resettlement when I took into my home Eritrean and Lao refugees; and I developed a sensitivity to the importance of having a home when I chaired the governor's efforts on affordable housing and homelessness.

Through a mutual interest in domestic problems, I developed a relationship with Bill and Hillary Clinton. In 1993 President Clinton announced my four-year appointment as ambassador to Austria. I was a diplomatic neophyte among international experts dealing with the war. My colleagues were foreign policy stalwarts whose names — Holbrooke, Gallucci, Vershbow, Fuerth — were on the most prestigious foreign policy rosters. Each stepped into his Balkan role with decades of experience charting our country's course in international affairs. I was younger (in my mid-forties), still learning to deepen my soft treble voice as I stood toe-to-toe in policy arguments with foreign ministers and four-star generals, cabinet members, national security advisors, and the president of the United States. The experience required every bit of self-confidence I could muster.

In contrast, among the women of Bosnia, I was at home. Instead of feeling drained by our encounters, I felt filled. Although our words often passed through an interpreter, we were close, having in common a love of home, a distrust of patriarchal politics, an almost desperate concern for our children, an understanding of the relationship of justice to inner healing, and the ability to communicate all this with our eyes or with touch when words failed. Most of the women I later interviewed had either known me or heard of me for years, since I'd become recognized as a friend of Bosnian women.

Still my role was complicated. I walked into a room with the imprimatur of the world's lone superpower, the hope or bane of Bosnians, depending on their politics. In contrast with European policy paralysis, the United States maintained the sheen of a forceful player pushing for action. To the extent that the United States was instrumental in bringing an end to a pointless, terrible war, we were appreciated across ethnic lines, including by Serb women with whom I met.

In addition to the policy assumptions inherent in my position, the high status of the ambassador role was a barrier, implying not only power but also responsibility. At least I didn't look, talk, or walk like the stereotypic diplomat—a help, since Bosnians' feelings against the international community were often vitriolic. After lightly armed UN troops stood by, instructed "not to take sides," as tanks and shells ripped apart lives and communities, many Bosnians had visceral disdain for the UN, sometimes spitting when a vehicle filled with "blue helmets" rolled by. They had similarly harsh criticism for international groups who housed and fed and transported thousands of staff to areas where citizens were still displaced, cold, and hungry. But as a relatively young woman, not wearing a gray suit, I was less a target of the distrust and frustration with which many of my diplomatic colleagues were received, rightly or wrongly.

I came for a week at the longest, then left again. My visits were high profile and often associated with a gift, such as a large collection of books for the burned National Library, or six tons of musical instruments to distribute among twenty-two schools, or fifteen hundred trees to replant the denuded parks. One day a young Bosnian took me aside on a Sarajevo street. "Those trees are more important to us than setting up the new central bank," she said—a comment I didn't pass on to the visiting delegation from the U.S. Treasury Department, which she was staffing. Since I wasn't posted to Bosnia, I was free from the responsibility of carrying out foreign policy; I had the luxury of going where I wanted to go, doing what I wanted to do, with whomever I wanted. Several Bosnians told me that because women had not been doing the shooting during the war, it was easier for them to cross the lines when the peace was signed. In the same way, no one had assigned me to Bosnia, so I didn't carry blame for foreign policy failures there. The Bosnians received my efforts as a gift from a visitor. My path had converged with theirs for a while, and I learned a lifetime of lessons on that stretch of journey. They, in turn, seemed glad for the company.

The Conversation

KRISTINA: *I can't describe it in words. It has to be lived.*

ALMA: *It's very hard to put into words how war creates craziness . . . with no one asking your permission.*

IRMA: *You know, it's really hard to talk about this, because I've been trying these last years just to forget. It's so strange. It's kind of like the whole war is collapsed into one day.*

MAJA: *I can't talk about myself. Where I come from, it's up to others to judge us. My responsibility is to work and act in the way I believe is right. But I agreed to do this interview, just because it's run by a lady.*

VESNA: *We're women, so we understand each other.*

As I gingerly escort the women of Bosnia and Herzegovina onto not only these pages but also the stage of international affairs, I must thank them. Their disclaimers aside, Kristina, Alma, Irma, Maja, Vesna, and twenty-one others offer extraordinary insights into the problems and possibilities of women confronting violent conflict. They've worked hard on this project, enduring raw remembering, as well as logistical hassles of travel to interviews, translation checks, more travel, more meetings, editing—all the while tolerating the inefficiencies of a first-time author.

We've spent many hours together, building our relationships, then recording our conversations. Back home, I stared at the pile of transcripts from scores of hours of taped interviews. My subjects had, in stream-of-consciousness mode, relayed stories from before, during, and since the war. They'd spoken without preparation; my job was to create the order. Determining the layout of this work, I vacillated between wanting to follow the dramatic narrative of each individual woman, as a self-contained unit, versus wanting to give the reader the experience I've repeatedly had in Bosnia over the years: sitting in a room with a few friends, trading memories and opinions.

Looking back over the literature coming out of Bosnia, I decided the "portraits of Bosnian women" books had already been written, although they were generally about life as refugees or other victim themes. (Some are listed in the bibliography.) This volume, instead, has been laid out as a thematic interaction among women who could agree or disagree with me, with each other, or with common wisdom about the Balkans. The dynamism of the conversations has hopefully compensated the reader for the lack of comfortable continuity in each individual's narratives. In fact, that same dynamism was reflected in my own process; over the years my outline shifted as insights seasoned and connections emerged from the ocean of words.

In the interview process, my early training in counseling psychology was immensely useful. I didn't compose a list of questions for each woman; my primary task was to create an environment of trust, then get out of the way, letting the woman across from me go wherever her thoughts pulled her. My second task was to keep up, to accompany her to unanticipated corners, take sudden turns, and not try to predict the course. Only then could I stand back and look at where she'd gone, comparing how her path crossed or diverged from those of the other travelers.

The process of striking up a conversation turned out to be simple. Often in a hotel room, or in her home, I sat in a chair opposite my subject as my interpreter held a video camera. Sometimes the setting felt unnatural, in the corner of a spartan meeting room, with a lonely glass of water on a bare tablecloth, like a stilted prop. But the intensity of the topics and the thick trust between us melted away hesitation. Listening to the tapes afterward, I realized our exchanges were those of friends: NADA: *My husband and I would really love you to visit us, if you possibly have the chance. We have a nice house.* SWANEE: *Thank you.* NADA: *So you could come, your family and your children.* SWANEE: *I'd like that.* NADA: *So really, you can be our guest. There's enough room for everybody. We can put you up. Not as a repayment for anything, but from my heart.* [A year later, reading Nada's text to her for accuracy, we both smiled—I was sitting at her kitchen table in Derventa, three hours north of Sarajevo.]

The friendship between us was based on mutuality.[2] I wasn't interested in maintaining an academic distance. Jet lag, plus a long series of interviews, left me, at the end of the day, with droopy eyes. Then my subjects kindly offered to put me to bed. We were that kind of friends. I took GALINA at her word when she said, straightforwardly, *I'm very fond of you. That's why I'm so open. I don't usually want to talk like this.* Still those comments surprised me when I heard them peppered throughout the recordings. I hadn't noticed as they were spoken but afterward realized they held a clue to our mutual trust and the depth of our conversations. Unsolicited affirmation came from MIRHUNISA. *You're the first woman to open my soul. I don't have a lot of time for emotions. In fact, given my work, I don't have a lot of time for me.* Mirhunisa's notion of an "open soul" was one I understood.

As free as I was from the role of diplomat, I was also free of the confines of a scholarly researcher. I could bring to the women a self beyond academic analysis. So when JELKA described to me her response to the death of her son, I felt tears rolling down my cheeks — but not from pity. I was joining Jelka, as I imagined losing my son Henry, or little Teddy. This wasn't therapy, and I felt no compunction to maintain a therapeutic boundary. Jelka and I were just being together. At the end of the interview, she remembered another meeting years earlier: *This is the second time I've seen you cry with me. It means so much.*

Reading through the transcripts, one particular exchange sums up our trust. KADA: *I feel like I've known you for years. If he were alive, my husband would say you're a lady, and I'd agree.* SWANEE: *Still, it's very hard for me to ask all these questions; because I feel like we're opening up more pain. And no matter how well I write, I can't capture the depth of your experience. On the other hand, you've said it's very important that your story be told, to get to the truth.* KADA: *Don't worry. You're like a very close friend, like a sister. Maybe you weren't with me through the worst, but you want to make it easier for me. That's what makes you my sister.*

That connection between Kada and me was reinforced by the provision that she, and all the others I interviewed, could edit out (or add) anything to the basic material from which I'd be drawing. Those were the terms of our conversations, and those are the terms of this book. In some cases, words spoken one year were edited as feelings mellowed over following years. For example, the cycle of fear became "difficult" to break instead of "impossible." "Ustasha forces" became "Croatian." The "Mujahadeen" who displaced a Serb tenant in a Sarajevo apartment became a "soldier from the Federation army." The "genocide" became "ethnic cleansing." The women understood that language not only describes; it also shapes the future.

Galina in particular was upset by the Bosnian edition of this book. She felt I unfairly described her as sometimes sounding like a Serb apologist. She said the book was one-sided and her words were taken out of context, and that much of her work to promote democracy, tolerance, and trust had been omitted. Disillusioned when she read that I had supported NATO's bombing of Serbia during the Kosovo conflict, she was unhappy that President Clinton had written the foreword to the book. We have remained friends, negotiating a number of changes in the manuscript for the English version.

For other women, some topics were too painful to see in print: a love affair broken off. *He went to his side, I went to mine. It was, after all, such a time.* One woman expunged a lengthy and dramatic description of her love affair with a married man. Another struck her allusions to domestic violence in Bosnian society. One deleted her description of political parties as being totally dominated by men. For another, the edits were necessary because of a political situation involving a family member for whose safety she feared.

As close as we might be during the interview, there were challenges our trust couldn't overcome. The husband of one of my early interviewees was an indicted war criminal, awaiting trial at The Hague. She was convinced of his innocence. I'd pushed long and hard for apprehension of those accused of atrocities; but as I listened to the woman across from me describe taking her two sons to visit their father in prison each month, I could connect. I told her I'd grown up in a family many demonized as right-wing extremist. In response, my new friend leaned forward and, staring at me intensely, said in a low voice, *"I will tell you, woman to woman. . . ."* Then she poured out her story. When he was convicted, she drove six hours to explain to me her decision not to be in the book.

In hundreds of such "woman-to-woman" hours, the topics of our conversations ranged widely: from philosophical tenets to plans for projects, from concerns about the economy to hollowing losses, from political questions to romantic memories. We might compare our husbands; other times we spoke of our children, sometimes commiserating, or exchanging advice, or encouraging each other. In one interview, three generations were present as we connected our lives across time and culture. VALENTINA: *I'm sorry, but I had to bring my son.* SWANEE: *I've done it a hundred times with my kids.* VALENTINA: *Mothers understand each other.*

"Mothers understand each other" turned out to be an element in my research method: the assumption of shared experience that allowed for confessions of success and failure, private hopes and grief—and a tremendous wealth of information. The crux was not actual mothering; several of the women were, in fact, not mothers. Mothering was more a metaphor for myriad ways we found to connect. Still, we had a division of labor. This was their story to tell, but mine to shape.

EMSUDA: *A lot of observers haven't understood, so they've said things that aren't right. They've hurt us because of their ignorance and misunderstanding.* SWANEE: *I'm afraid of that with this book.* EMSUDA: *That's OK. We're used to it. We won't take of-fense.* I must rely on Emsuda's offer of understanding, and even forgiveness, as I accept the task of telling her story and others'. However creative the framework, how does one capture, in a logical progression, "accessible" for the reader, the onslaught of madness? How to edit into convincing and concise prose the terror of trying for months to protect a young daughter from gang rape in a concentration camp? As Emsuda says, simply: *It's very hard to describe. Almost every day was like a novel. It can't be summarized in a few sentences. There's always something very important that remains unsaid. That's why it's very difficult for me to speak about my experiences. Some things just have to be lived.*

As I moved around the pieces of the mosaic to organize the women's words into a pattern for the reader, something else happened for the women. Whenever I reviewed with them passages in the manuscript, they often cried as memories were reawakened. But in our final review, when I showed them the outline I had now imposed, their responses caught me off guard. JELKA's was typical: *You've taken my experience and put it in a framework. I couldn't make sense of all this, but you have. What a gift. Thank you. . . . Thank you more than I can say.* I wondered for a moment at Jelka's emotionality as she spoke, then I realized she was trying to tell me that this book isn't just an arrangement of various accounts. The words on paper represent a heavy, dense burden. They are loaded with questions of fidelity in relationships, of religious values, of good and evil, of place in the world, of purpose in life. This book repackaged that burden, making it easier to carry. That was the gift I could give back to the women. And that's a great satisfaction.

KADA: *Thank you for telling my story. What's written down will last. What we try to remember will probably just disappear with us one day.*

Acknowledgments

I've wondered why some authors carry on about all the people who helped them with their books. Until now. Far beyond the twenty-seven of us who speak directly in this book, this work has been a team effort.

It was an honor to work in partnership with Tarik Samarah, who is not only a friend but also a brilliant photographer, able to capture on film the mix of beauty, strength, whimsy, sadness, and hope of the speakers in this book.

In the text preparation, I was especially aided by Ariane Bradley and Maria Carroll, two bright young women who contributed to almost every aspect of this book. Their help across the years ranged from broad suggestions to minute editing, conducting follow-up interviews, and coordinating a diverse research team. More thanks also to Guy Edmunds, Kessely Hong, and Michael Szporluk, intelligent and idealistic Harvard graduate students, who could be bribed with pizza and margaritas to read through the original transcriptions and pull out themes that grabbed their attention, helping me create an outline from the women's narratives. Michael Sullivan contributed excellent research on gender questions. Rina Amiri was always a source of research help and inspiration. Birgit Radl helped with German to English research and translations.

Chris Vaudo, Kathy Jankiewicz, Gina Feuerlicht, A. Greeley O'Connor, Jan Smith, Susan Gluss, Nick Beckman, and Carol Edgar joined other friends suffering through tedious editing, poring over the manuscript as intelligent outsiders. Advice on contextual details came from Ivana Vuko, Miki Jacevic, Ivana Krizanic, Branka Peuraca, and Carrie Coberly. Help on the media issues came from Tanya Domi, former press spokesperson for the OSCE in Bosnia.

Similarly, I received help from Cristina Posa, a promising Harvard Law School graduate who later worked at the International Criminal Tribunal in The Hague. The last major tightening and reorganization was recommended by Valerie Millholland, my able editor at Duke University Press. An otherwise daunting chore became tolerable as I watched with awe one spunky Julia Appell, an extraordinarily gifted Harvard undergrad with a ruthless red pen. And Annemarie Brennan was insightful and meticulous in the final review.

Expert advice came from diplomats who have encouraged me over the years: John Kenneth Galbraith, the late Warren Zimmermann, and Miomir Zuzul. Louis Sell, in particular, provided essential advice from his many years in the region and his scholarship on the rise and fall of Milosevic. Help with overall structure and style came from Catherine Bateson, whose own volumes giving voice to groups of women rendered her suggestions extremely helpful; Jane Mansbridge, an authority in gender and great friend to me through the Women and Public Policy Program of the Kennedy School; and Tom Butler, South Slav specialist at Harvard, who, happily for me, couldn't help but line edit as he read, and reread, for content suggestions.

My Harvard context provided a marvelously stimulating and free environment in which to work. Dean Joseph Nye, no stranger to the conundrums of war and peace, was always encouraging. Victoria Budson, executive director of the Women and Public Policy Program (which I lead), kept that office humming when I secluded myself for weeks at a time to write. War chroniclers Samantha Power, Michael Ignatieff, and the late Elizabeth Neuffer all had grappled with the same tension between describing real horror and respecting the privacy of the horrified. They also understood the trials of publication, and they offered inspiration laced with commiseration.

There were those in the U.S. government whose high position gave me entrée, and whose encouragement emboldened me to stand up to critics who wanted to be sure I didn't rock their boat. Key among those leaders was President Clinton, who promoted my work on the empowerment of Bosnian women with a spontaneous "I love this stuff!" First Lady Hillary Clinton consistently advocated for my work with women—anywhere, anytime. Both Clintons tolerated my insistent pushing that our U.S. troops should be picking up indicted war criminals. Across The Pond, European Commissioner Emma Bonino, Her Majesty Queen Noor of Jordan, and former Italian Foreign Minister Susanna Agnelli were at my side whenever I needed their help in my work with Bosnian women.

I had encouragement from other Washington quarters, particularly Senator Joe Biden on the Senate Foreign Relations Committee. Similar personal and professional help has come from Senator Ted Kennedy. At the State Department, in addition to Madeleine Albright and Dick Holbrooke, under-secretaries Peter Tarnoff, Dick Moose, and Tim Wirth aided me with advice as well as example. In Bosnia, I was welcomed not only by wartime American ambassadors Jackovich and Menzies but also by diplomats Bob Beecroft, Mike Parmly, Tom Miller, Daniel Serwer, and Jacques Klein, several of whom fed and housed me (as I did them in Vienna). Peter Galbraith, U.S. ambassador to Croatia, sparked my interest in women's experience of the war, gathering about forty Croatian women for me to meet with in his backyard in April 1994. At the Pentagon, my strongest encouragement came from Joe Kruzel, who lost his life on Mount Igman in the summer of 1995. Among military officers, my work was aided by commanders on the ground, particularly General Bill Nash, but also a string of NATO commanders: John Galvin, George Joulwan, and Wes Clark. Wes has been as relentless in his encouragement of my work as he was driving Milosevic's army out of Kosovo.

In Vienna, my forays into Bosnia were not only supported by Foreign Minister Alois Mock but also generously covered by competing newspapers run by Bibi Dragon and Oscar Bronner. Herbert Bammer (Austrian Airlines) and Horst Breitenhurst (IBM) were key allies, among many others. Journalist/scholar Cristina von Kohl and Green parliamentarian Mirjana Granditz pushed me constantly to do more for the Balkans. Inside the embassy, those who put their shoulders behind the Bosnia wheel were led by our public affairs officer Helena Finn with her able deputy Karen Czerny, political officers Debbie Cavin and Tim Savage, agriculture liaison Allen Mustard, military attachés John Miller and Dale Holrah, as well as my own front office "air traffic controller," Susan Ray. My deputy chief of mission, Joan Corbett, kept the embassy moving forward whenever I was off in Bosnia again.

I was also fortunate to have blessedly competent Bosnian colleagues. My Sarajevo-based office was staffed first by Amira Ferand, Nermina Kadic, and Vjeko Saje (Irma's father). Later, Sunita Samarah took the helm, assisting me with the initial selection of the women, endless logistical arrangements, and, years later, the last bits and pieces of the wrap-up for the Bosnian version of this book. She was an invaluable on-the-ground conduit between me and the twenty-six women. Help also came from Emina Ganic, Fahrija's daughter, whose fine-tuned language was partly from her Oxford education, her years in the United States and Vienna, her refugee experiences, and her work at the U.S. Embassy and Council of Europe — all before her twenty-third birthday!

For seven years, a spectacular partner helped me mold practice out of passion. In Vienna, I had the good fortune of crossing paths with Valerie Gillen, who went on to work with me extensively throughout the Balkans, where she became a trusted friend to many. Val gave support to the first postwar women's conference in Sarajevo, assisted survivors from Srebrenica, helped launch the League of

Women Voters at Eagle Base outside Tuzla, planned Bosnian women's political conferences in Washington and Sarajevo, and oversaw our foundation's office in Sarajevo. Val's deputy at the time was Sarah Gauger, whose carefulness and wisdom balanced my reckless ways, as she managed the details that made impossible events merely difficult.

But ultimately this book was a family affair. In her last years of life, my mother frequently said how proud she was of what I was doing for the women in Bosnia, a country she could not have located on a map, but which she recognized as part of my inner landscape. My brother's management of our family company allowed me to be philanthropically involved in the Balkans. My sisters, Helen and June, rooted and prayed for me in my forays. Son Henry gave emotional support from a distance; but my two younger children gave up their mother scores of times as I visited Bosnia over a seven-year period. When I returned from those trips, my children knew I was preoccupied with the stories I'd heard, and at one point they let me know that they were "tired of competing with refugees." Fair enough. The price they paid during my research years made me all the more gratified when Lillian and Teddy, teenagers as this text was being completed, helped with insightful, if brutal, editing suggestions.

Finally, I don't know if I could have ever let this book out of my clutches had it not been systematically examined by my resident editor, Charles Ansbacher. He listened to me read it line by line for weeks — in the car, in bed every morning and night, and over the phone when one of us was traveling. We were partners in Bosnia. My research trips were often built around his engagements as the principal guest conductor of the Sarajevo Philharmonic. After a long day — his in the rehearsal room of the National Theater, mine in a hotel room with one interview after another — we'd compare notes over midnight pasta in a bustling Sarajevo cafe. I'd often cry as I relayed a story I'd been told. He'd wonder at his emotional wife, then remember to whisper to me that he was proud. After nineteen years, we've developed the sort of partnership Kada describes in a scene with her husband, swimming in the stream and collecting mushrooms in the woods outside Srebrenica. Our relationship has become fluent. I don't remember exactly. Starting this book was probably his idea. Finishing it definitely was.

February 2004   Cambridge, Massachusetts

Notes

Preface

1   The last American ambassador to Yugoslavia, before it fell apart, describes Sarajevo as "a haven for diverse ethnic groups . . . a city of chestnut trees and minarets, streetcars trundling along . . . and the swarming fifteenth century Turkish market." Warren Zimmermann, *Origins of a Catastrophe*, 197. But I arrived just after the *Survival Guide* was written, between 1992 and 1993. The book is a parody on the Michelin guides, complete with advice about how to collect water, find the best cemeteries, etc. A typical entry, under "Recreation," is in the paragraph on "Running," "That is the favorite sport, practiced by everyone in Sarajevo." Miroslav Prstojevic, FAMA: *Sarajevo Survival Guide*, 51.

2   Peter Galbraith, then on the staff of the Senate Foreign Relations Committee and later the Clinton administration's ambassador to Zagreb, concluded that America's record in the face of the Serb onslaught was "sorry and sordid." He noted that there was not one addition to the staff of the Zagreb embassy in August 1992. The embassy would have been the obvious base from which to gather intelligence if a desire to do so had existed. Muslim refugees were fleeing, in large numbers, westward toward Croatia. "We did not want to know what was going on, did not want to confront it, and did not want to act," Galbraith said. "This was the last issue the Bush administration wanted to deal with in August 1992." Roger Cohen, *Hearts Grown Brutal*, 220–21.

3   "Biljana Plavsic, the former professor of biology from Sarajevo University, . . . liked to expound on the Muslims' sexual proclivities. In September 1993, she wrote in the Belgrade newspaper *Borba (Struggle)* that 'alas, rape is the war strategy of the Muslims and some Croats against the Serbs. Islam considers this something normal since this religion tolerates polygamy. Historically, during the five centuries of the Turkish occupation, it was quite normal for Muslim notables to enjoy *jus primae noctis* with Christian women. It should be stressed that Islam considers that the national identity of the child is determined by the father.'" Cohen, *Hearts Grown Brutal*, 222. Plavsic turned herself in to the war crimes tribunal in January 2001, apologizing to the victims and pleading guilty to persecutions on political, racial, and religious grounds. Mirko Klarin, "Plavsic Plea 'Bolsters' Reconciliations," *Institute for War and Peace Re-*

porting, Tribunal Update, No. 294, January 8, 2003, http://www.iwpr.net (last accessed January 2004).

4 Plavsic relayed this with considerable sadness in a side conversation in my home in 1997. Karadzic's anger at her not toeing his line led to threats against her safety. Indeed, according to Elizabeth Rubin, a joke in Republika Srpska had "Radovan Karadzic, the indicted wartime leader, pulling the trigger on his former comrade in arms, the Bosnian Serb President, Biljana Plavsic." Elizabeth Rubin, "The Enemy of Our Enemy," *New York Times*, September 14, 1997. Although a hard-liner during the war as Karadzic's vice-president, Plavsic went on to be elected president of Republika Srpska in 1996, "shed[ding] her image as his marionette, publicly accusing him and the ruling party bosses of state-sponsored corruption" (ibid).

5 Victor Jackovich was the first U.S. ambassador to Bosnia. Because of the danger in Sarajevo, I hosted the U.S. embassy to Bosnia in my embassy in Vienna—turning over to their tiny staff several rooms one floor above my office for about a year and a half. This is the only time in diplomatic history an embassy has been located in a third country. Although his time was divided between the besieged capital and Vienna, Vic was beloved by the people of Sarajevo, who felt empathy for and from him, given not only his commitment but also his Yugoslav parentage.

6 John Menzies was the second U.S. ambassador to Bosnia. A man of extraordinary sensitivity and intelligent commitment, he lived in Sarajevo despite the siege. In the nonsensical distortions of government policy, although this conflict was devouring the time of Washington experts, the State Department assigned only a skeletal crew to the field. During much of his tenure, Ambassador Menzies had only one political officer, Karen Decker, for first-hand reporting on the evolving crisis.

7 Also present were the indefatigable Croat-American businesswoman Zdenka Gast, National Security Council European Director Jennone Walker, and aide to Senate Majority Leader Bob Dole, Mira Barata.

8 For a detailed insider account of the events leading to the largest military action in NATO history up to that point, see Holbrooke, *To End a War*.

9 Pauline Neville-Jones headed the British delegation; the U.S. host group included no women.

10 The *Rocky Mountain News* published my five-part description of those meetings in January 1996.

11 Gutman won the Pulitzer Prize for international journalism for his reports in *Newsday*. He since has coedited with David Rieff *Crimes of War: What the Public Should Know*. Omarska is part of the story of Emsuda, in this book. CNN correspondent Amanpour was persistent in her coverage of Srebrenica, described later in this book by Kada.

12 Steiner went on to become Germany's ambassador to the Czech Republic, then the primary foreign policy advisor to Chancellor Schroeder, and eventually the special representative for the UN secretary general in Kosovo.

13 Eventually, California attorney Mark Steinberg led the push to organize an "initiative for the missing" led by former Senator Bob Dole. Queen Noor of Jordan joined

the effort in 2001. This eventual international response was laudable but out of sync with the urgency of the women's pleas for help finding their men and boys, who they feared were in forced labor in Serbian mines.

14 Assistant Secretary of State (for Refugees, Population and Migration) Phyllis Oakley insisted that the fund be managed through the UN High Commission for Refugees, an affiliation that meant a slow, bureaucratic start. Still, the model was successful enough to be replicated by the UNHCR in Rwanda and Burundi, as well as Kosovo.

15 See "Bosnia-Herzegovina. Families Have the Right to Know about Relatives Unaccounted for," ICRC News 96/4, January 31, 1996 (available at http://www.icrc.org, last accessed January 2004); and David Rohde, *Endgame*, 344–45.

16 This project, along with many others in Bosnia, I funded from my private foundation, Hunt Alternatives Fund.

17 Through the Star Network, an American NGO, codirected by an extraordinarily committed Lael Steagell.

18 Leadership of the Mission to Bosnia was provided by Robert Frowick, then Robert Barry.

19 General Clark called for military intervention when "ethnic cleansing" began to be directed against ethnic Albanians in Kosovo, whose Tito-granted autonomous status was revoked by Milosevic. Clark alienated Pentagon leaders not willing to "fight for the right," as he said. Although he won the war, in 2000 Clark was relieved three months early, according to official Pentagon statements. In fact, the forced retirement was years premature, based on historical tenures. A *Washington Post* editorial on July 29, 1999, lauded Clark's performance as the Supreme Allied Commander during the Kosovo campaign and questioned the timing of the abrupt announcement of his retirement, concluding that Clark was perceived as being "too political. . . . Clark wanted to use his authority to actually accomplish something." In the final analysis, the only battle that defeated Clark was against the Pentagon power structure itself. See *Waging Modern War* for Wesley Clark's account.

20 Charles and Wes, both White House Fellows, became friends when Wes was stationed in Colorado Springs, where Charles was the symphony conductor.

21 Although grievances between ethnic Albanian and Serb communities there date back much further, Kosovo was in a state of tension from the early 1980s. The Albanian language was disallowed, massive numbers of professional ethnic Albanians lost their public-sector jobs, health care and schooling were cut off, and a harsh system of apartheid was instituted. Rumors of vandalized Orthodox churches and graveyards fed Serbs' fears that they were in danger. In 1998, the situation escalated into open war. The infamous warlord Arkan moved in his paramilitaries, and hundreds of thousands of Kosovars were expelled from their homes by Serb forces. As in Bosnia, the international community delayed intervention. Finally, rallied by Supreme Allied Commander Clark, in 1999 NATO bombed Serbia after Milosevic's forces massed on the Kosovo border and every indication was that the carnage was about to be repeated.

22 NGOs are a new feature of Bosnian civil society since the demise of communism. Dur-

ing the war, when BOSFAM, a major humanitarian organization, decided to pull out because of risk to its employees, Beba Hadzic from Srebrenica was told they could allow a local person to take over the NGO. "I'll run the NGO," she replied—then added, "What's an NGO?" Repeatedly, I've seen Bosnian women assume responsibility for a future they can neither describe nor imagine.

23 NATO began seventy-eight days of air strikes on March 24, 1999, to counter Serbia's actions against ethnic Albanians in Kosovo. After the bombing stopped in the first week of June 1999, NATO soldiers moved in as Serb forces withdrew and Kosovar Albanians began returning, in massive numbers, to their homes. Despite NATO's claim to have exclusively military intentions, a number of civilian targets were hit, among which were the Chinese embassy in Belgrade, "Zastava" auto factory, industrial and communication facilities, and bridges. Sixteen young people were killed the night Radio-TV Belgrade was hit. The NATO military campaign was not limited to Kosovo; Novi Sad, Yugoslavia's second largest city, was repeatedly bombed. Its three bridges across the Danube were destroyed early in the war, but the bombing of economic targets in and around the city continued throughout the conflict.

24 "After university, Karadzic became a psychiatrist whose clients included the Sarajevo soccer team, which he tried to pull out of a slump by using group hypnosis. In his spare time, he was a poet whose talents were modest, at best, and he existed on the margins of Sarajevo's rich cultural life. He was, according to some accounts, snubbed by the literary elite, and this, the theory goes, contributed to his desire to punish the city that turned its back to him. . . . In 1985, Karadzic spent eleven months in jail on fraud charges related to a home loan. After that, he dabbled in politics but was not known as a nationalist; he joined the Green party before taking charge, in 1990, of the Serbian Democratic Party (SDS)." Peter Maas, *Love Thy Neighbor*, 159.

25 Steven Erlanger, writing about the effect of the Kosovo bombing on Milosevic's eventual downfall, quotes Milan Bozic, professor and politician in Belgrade: "If in 1996, the West had wanted to push harder, [Milosevic] would have been out." The article ends by reluctantly agreeing with Emsuda's assessment of the value of a "radical response," with Bozic saying, "The war in Kosovo finally ended Milosevic's symbiotic relationship with the West. It was an important leg of his stool and it was gone, and it helped unseat him." American leadership on Balkans matters has been spotty, at best, with policies waxing and waning according to U.S. perception of its own interest. Erlanger cites Dragor Hilber, a leading opponent of Milosevic, as concluding that "the Americans and the West, desperate to push out Mr. Milosevic, finally [in 2000] . . . provided much more help than before, pouring money into Serbia—to the opposition, the media, to student protesters, almost everyone who could claim to be anti-Milosevic." *New York Times*, December 25, 2000.

26 The last U.S. ambassador to Yugoslavia, describing his interaction with Izetbegovic in the period leading up to the war, says, "I detected no inkling on his part of the massive aggression that the [Yugoslav National Army], together with Milosevic and Karadzic, was mounting against him." Warren Zimmermann, *Origins of a Catastrophe*, 191.

Introduction

1   Victims finding their voice is not simply a variation of the women's movement, or "power to the people." It is an exquisitely sensitive psychological balancing of the need to forget and the need to remember, described by Martha Minow, *Between Vengeance and Forgiveness*, 4.

2   "Over eight thousand people had been killed in Sarajevo and more than fifty thousand injured. . . . Of the one million Muslims who once lived in the 70 percent of Bosnia controlled by the Serbs since the first months of the war, no more than fifty thousand remained by early 1995. Reams of United Nations resolutions and endless diplomatic minuets had not brought the parties noticeably closer to an agreement to end the war." Roger Cohen, *Hearts Grown Brutal*, 362.

3   While estimates on the percentage of women vary, in every informal reference I've heard from policymakers, women are figured to be substantially over 50 percent.

4   From the foreword in Janja Bec, *The Shattering of the Soul*, 9.

5   For an excellent discussion of Bosnian Muslim identity over centuries, see Francine Friedman, "The Bosnian Muslim National Question," in Paul Mojzes, ed., *Religion and the War in Bosnia*, 1–19.

6   The words "nation" and "nationalist" are confusing because "a nation refers to a group of people who believe they are ancestrally related. . . . Nationalism . . . does not connote loyalty to the state; that loyalty is properly termed patriotism. Loyalty to state is sociopolitical in nature, and is based in large part on rational self-interest. Loyalty to nation is intuitive rather than rational, and is predicated upon a sense of consanguinity." Walker Connor, from an address in Bonn, December 2000. "Nationalist" refers to chauvinistic attitudes toward an ethnic group, but the use of "nations" to refer to those groups is not used in this book, so as not to confuse readers (particularly Americans) who think of a nation as a sovereign state. See Benedict Anderson, *Imagined Communities*, 6–7.

7   See Cynthia Cockburn, *Gender and Democracy in the Aftermath of War: Women's Organization in Bosnia-Herzegovina*, 7.

8   That solution creates its own problems: since a hundred years earlier "Bosniak" was used to denote all Bosnians (Irma insists on that broader usage still), the current use of the word exclusively for Muslims leaves open the possibility that nationalist Bosnian Serbs and Bosnian Croats may happily distinguish themselves from "Bosniaks" and demand that the regions in which they are the majority be annexed by Serbia and Croatia, respectively.

Part I. Madness

1   Yugoslavia, and Bosnia in particular, had a thriving Jewish community until World War II, and Sarajevo was known around the world as the home of the "Sarajevo

Haggadah," a fourteenth-century Spanish illuminated manuscript. Noel Malcolm, *Bosnia: A Short History*, 112.

2   Warren Zimmermann, *Origins of a Catastrophe*, 7.

3   For a detailed portrait, see Louis Sell, *Slobodan Milosevic and the Destruction of Yugoslavia*. George Bush's secretary of state describes the Serb leader in mid-1992: "His whole life has been built on using the past to inflame the present. On first appearance, a friendly charmer in a well-tailored suit with a short-cropped haircut, Milosevic is at heart a tough and a liar. . . . At times, I felt I was talking to a wall with a crew cut." James Baker, *The Politics of Diplomacy: Revolution, War and Peace*, 481. See also the *New Republic*, April 12, 1999.

4   Zimmermann, *Origins of a Catastrophe*, 183–84. In addition, Miomir Zuzul, Croatia's ambassador to the United States, later named foreign minister in 2003, confirmed that "Tudjman would talk to whomever would listen about why Bosnia could not exist. . . . For him Muslims were only Croats of a different religion." Private conversation, Washington, June 2001.

5   See Misha Glenny, *The Fall of Yugoslavia*, 90; Zimmermann, *Origins of a Catastrophe*, 199; Laura Silber and Allan Little, *Yugoslavia: Death of a Nation*, 98–99, 107.

6   Sabrina Petra Ramet, *Balkan Babel*, 37.

7   At the end of August, the movement was still strong; forty busloads — mostly mothers — arrived at the Yugoslav National Army headquarters in Belgrade. Demonstrations continued in Sarajevo, where the women interrupted a session of parliament to demand that their sons be discharged. Cynthia Cockburn, *The Space between Us*, 166. The story is retold by Brian Hall, who also describes the "mother's movement": "Serb mothers had been invading the Serbian Parliament, Croat mothers the Croatian Parliament, each group chanting that nationalism was nothing to them compared to the lives of their sons. 'Idiocy!' they cried. 'A men's war!' 'Listen to the mothers!' " But speaking with one voice was a challenge: The Serb and Croat mothers decided to "descend on the Federal Parliament, an irresistible tide of black-clad women." They rented buses for the journey from Zagreb to Belgrade through battle zones, picking up mothers along the way. The convoy stopped after two hours; Serb and Croat mothers were fighting. They eventually resumed their journey — Serb mothers in one set of buses and Croat mothers in the other. Hall, *The Impossible Country*, 292.

8   Over the next four years, Croatia would quietly collect arms (some from their share of U.S.-approved covert arms shipments to Bosniaks) in spite of the UN-imposed embargo, so that in 1995 Tudjman and his forces, in a stunningly successful blitzkrieg, could regain the purged territory, driving out Croat Serbs.

9   Ramet, *Balkan Babel*, 244. See Steven Burg and Paul Shoup, *The War in Bosnia and Herzegovina*, 28, for a map of ethnic majorities in 1991.

10 The question of why so many people stand by in the face of evil is at the crux of Peter Maas's *Love Thy Neighbor*.

11 Reports coming from refugees were gruesome: a son forced to eat his father's testicles, mothers gang-raped in front of their children, a grandfather forced to eat his

slain grandson's liver. But a *New York Times* reporter adds a keen observation: "The Serb bombardment of Sarajevo looked like mindless barbarity in that, over more than three years, it took thousands of innocent lives and was a colossal public-relations disaster. In the early months of the conflict, however, it served one important purpose. It distracted the international community from the real business of the war." Cohen, *Hearts Grown Brutal*, 168.

I. Hell Breaks Loose

1   For an excellent window on rural life in Bosnia and a moving selection of ten transcripts of interviews with Muslim survivors of atrocities, see *The Shattering of the Soul*, by Janja Bec.

2   See Andras Riedlmayer, *A Brief History of Bosnia-Herzegovnia*, 1993, http://www.kakarigi.net/manu/briefhis.htm (last accessed January 2004); and United States Congress, Commission on Security and Cooperation in Europe, "The Referendum on Independence in Bosnia-Herzegovina, February 29–March 1, 1992" (prepared by the staff of the Commission on Security and Cooperation in Europe) (Washington: The Commission, 1992), microform.

3   Confronted with evidence of Arkan's atrocities at the beginning of the Bosnian war, Milosevic said to the U.S. ambassador, "I've checked, and I've discovered that Arkan was in Bosnia only as a bodyguard for one of the Bosnian Serb politicians." Warren Zimmermann, *Origins of a Catastrophe*, 198.

4   Laura Silber and Allan Little, *Yugoslavia: Death of a Nation*, 224.

5   The White Eagles were a paramilitary group led by Vojislav Seselj, Serbian deputy prime minister and head of the Serb Radical Party, which had a branch in the Republika Srpska. (The Radical Party was banned by the OSCE in Bosnia in March 2000, citing its continued obstruction of the Dayton Peace Agreement.) During the war, the White Eagles and other groups like "Arkan's Tigers" roamed Eastern RS with impunity—killing, ravaging, plundering, and raping, as they "ethnically cleansed" Bosnia and Herzegovina. "The entire region has been roasted alive on an open fire." Misha Glenny, *The Fall of Yugoslavia*, 182.

6   A ski village, Pale had a mixed prewar population of 6,000 to 7,000 Serbs and Bosniaks. During the war it grew to nearly 14,000 Serbs exclusively. The Serbs built new offices for its government and used the rundown Panorama Hotel for meetings with representatives of the international community and the media during the early post-Dayton period. In 1997, Biljana Plavsic moved the capital of Republika Srpska to Banja Luka.

7   Zagreb, the capital of Croatia, is about a five-hour drive from Vienna. In April 1994, Peter Galbraith, the first U.S. ambassador to Croatia, hosted Charles and me as his guests for a dinner with local political figures. In addition to visiting nearby refugee camps with Peter, and viewing the damage on the front lines, I took the occasion to

meet with about forty women leaders in his backyard, to hear about the important work they were doing in the midst of the conflict in their country.

8 Slavenka Drakulic, a well-known interpreter of the Balkans, was my guest several times in Vienna, and I was with her in New York at Gloria Steinem's apartment in March 2000, for a meeting of the Network of East-West Women. Her account of becoming a refugee fleeing the violence in Croatia includes this powerful litany: "I know these symptoms of denial by heart now: first you don't believe it, then you don't understand why, then you think it is still far away, then you see war all around you but refuse to recognize it and connect it with your own life. In the end it grabs you by the throat, turning you into an animal that jumps at every piercing sound, into an apathetic being trudging from one side of the room to the other, into the street and to the office where you can do nothing but wait for something to happen, to hit you at last. You learn to breathe in death, death becomes your every second word, your dreams are impregnated by dismembered bodies, you even begin to picture your own end. In the morning you don't recognize your face in the mirror, the sickly gray color of the skin, dark circles under the eyes and the pupils unable to focus on any one thing for longer than a second. The war is grinning at you from your own face." Slavenka Drakulic, *The Balkan Express*, 28–29.

9 A beautiful city, Mostar is "famous above all for its Ottoman architecture symbolized by the [now destroyed] old footbridge that arches high over the Neretva River." Glenny, *The Fall of Yugoslavia*, 158. Many of Mostar's architectural beauty spots eventually took on the appearance of the previously destroyed Vukovar in eastern Slavonia, harkening back to Dresden and Stalingrad from the World War II era.

10 Silber and Little, *Yugoslavia: Death of a Nation*, 27.

11 According to Vjeko Saje, Irma's father, most of the sixteen-year-old boys were killed, not because they were officially drafted, but as each street tried to defend itself against encircling tanks. All the men in Sarajevo had to dig trenches or go to the front. Irma's father, an architect working in an engineering company, dug for one week, then worked at his office for three.

12 A popular resort town and ancient port city on Croatia's Dalmatian Coast, Split became a destination spot for fleeing Bosnian refugees from the war and a key transport hub during the war. It is up the coast from Dubrovnik, where the affable mayor remarked to me in 1994, "I don't understand why the tourists aren't back. It's safe now; we have all the big guns in place." He also complained that the hotels were all full — but full of refugees.

13 See Tone Bringa, *Being Muslim the Bosnian Way*.

14 The Serb-led assault in Croatia's industrial region of eastern Slavonia was brutal. Moving, although horrific, accounts of Vukovar and other sites of atrocities described by children who survived the invasion are found in *Sunflowers in the Sand*, by Leah Curtin, with pictures drawn by the children. "By the end of October [1991], it had been shelled from land and bombed from the air to such a degree that scarcely a building was intact. Vukovar assumed enormous symbolic importance to both sides. Without

it, Serbia's territorial gains in eastern Slavonia were threatened. To the Croats, the unexpectedly fierce defense of the town against overwhelming odds inspired hopeful, if unrealistic, talk of a 'Croatian Stalingrad,' " Marcus Tanner, *Croatia: A Nation Forged in War*, 256. Simultaneously, the Yugoslav National Army (JNA) had begun its operations on Dubrovnik, encircling it and shelling the 12th century city on the Adriatic, the crown jewel of the former Yugoslavia. This act by the Serbs shocked all of Europe and set off alarms through Bosnia and Herzegovina. December 6, 1991, despite a local cease-fire agreement, "troops surrounding Dubrovnik . . . launched a merciless ten-hour attack on all parts of the port, including the historic buildings of the old town." Glenny, *The Fall of Yugoslavia*, p. 135.

15 This area was strategically essential to the Serbs. Without control of this corridor, they would be cut off from the Eastern portion of their self-proclaimed "Republika Srpska," as well as the lands they had taken over in Croatia.

16 On a per capita basis, the Austrians took in more than twice the number of Balkan refugees as did Germany, which was the next largest host country. As the years went by, both governments initiated policies to return refugees to their homeland. Those policies were driven by domestic concerns, and refugees were sometimes sent back into destroyed villages. The Austrian experience contains several lessons. Of some 84,000, approximately 60,000 were integrated into the Austrian workforce. The GOA adopted a program in March 1997 to motivate the 10,700 Bosnian refugees still in government care to return home, and to help potential returnees start a new existence. The government gave each family $2,500 for support programs. In most of the cases, however, cash-in-hand was only part of a more complex program aimed at helping local Bosnian communities to which the refugees returned, in many cases linked with EU projects. Only about half of the refugees in government care made use of the offer. Summary of a March 1997 embassy cable to the State Department.

17 See Manfred Nowak's report, "Mission für Sicherstellung von Beweisen," December 1992.

18 See Wolfgang Libal and Christine von Kohl, *Der Balkan*, 91.

19 Oliver Hoishen, "Wächst aus der Krise etwas Hoffnung?" *Frankfurter Allgemeine Zeitung*, December 14, 1999; Südosteuropäischer Dialog, *Balkan*, Heft 3, 13.

20 Dan DeLuce, "Some Serbs Secretly Helped Moslems — Bosnian Mufti," Reuters, January 30, 1996.

21 Michael Sells, *The Bridge Betrayed: Religion and Genocide in Bosnia*, 22.

22 Vesna Nikolic-Ristanovic, editor and author of the following listed pages (Borislav Radovic, trans.), *Women, Violence and War: Wartime Victimization of Refugees in the Balkans*, 41–83.

23 Ruth Seifert citing Rolf Pohl, "Mannlichkeit," in Stiglmayer, *Mass Rape*, 60.

24 See Südosteuropäischer Dialog, *Balkan*, Heft 2, 10; and also Seifert, "Mannlichkeit," in Stiglmayer, *Mass Rape*, 55.

25 Vera Folnegovic-Smalc, "Psychiatric Aspects of the Rapes," in Stiglmayer, ed., *Mass Rape*, 175–76;

26 *Calling the Ghosts* (an award-winning documentary by Women Make Movies), released in 1996, offers a gripping portrayal of a camp in Omarska, with actual footage from the camp. (The school in which Emsuda was held was Trnopolje, in the
same area, and she witnessed and experienced much of the same brutality.) The hour-
long documentary is narrated by attorney Jadranka Cigelj and civic judge Nusreta
Sivac, who were among several dozen women incarcerated there, victims of and witnesses to horrific atrocities for two months. "Whatever we say is nothing compared
to what we went through." The words of Emsuda (who is thanked in the film credits)
should be read with that reminder. The difficulty of reporting on an experience such
as hers is summed up as one of the women gathers critical, extensive testimony for
the war crimes tribunal at The Hague: "To expose the crime, you violate the witness."
See Gayle Kirshenbaum, "Women of the Year: Jadranka Cigelj and Nusreta Sivac,"
Ms. Magazine, January–February 1997, 64–68.

27 "Occupations in BIH have always been gender-typed . . . women workers were primarily concentrated in industry. This is significant in that the collapse of the economy
due to the war has destroyed a significant part of this sector. Moreover, wages were
lower in the predominantly 'female' sectors such as textiles and tobacco manufactur-
ing, compared to predominantly 'male' sectors such as mining and the steel industry."
International Human Rights Law Group, *A National NGO Report on Women's Human
Rights in Bosnia and Herzegovina*, 155.

28 In camps like Trnopolje, "those . . . judged to have been leaders of the Muslim community . . . most of these were killed." Silber and Little, *Yugoslavia: Death of A Nation*,
250–51.

29 Western recognition of Croatia and Slovenia has drawn much blame for causing the
wars in the former Yugoslavia (for example, see Misha Glenny, *The Fall of Yugoslavia*,
112). Others assert that this blame is misplaced, in that war had begun months before EU recognition. However, "once Western powers began an explicit attempt at
mediation in May 1991, they sped up this process [of disintegration] by accepting the
nationalists' definition of the conflict. . . . The longer the fighting went on, the more
involved they became, but they never stopped to alter their original reluctance, re-
duce their contradictory messages, recognize the role they were playing in the conflict
itself, or formulate a policy." Susan Woodward, *Balkan Tragedy: Chaos and Dissolution
after the Cold War*, 147.

30 Zimmermann, *Origins of a Catastrophe*, 172.

31 Ibid., 242.

32 See Stiglmayer, ed., *Mass Rape*, 23–24.

33 Silber and Little, *Yugoslavia: Death of A Nation*, 274. See also Bisera Turkovic, *Bosnia and
Herzegovina in the Changing World Order*, 68–69, for a discussion of the UN authoriza-
tion to use force to ensure UNPROFOR's mandate, which included not only delivering
aid but also deterring attacks against the "safe areas."

34 See especially Rohde, *Endgame*; and Jan Willen Honig and Norbert Both, *Srebrenica:
Record of a War Crime*. The UN critiques itself in its Report of the Secretary-General

Pursuant to General Assembly Resolution 53/55: The Fall of Srebrenica. See http://www.us-israel.org/jsource/un/unga53_55.html (last accessed January 2004).

2. Love in the Crucible

1 A Montenegran Serb notes how "in wartime, hope takes refuge in the body and in the unconscious; for the same reason it leaves them in peacetime. Physically as well as psychically, the man of peace and the man of war are absolutely different beings. In wartime the weaknesses and even illnesses of peace vanish. Bodies suddenly regain their youth. . . . The person you were before the war remains familiar but is becoming transformed into a stranger, who moves silently and inevitably away, creating inside you the unbearably painful atmosphere of a passionate parting." Stanko Cerovic, "How Does One Go To War?," in *Autodafe, The Journal of the International Parliament of Writers* 1 (Spring 2001): 127–28.

2 For a powerful account of a neighbor/rapist, see Julie Mertus et al, *The Suitcase*, 28–30.

3 For discussion of gender differences in this regard, see Carol Gilligan, *In a Different Voice*, 62–63.

4 Gorazde was, for the Serbs, one of three "unwelcome ethnic stains on an otherwise pure Serb tableau." Laura Silber and Allan Little, *Yugoslavia: Death of a Nation*, 257, also 324–25.

5 An award-winning film was made about this family, directed by Nadia Mehmedbasic, documenting the ordeal and subsequent birth of two more children.

6 A poor road down the mountain was the scene of numerous fatal accidents, including the overturned APC of three American diplomats in summer 1995, increasing the resolve for American intervention a few weeks later.

7 " 'I am so tired of saying thank you,' a woman named Amela Simic told me one evening in Sarajevo. 'I think what I look forward to most in peacetime is never having to say thank you again . . . I think I will send my friends envelopes with money in them and boxes of chocolates . . . I will be myself again.' " David Rieff, *Slaughterhouse: Bosnia and the Failure of the West*, 134.

3. Reasons for the War

1 Although the ground offensive led by Croat and Bosnian forces was the most important factor in ending the war, there was plenty a committed United States could have done to move NATO and the UN to action. Instead, only after Srebrenica was overrun, "NATO planes flew 3,400 sorties and over 700 attack missions in the bombing campaign that started on August 30 and ended September 14. The use of force laid the basis for the end of the war. Would it have done so three years earlier, when the Serb camps were discovered and the Muslims of Bosnia were suffering genocide? I see no

reason to believe that earlier bombing would not have been equally effective." Roger Cohen, *Hearts Grown Brutal*, 455. Warren Zimmerman agrees. *Origins of a Catastrophe*, 241–42.

2 Warren Zimmermann, *Origins of a Catastrophe*, 39.

3 Ibid., 7. "As the Communist *pterodactyl* perished and left the nest empty, the eggs hatched an entire flock of birds of prey who are now viciously pecking at each other in the fight to dominate the nest or at least a segment of the nest." Paul Mojzes, *Yugoslavian Inferno*, 126.

4 Bisera Turkovic, *Bosnia and Herzegovina in the Changing World Order*, 109ff.

5 From a small group conversation with Silajdzic in 1996. See also Paul Parin, "Open Wounds: Ethnopsychoanalytic Reflections on the Wars in the Former Yugoslavia," in Alexandra Stiglmayer, ed., *Mass Rape*, 43–44. An eloquent treatment of these themes is also laid out by Bisera Turkovic, who served as the Bosnian ambassador to Hungary while I was representing the United States in Vienna; see *Bosnia and Herzegovina in the Changing World Order*.

6 Laura Silber and Allan Little, *Yugoslavia: Death of A Nation*, 26.

7 Wesley Clark, *Waging Modern War*, 68.

8 Francine Friedman, *The Bosnian Muslims*, 159–68.

9 See Tone Bringa, *Being Muslim the Bosnian Way*, 9–10.

10 Noel Malcolm, *Bosnia: A Short History*, 208, 218–19.

11 In addition to the Louis Sell, *Slobodan Milosevic and the Destruction of Yugoslavia*, for a particularly insightful, firsthand view, see Zimmermann, *Origins of a Catastrophe*. Silber and Little, *Yugoslavia: Death of a Nation*, provides a detailed account. Misha Glenny, *The Fall of Yugoslavia*, and Malcolm, *Bosnia: A Short History*, are excellent scholarly sources. Cohen, *Hearts Grown Brutal*, also gives a strong on-the-ground account.

12 Glenny, *The Fall of Yugoslavia*, 31.

13 Parin, "Open Wounds," in Stiglmayer, ed., *Mass Rape*, 45.

14 The Bosnian Serb was "like a punch-drunk fighter; [he] flailed about him with flurries of distortions and lies." Zimmerman, *Origins of a Catastrophe*, 202.

15 Psychologist Miomir Zuzul was key to negotiations I hosted (with Ambassador Chuck Redmond as negotiator) to stop fighting between the Croats and Bosniaks and to create the Federation in 1994. Zuzul subsequently became Tudjman's ambassador to the United States. "For the biggest part of the war in Bosnia, Milosevic was united with his 'brother in arms' Karadzic, another obvious criminal. But in contrast to Milosevic's pragmatism, Karadzic was a kind of romantic who believed myths from (Serbian) history, and who was 'fighting the 600-year-old war for survival of Serbs and the Serbian Orthodox Church.' For him and a surprisingly big number of Serbs both in Serbia and BiH, the war started with a battle at Blackbird Field (Kosovo Polje) at the end of the 14th century, when the Ottomans defeated the Serbs. For Karadzic and his supporters, Muslims were enemies whose existence endangered the survival of the Serbian nation. From that paranoiac perspective (I do not have any

doubts that Karadzic can be diagnosed as a person with serious psychical disorders) there is no other way but to fight and eventually kill or expel all Muslims. So what we had in Bosnia was a combination of romantic nationalistic fantasy (almost a kind of collective madness) and pure pragmatism without any moral or human restrictions. To implement the . . . 'sacred mission' they needed somebody like Ratko Mladic, war criminal par excellence, a person who could kill in 'cold blood'—and without any particular reason—a person, or a village, or an entire nation. Unfortunately for us Croats, Tudjman, who certainly did not belong to this group of notorious criminals, did not do enough to distinguish himself from them, their ideology, and their goals. To understand at least the basics of what was going on in Bosnia, one needs to add to this gallery of leaders at least one more—Alija Izetbegovic. He was somehow captured in between his own Islamic ideology and (in my opinion) personal inability to do anything concretely. I do not want to say that Alija is responsible for the tragedy in Bosnia, but he certainly was not a person who could prevent or stop that tragedy." From an e-mail dated August 4, 2001, quoted with Miomir Zuzul's permission.

16 Zimmermann, *Origins of a Catastrophe*, 175.

17 Ibid., 116.

18 In one particularly mundane scene, Tudjman, attending the fiftieth anniversary of the V-Day celebration in England, drew on his napkin his proposed partition of Bosnia for Paddy Ashdown, then the leader of the Liberal Democrat Party in Britain. Silber and Little, *Yugoslavia: Death of a Nation*, 25.

19 See Glenny, *The Fall of Yugoslavia*, 148–49.

20 See Wolfgang Libal and Christine von Kohl, *Der Balkan*, 89ff.

21 See Silber and Little, *Yugoslavia: Death of a Nation*, 246.

22 Malcolm, *Bosnia: A Short History*, 204–6; he also cites Branka Magas, *The Destruction of Yugoslavia: Tracking the Break-Up 1980–92*, 50. Another particularly clear example of this theme is a collection of 256 poems, plays, short stories, excerpts from novels, epistles, war reports, essays, and travel accounts replete with dramatic passages: "The Turks used to impale them, trying for centuries to convert them to Islam . . . the Austrian-Hungarian Empire used to sterilize them, the Ustasha massacred them, they were sold cheap to communism at the Yalta Conference after being beheaded by the Croatian dictator Tito. . . . Philosophers, intellectuals, professional humanitarians; governments, the United Nations, the Hague Tribunal, are all pressuring the Serbs, killing or slandering them." Jean Ditour, "The Stigma of Virtue," in Damjanovic, Tomic, and Cosic, eds., *Serbia in the Works of Foreign Authors*, 246.

23 Sabrina Petra Ramet, *Balkan Babel*, 213.

24 Malcolm, *Bosnia: A Short History*, 204.

25 The most glaring examples were in Croatia. "In 1969 Serbs, who made up 15 percent of the population in Croatia, occupied 54 percent of all positions in the police and composed 27 percent of the members in the Croatian party organization." Felix Niesmann, *Im Spannungsfeld von Zentralismus und Selbstverwaltung*, as cited in Stiglmayer,

Mass Rape, 31. Similarly, "in 1961, the Serbs made up 42 percent of the population of Yugoslavia, but they represented 84 percent of the ministers, officials, and functionaries active in federal institutions, 8 percent of the federal judges, 70 percent of officers, and 65 percent of generals in the Yugoslavian Federal Army, as well as 57 percent of all party members." Robert K. Furtak, "Jugoslawien," and Othmar Nikola Haberl, "Parteiorganisation," as cited in Stiglmayer, ed., *Mass Rape*, 31. "The reasons for this were complex, but part of the explanation lies in the high percentage of Serbs in the Communist Party." Glenny, *The Fall of Yugoslavia*, 13.

26 "The Serbs, like members of other small nations, have a tendency to stretch their admirable history beyond its true dimensions. More than one Serb has told me, 'My ancestors were eating with golden forks while the French were still using their fingers.'" Zimmermann, *Origins of a Catastrophe*, 11.

27 Malcolm, *Bosnia: A Short History*, 204.

28 Silber and Little, *Yugoslavia: Death of a Nation*, 62.

29 Ibid., 98–99.

30 Cohen, *Hearts Grown Brutal*, 273–74.

31 Turkovic, *Bosnia and Herzegovina in the Changing World Order*, 8–21.

32 Former U.S. Foreign Service Officer Louis Sell argues strongly that such perceptions by Emsuda and Greta are indicative of postwar anti-Serb reaction. From a personal conversation, February 2003.

33 See Turkovic, *Bosnia and Herzegovina in the Changing World Order*, 76.

34 Sabrina Petra Ramet speaks for many influential policymakers: "Since 1918, there has been a constant tension between Serbs and non-Serbs in this polyglot country. . . . This struggle . . . lies at the heart of the instability for which Yugoslavia was famous. . . . I was always pessimistic about Yugoslavia." *Balkan Babel*, 1, 3. In contrast, Ambassador Zimmermann insists, "The Yugoslav catastrophe was not mainly the result of ancient ethnic or religious hostilities, nor of the collapse of communism at the end of the cold war, nor even of the failures of the Western countries. . . . My most difficult task has been to convey the conviction that all Yugoslavs weren't the bloodthirsty extremists so ubiquitously visible in Western news accounts." *Origins of a Catastrophe*, vii, xi.

35 Bringa, *Being Muslim the Bosnian Way*, 13–14.

36 "On 28 June 1989 several hundred thousand Serbs assembled at the battlefield site of Gazimestan, outside the Kosovar capital, Prishtina, to celebrate the six-hundredth anniversary of the Battle of Kosovo. For many weeks a ferment of national feeling had been created inside Serbia; the bones of Prince Lazar, who died at the battle, had been on a tour of the country, becoming an object of pilgrimage wherever they were. . . . Milosevic told the crowd, 'We are again engaged in battles and quarrels. They are not armed battles, but this cannot be excluded yet.' The crowd roared its approval." Malcolm, *Bosnia: A Short History*, 213. Meanwhile, in Bosnia, Karadzic was explaining to the U.S. ambassador, "'You have to understand Serbs, Mr. Zimmermann. They've been betrayed for centuries. Today they can't live with other nations. They must have their own separate existence. They're a warrior race, and they can trust only them-

selves to take by force what is their due. But this doesn't mean that Serbs can hate. Serbs are incapable of hatred." Zimmermann, *Origins of a Catastrophe*, 203.

37　With heavy lobbying from the United States, an economic embargo was imposed by the UN against Yugoslavia in May 2000. James Baker, *The Politics of Diplomacy*, 645–48. The sanctions had some effect: "Lord Owen insisted that Milosevic had been moved [to accept the Vance-Owen peace plan] by the international coalition that was lining up against him. . . . He knew how damaging the new package of sanctions would be to an economy already ruined by the cost of waging war. . . . 'This was a clear economic decision' Owen said later." In addition, "the Federal President, Dobrica Cosic, later complained that they placed rump Yugoslavia 'in a kind of concentration camp whose borders are guarded by the NATO air force and fleet and the international police.' " Silber and Little, *Death of a Nation*, 277–78. Bosnian Serbs insisted on the lifting of sanctions first before they would accept a peace plan, in contrast to the Contact Group mediators who insisted on peace first, then the lifting of sanctions. Ibid., 337. Milosevic, speaking to representatives of the European Union in Geneva on December 9, 1993, attacked international trade sanctions on Serbia: " 'I do not know how you will explain to your children, on the day when they discover the truth, why you killed our children, why you led a war against three million of our children, and with what right you turned twelve million inhabitants of Europe into a test site for the application of what is, I hope, the last genocide of this century.' " Cohen, *Hearts Grown Brutal*, 169.

38　Marlise Simons, "Crossing Paths: Albright Testifies in War Crimes Case," *New York Times*, international ed., December 18, 2002.

39　See Zimmermann, *Origins of a Catastrophe*, 117–22.

40　Committee to Protect Journalists, www.imcbih.org, August 29, 2000 (last accessed January 2004). A majority of the radio and television stations were later licensed according to regulations instituted by the Independent Media Commission. For more about media behavior, readership surveys, and public opinions, see Ramet, *Balkan Babel*, 66–85.

41　In the fall 2000 presidential election, the tabloid *Vacerni Novosti* ran a "computer-distorted photograph of the crowd at Mr. Milosevic's rally . . . clearly extended by at least a third of its length by adding another photograph of the same crowd taken at a different moment." Steven Erlanger, *New York Times*, September 22, 2000.

42　See Bringa, *Being Bosnian the Muslim Way*, 13–14.

43　Glenny, *The Fall of Yugoslavia*, 44, as well as conversations with Tanya Domi, former press spokesperson for the OSCE in Bosnia, August 2000, and Dejan Anastasjvic, journalist with *Vreme*, winter 2002.

44　See Zimmermann, *Origins of a Catastrophe*, 174.

45　"In the battle over control of television, TV relay towers became much-sought-after prizes. Serb seizure of several key TV relay installations meant that Sarajevo TV could reach only a relatively small part of Bosnia by spring 1992. Yutel [European Satellite company] stopped broadcasting in mid-May when its transmissions were limited to the city of Sarajevo." Steven Burg and Paul Shoup, *The War in Bosnia Herzegovina*, 64–65. The war over transmitters continued without abatement after the signing of the Accords—well into the 1998 national elections—when the international community took its first steps to address the problem through the OSCE Media Experts Commission. The commission found overwhelming evidence of disproportionate coverage of the nationalist Croat party (HDZ) on Croatian Radio Television, in violation of the Bosnian election rules and regulations. Not until the establishment of the Independent Media Commission in 1998 did the international community have and enforce regulatory protocols for the frequency spectrum in accordance with international law. Independent Media Commission, press release, February 17, 2000. See also Kemal Kurspahic, *PrimeTime Crime: Balkan Media in War and Peace*, 195.

46 "Throughout the war, there was a mirror at work in the Serb mind. Their psyche had become infected, like that of the policeman who has worked all his career on wiretaps and goes insane because he is convinced that people are listening to him at every moment." Cohen, *Hearts Grown Brutal*, 222.

47 The August 28 market shelling in Sarajevo was the "final outrage," coming immediately after the diplomatic shuttle tragedy on Mount Igman. The mortar shell killed at least thirty-five civilians, filling television screens with scenes of carnage. Bosnian Serbs accused the Bosnian Muslims of staging the incident to draw NATO into the war. Richard Holbrooke, *To End a War*, 91–93.

48 Catherine A. MacKinnon, "Turning Rape into Pornography: Postmodern Genocide," in Stiglmayer, ed., *Mass Rape*, 76.

49 "The Serbian media were central in the process of defining the Serbian nation as a community under threat in a variety of ways. Through the 1980s, but especially since late 1987, Serbian state- and Church-controlled media published and broadcast materials which stressed 'the victimization of Serbs in Yugoslavia' and 'the danger faced by the Serbian nation if the Federation (Yugoslavia) continued to ignore its plight.'" Spyros Sofos, "Media and the Politics of Disintegration and Ethnic Division in Former Yugoslavia," in Tim Allen and Jean Seaton, eds., *The Media of Conflict*, 162–75.

50 Burg and Shoup, *The War in Bosnia Herzegovina*, 64–65.

51 "Serbs were brainwashed by television. Please do not be put off by the simplicity of this assertion: it is a reasonable explanation of how an entire nation composed of generally sensible citizens . . . would follow their leader into an abyss of war and ruin. . . . Milosevic controlled television absolutely, refusing to let independent stations have any national frequencies. . . . Milosevic, a well-trained Communist who understood the power and importance of propaganda, met or talked on a daily basis with the director of Radio-Television Serbia, whom he appointed and replaced as necessary. Newspapers and magazines were largely irrelevant because few people could afford to buy them anymore. The most amazing thing about the role of television was that it not only had the power to form people's opinions, it could change those opinions overnight. . . . [For example,] at the start of 1993, Milosevic opposed the Vance-Owen peace plan, which would have split Bosnia into ten autonomous provinces, giving the

largest amount of territory to the Serbs, but not in contiguous pieces. State television reported, ad nauseam, that the plan was unfair. In April 1993, opinion polls showed that only one third of Serbians favored it. However, Milosevic changed his mind when he sensed that America might intervene if Serbs in Bosnia refused the plan. Suddenly, Milosevic was in favor of it. Suddenly, state television was in favor of it. And suddenly, Serbians were in favor of it. Opinion polls showed that in early May nearly two thirds of Serbians supported Vance-Owen, virtually the reverse of what polls showed a month earlier. Milosevic, like a drill sergeant, could shout 'About face!' over the airwaves, and his subjects would turn on a dime." Peter Maas, *Love Thy Neighbor*, 227.

4. The Lie of Intractable Hatred

1   In addition to the physical destruction, sixty-two imams (Muslim religious leaders) were killed throughout Bosnia during the war. Robert Fisk, "One Candle in the Heart of Darkness," *The Independent* (London), October 27, 1996.

2   See Warren Zimmermann, *Origins of a Catastrophe*, 4, 196–97.

3   "What the diplomats often failed to realize is that despite the appearance of chaos, the wars have been prosecuted with terrifying rationality by protagonists playing long-term power games." Laura Silber and Allan Little, *Yugoslavia: Death of a Nation*, 27.

4   See Samuel Huntington, *The Clash of Civilizations*, 281. This was Franjo Tudjman's favorite book (from a private conversation with Miomir Zuzul, Croatian ambassador to the United States, June 2001). The book was also praised by Croatian state-run media, for providing a rationale for nationalistic goals of ethnic purity. Huntington's worldview included harsh criticism of U.S. political leaders in the 1990s who "have not only permitted but assiduously promoted the diversity rather than the unity of the people they govern" (306).

5   See Silber and Little, *Yugoslavia: Death of a Nation*, 25.

6   See Kumar Rupesinghe, "What Is Co-existence?" in Paul van Tongeren, ed., *People Building Peace*, 69.

7   Milosevic knew how to tap into the nationalistic feeling of fraternity, calling for unity among Serbs. In his speech at the battlefield in Kosovo in 1989, he cited disunity as "pulling Serbia backwards" and making Serbs inferior. Roger Cohen, *Hearts Grown Brutal*, 272. "Milosevic and the ideologues of his Serbian revolution took their people back to the womb of their unreason. A place where defeat was victory, death a kingdom of heaven, suicide redemption, suffering vindication, and exile a homeland." This nationalism gave Serbs the "solace of a glorious past and their mirage of a glorious future." Ibid., 188.

8   UN Security Council Resolution 713. Bisera Turkovic, *Bosnia and Herzegovina in the Changing World Order*, 42.

9   "An irony of the Bosnian war was that it broke out at a time when the end of super-power rivalry had opened new, fluid possibilities for limited intervention, but also

at a time when the Gulf War had given new credence to the Powell Doctrine—the notion that the United States should act militarily only when its vital interests are clearly threatened and overwhelming force can be used, preferably with impunity." Cohen, *Hearts Grown Brutal*, 242.

10 An inside view of Bush's Balkan policy is found in the memoirs of Jim Baker, his secretary of state from 1989 to 1992. James Baker, *The Politics of Diplomacy*, 634–51.

11 Private conversations with Warren Zimmermann, July 2001.

12 See Charles Lane, *New Republic*, April 12, 1999.

13 Bisera Turkovic, "US Response to the Bosnian Crisis," in *Bosnia and Herzegovina in the Changing World Order*, 50–66.

14 In *Balkan Ghosts: A Journey through History*, Robert Kaplan crafted a well-written travelogue in 1989 and 1990 that winds its way through the Balkans. *Balkan Ghosts* purportedly shaped President Clinton's thinking on the limitations of intervention in the Balkans. "The President reportedly inferred from the book that the peoples of the region had never peacefully coexisted for very long." Michael T. Kaufman, *New York Times*, May 22, 1999. Kaplan says he never meant the book to be used as a policy tract and declared himself as an "unambiguous, public interventionist" [since 1992]. Robert Kaplan, *New York Times*, June 13, 1999. Along the same lines, Secretary of State Warren Christopher testified before Congress in May 1993 that "all sides" were responsible for atrocities in the Balkans. Michael Scharf, *Balkan Justice*, 31.

15 My data are more one-sided than that of cultural anthropologist Tone Bringa, who notes that "in the media coverage of the war there seem to be two approaches. The first is that the people in Bosnia-Herzegovina have always hated each other and whatever tolerance and coexistence there was had been imposed by the communist regime. The other is the idealized approach that Bosnia-Herzegovina, with its potent symbol Sarajevo, was the ideal example of a harmonious and tolerant multicultural society, where people did not classify each other in terms of 'Serb,' 'Muslim,' or 'Croat.' Neither of these approaches reflects the Bosnia I experienced during the five years before war broke out in April 1992. There was both co-existence and conflict, tolerance and prejudice, suspicion and friendship." Tone Bringa, *Being Muslim the Bosnian Way*, 3.

16 See Baker, *The Politics of Diplomacy*, 644–45. In the Clinton administration, Bob Frazure, deputy to Assistant Secretary of State Richard Holbrooke, referred to a Contact Group meeting as "kabuki theater," with each representative playing a completely predictable part. (From a private conversation in Vienna as we were going into a Contact Group meeting, soon before Frazure died in an accident on Mount Igman.)

17 "In Bosnia-Herzegovina consciousness of a 'Yugoslav' identity was strongest among generations who had been educated in the 1950s and 1960s." Bringa, *Being Muslim the Bosnian Way*, 4.

18 Noel Malcolm, *Bosnia: A Short History*, 194–96.

19 From a private conversation, Danis Tomovic, filmmaker (*No Man's Land*), February 2003.

20 After hearing endless hours about why limited military intervention could not be effective in '92, '93, or '94, I find these words ring true: "On August 30, [1995] NATO warplanes began the largest air attack in the alliance's history, more than 3,500 sorties in two weeks, wave after wave of the world's most advanced . . . munitions. A salvo of Tomahawk Cruise missiles was even thrown into the assault. This was exactly the kind of intervention that, for more than three years, the West's leaders had said would not work, could not work. Of course it worked." Peter Maas, *Love Thy Neighbor*, 271.

21 See Dzevad Karahasan, *Sarajevo, Exodus of a City*, 2–16.

22 See Bringa, *Being Muslim the Bosnian Way*, 13.

23 The highway stretching from Zagreb to Belgrade was named by Tito the "Brotherhood and Unity Highway." Connecting two republics, it gave a physical reality to his philosophical and political ideal.

24 Bringa, *Being Muslim the Bosnian Way*, 8–10.

25 Spoken in the homes of Sarajevo's Jews as late as World War II, Ladino, a blend of Hebrew and Spanish, was written with Hebrew characters. See also Karahasan, *Sarajevo, Exodus of a City*, 92–97.

26 Along the same lines, I was impressed that when I, as the U.S. ambassador to Austria, was asked to have a two-hour lunch with staff at the Holocaust Museum in Washington, the questions were not about the rising political right wing in Austria, but rather my understanding of what Muslims in Bosnia were experiencing. That being said, Jews internationally, in fact, did not rally their powerful forces to demand intervention to stop the genocide. An exception was Elie Wiesel, survivor of the Holocaust, Nobel peace laureate and writer. In an op-ed piece, Wiesel described his visit to the Manjaca camp, administrated by Serb forces outside Banja Luka. Although the commandant of the camp assured Wiesel that Manjaca was "in good order," he found the prisoners to be "living in deplorable conditions: crowded, 600 in a barracks, with no heat and poor clothing; they were lying on the ground, pressed against one another, like human shadows." Wiesel urged "an imaginative, spectacular gesture, from the international community." He suggested that President Clinton call for a summit in the heart of besieged Sarajevo and call Balkan leaders to join him, insisting that they not leave until an "agreement had been reached." *New York Times*, February 25, 1993.

27 Valeria Heuberger, in Südosteuropäischer Dialog, *Balkan*, Heft 2, 13.

28 There was great concern among the Western international community that the hardships of war would give Iranian extremists, operating under cover of humanitarian missions, a foothold in Bosnia, and, therefore, Europe. That fear wasn't strong enough, of course, to make the Western powers do much to stop the war in the first several years. Turkovic, *Bosnia and Herzegovina in the Changing World Order*, 91.

29 Fahrija is clear about her regret at leaving "this great, great organization we had created. They still send me letters from time to time, to let me know how things are going. They were recognized by President Clinton as the best-run humanitarian organization, and the First Lady held a reception for them."

Part II. To Heal History

1 Laura Silber and Allan Little, *Yugoslavia: Death of a Nation*, 25.

5. Challenges

1 Jaroslava Moserova, vice president of the Czech senate, Vital Voices: Women in Democracy conference, Vienna, Austria, July 1997.

2 See International Human Rights Law Group, *A National NGO Report on Women's Human Rights in Bosnia and Herzegovina*, 170.

3 Sabrina Petra Ramet, *Balkan Babel*, 319–20.

4 Shelley Anderson, from the Women Peacemakers Program of the International Fellowship of Reconciliation, asks, rhetorically, "What is the exact difference between 'peace time' and 'war time' to a woman being beaten by her male partner or a girl being sold into prostitution?" *Women Building Peace*, 241–42.

5 Cynthia Cockburn, *The Space between Us*, 171.

6 As reported by Infoteka, a project within Medica Zenica, in *To Live With (out) Violence: Final Report [on] Violence against Women [in] Zenica, Bosnia-Herzegovina*, 61, and as described in International Human Rights Law Group, *A National NGO Report on Women's Human Rights in Bosnia and Herzegovina*, 169–72. See also the discussion of alcohol in Folnegovic-Smalc, "Psychiatric Aspects of the Rapes in the War against the Republics of Croatia and Bosnia-Herzegovina," in Alexandra Stiglmayer, ed., *Mass Rape*, 175. Other observers attributed the increase in beatings to men's upset over disruption of the patriarchal system. See Cockburn, *The Space between Us*, 158.

7 Alma's hometown, after the war: "The utter devastation of Mostar was stunning. Pockmarks in ruined buildings gave mute testimony to the violence—there was not one square foot undamaged. Most of the roads had craters surrounded by the stereotypical marks of rocket and mortars and bombs. . . . School buildings, apartments and many shops were rubble. . . . However, many people were out—some sitting under colorful umbrellas in outdoor cafes, chatting and drinking Turkish coffee and soft drinks." Leah Curtin, *Sunflowers in the Sand*, 66.

8 In addition to Richard Holbrooke's detailed description of the Dayton process, in *To End a War*, a disheartening window into the ineffectual U.S. effort is provided in the memoirs of the secretary of state, Warren Christopher, in *Chances of a Lifetime*, 251ff.

9 Private conversation with John Menzies, 2002.

10 Wolfgang Libal and Christine von Kohl, *Der Balkan*, 80. Corroborated in conversations with Croat Ambassador Zuzul.

11 "[At Dayton], the leaders who had sent these people to premature graves and spread such misery were treated with respectful deference." Roger Cohen, *Hearts Grown Brutal*, 461.

12 While "there are no obvious legal obstacles to women becoming economically in-

dependent . . . opening their own businesses . . . in practice, women encounter obstacles . . . due to their lack of adequate financial resources for start-up and inability to obtain credit. Twenty-four percent of those who experienced discrimination reported that they had been discriminated against in accessing credit." International Human Rights Law Group, *A National NGO Report on Women's Human Rights in Bosnia and Herzegovina*, 155.

13   Informal account from a Sarajevo journalist, July 2001; and ICG, *After Milosevic*, 137.

14   International Human Rights Law Group, *A National NGO Report on Women's Human Rights in Bosnia and Herzegovina*, 203.

15   UN High Representative Carlos Westendorp announced in fall 1997, as reported by *Deutsche-Presse*, that "an important part of international aid to Bosnia is disappearing into corrupt channels, including extremists who use it to purchase arms." In August 1999, *Deutsche-Presse* cited a *New York Times* article claiming that money that should have gone directly to purchasing agricultural equipment and feed was given by the mayor of Sanski Most to his brother to start a bank.

6. Women Transforming

1   "When we think of war, we do not think of women. Because the work of survival, of restoration, is not glamorous work. Like most women's work, it is undervalued, underpaid, and impossible. After war, men are often shattered, unable to function. Women not only work, but they create peace networks, find ways to bring about healing. They teach in home schools when the school buildings are destroyed. They build gardens in the middle of abandoned railroad tracks. They pick up the pieces, although they usually haven't fired a gun." Eve Ensler, *Necessary Targets*, xiv.

2   Hannah Arendt, in *The Human Condition*, speaks of action as being closely connected "with the human condition of natality; the new beginning inherent in birth can make itself felt in the world only because the newcomer possesses the capacity of beginning something anew, that is, of acting" (9).

3   From 1987 to 1994, the percentage of women in parliament in Albania dropped from 28 to 6, in Romania from 34 to 4, and in Hungary from 21 to 11. Parliament was 33 percent female in the Soviet Union; in many of the newly independent states, that figure is now under 3 percent. The same trend exists for women in top ministerial posts: percentages in Albania, Romania, and Hungary declined from 6, 12, and 4, respectively, to 0. Swanee Hunt, "Women's Vital Voices."

4   Barbara Jancar, "The New Feminism in Yugoslavia," in Pedro Ramet, ed., *Yugoslavia in the 1980s*, 203, 204. See also Tanya L. Domi, "Advancing Women's Political Rights in Bosnia-Herzegovina," *Harriman Review* 14 (November 2002): 36–46.

5   *New York Times*, May 20, 1999. See also Swanee Hunt, "Raising their Voices: Women in the New Democracies," *Ambassadors Review;* also see Jennifer Griffin, *Surviving Democracy: Where Women Fear Freedom.*

6   See the International Crisis Group (ICG) report *After Milosevic* for an excellent discussion of the political scene.

7   In 1996 the League of Women Voters Education Fund opened a U.S. coordination office for absentee voting in the Bosnian elections. Through the "Bosnian Citizen Get-Out-The-Vote Campaign," the League worked with the OSCE to enfranchise Bosnian refugees and displaced persons residing in fifty-five countries around the globe for elections in 1996, 1997, and 1998. http://www.lwv.org/elibrary/pub/impact/impact00_02_2d.html (last accessed January 2004). See also Tanya L. Domi, "Bosnian Women Take Their Place at the Negotiating Table," *OSCE Newsletter* 9 (December 2002): 11–13.

8   The Red Crescent, federated with the Red Cross, is often sent into Islamic countries in place of the Red Cross. Their mission is "to improve the lives of vulnerable people by mobilizing the power of humanity." Among the many activities of the Red Crescent is refugee assistance. www.ifrc.org (last accessed January 2004).

9   George Soros took the lead in Bosnia among private philanthropists worldwide. A Hungarian American investor, with the implosion of communism he was quick to open offices throughout the former communist world to try to stabilize newborn democracies. Soros made a huge investment, not only financially but with time and attention. During the Bosnian war, he was utterly practical, funding projects like a water system to keep Sarajevans from being sitting ducks for snipers as they waited by public faucets. He gave $25 million from 1995 to 1999 through his cutting-edge Open Society Institute, focusing on education, women's rights and leadership training, civil society building, media reform, arts and culture, economic reform, public administration, health and medical services, and the environment, among others. See Jakob Finci, *Annual Report*, Soros Foundations Open Society Fund B-H, 1995–1999.

10   On May 7, 1993, the Ferhadija mosque was leveled by Bosnian Serb forces. Built 400 years earlier, it was one of the most beautiful examples of Islamic architecture in the Balkans. Eight years after its destruction, a ground-breaking ceremony was organized in Banja Luka to begin rebuilding the mosque. A violent mob of several thousand Bosnian Serbs protested, throwing rocks and setting buses and cars on fire. Over 600 Muslims and diplomats were trapped in an Islamic center for six hours. A smaller ceremony was planned six weeks later, on June 18, but it too was disrupted by violence.

11   Though the Serbs shelled Mostar, the majority of the destruction was at the hand of nationalist Croats.

12   Zelene Beretke (in English, "Green Berets") was a paramilitary organization founded in Sarajevo in early 1992. It was, along with a handful of other paramilitaries like the Patriots' League and Bosnia 22, a predecessor to the official army of Bosnia-Herzegovina. Its allusion to the green color of Islam was intended to attract primarily a Bosnian Muslim population. From an informal conversation with Ivana Vuko.

13   That large discrepancy continued until 2000, when large numbers of Bosniaks began returning to Republika Srpska.

14   Kolo Srpskih Sestara, the Association of Serb Sisters (or Serb Sisters' Circle), was

founded in Belgrade in 1903 as a women's voluntary, cultural, and educational association. Its primary role — to assist the Serb population in southern Serbia and in Mace-
donia after the failed rebellion against the Ottomans — was modified in subsequent
years. From 1993 until 2000, the association was most active in organizing fundraising
and in collecting donations of food, clothing, etc., primarily for Serb refugees from
Croatia and Bosnia. Its Web site (http://www.arandjelovac.com/latinica/organiza
cije/sestre.htm) notes that members "cherish Serbian cultural heritage and traditions." Although registered as a humanitarian organization (1997 *Directory of NGOs*),
the group is considered by many to be nationalistic. It supported the most right-
wing parties, such as Seselj's Radical Party, Milosevic's Socialist Party of Serbia, and
Arkan's Party of Serbian Unity, and its offices were on state premises. (From an informal conversation with Zorica Trifunovic, cofounder of the war-resisting organization
Women in Black.)

15 The Open City program of the international community rewarded communities
with funding. According to locals, the program ended in failure, with authorities,
instead of the returnees, taking the money.

16 Richard Holbrooke's *To End a War* makes no mention of the media as a negotiating issue.

17 Informal conversation with presidential aide Mirza Hajric, March 2001.

18 Emina, our interpreter (and Fahrija's daughter), has similar memories: "I left Sarajevo in '92, really days before the war started. Let me tell you about the textbooks.
In our primer, if there was a Muslim name, let's say Emir, he's collecting hay. If it's
a Serb name, like Milan, Milan is reading a book. At school I was told I have an old-
fashioned name. 'Emina' was too Muslin to be cool. That in itself is propaganda,
starting somewhere, so, so far off, somewhere you think politics doesn't penetrate
the minds of little kids." From a private conversation, 2001.

19 Svetlana Broz, granddaughter of Tito, is writing a book on inter-ethnic couples who
married during the war. Private conversation, spring 2001. She has also written *Good
People in an Evil Time: Participants and Witnesses*, in which she brings together the
stories of Bosniaks, Serbians, and Croats to demonstrate that the war in Bosnia was
not caused by inter-ethnic hatred and to show that relationships within and among
the different groups continued throughout the war.

20 Mostar's troubles are long-lasting. On April 6, 2001, UN peacekeepers and Bosnian
police, backed by NATO troops, seized control of a major Croatian bank being used
to finance illegal security forces of the hard-liners. A riot ensued. *Dominion Post*,
April 7, 2001.

7. The Road to Reconciliation

1 ICG, *After Milosevic*, 136–37.

2 http://www.freemedia.at/Boston%20Congress%20Report/boston7.htm (last accessed January 2004).

3   Donna Pankhurst, "Issues of Justice and Reconciliation in Complex Political Emergencies," 239.

4   Adam Heribert, *Royal Institute of International Affairs* (January 1998): 5.

5   Reflecting on the Holocaust, Robert Coles speaks of "how often many of us who profess the Christian ethic of forgiveness succumb to smugness, arrogance, propentiousness, a cocky self-importance that is utterly incompatible with the kind of absolution and reconciliation implied in the act of forgiveness: no exculpation for wrong, but an acknowledgment that a long, tenaciously critical look inward justifies a whole-hearted response of merciful grace, for which one prays." Robert Coles in Simon Wiesenthal, *The Sunflower: On the Possibilities and Limits of Forgiveness*, 128.

6   Heribert, *Royal Institute of International Affairs* (January 1998): 5.

7   Bureau of Democracy, Human Rights, and Labor, "Implementing the Peace Accords: The War Crimes Tribunal," May 28, 1997, www.state.gov/www/regions/eur/bosnia/bosnia_war_crimes.html (last accessed January 2004). The first indictment, in February 1995, was against two Serbs connected to the Omarska concentration camp, where Emsuda was held. In addition, in February 1998, the U.S. Institute of Peace created a joint Bosniak-Croat-Serb truth and reconciliation commission to establish consensus on abuses suffered by victims from all ethnic groups in the recent war. U.S. Institute of Peace, "Bosnia to Form a Single Truth Commission," February 1998, www.usip.org/pubs/PW/298/truth.html (last accessed January 2004). The commission was tasked not only with establishing culpability but also with documenting acts of heroism by ordinary citizens; no other truth commission in the world had incorporated this task. Meanwhile, Yugoslav President Vojislav Kostunica established a truth and reconciliation commission in March 2001, regarded by outsiders as a whitewashing of Serb responsibility, but ostensibly to investigate war crimes in Slovenia, Croatia, Bosnia, and Kosovo. The truth commission can be transformative: "When I witnessed victims reaching out to perpetrators who had shattered their worlds, and offering them forgiveness, I was filled with hope. It became clear to me that the . . . process had far-reaching consequences, not only for individual victims and perpetrators encountering each other . . . but also as a model for uniting groups of people struggling with a history of conflict." Pumla Gobodo-Madikizela, "The South African Truth and Reconciliation Commission."

8   Sven Alkalaj in Wiesenthal, *The Sunflower*, 102–3.

9   See Martha Minow, *Between Vengeance and Forgiveness*, 5.

10 See Gobodo-Madíkizela, "The South African Truth and Reconciliation Commission."

11 Estimates of the number of murdered men and boys range between 7,000 and 10,000. Almost seven and a half years later, two-thirds of the bodies unaccounted for had yet to be found. Daniel Simpson, "DNA Tests Help Some Families of Bosnia Victims, but Not Most," *New York Times*, international ed., December 23, 2002.

12 For a thorough account of the role of the Dutch UN battalion in the Srebrenica massacre, see Jan Willem Honig and Norbert Both, *Srebrenica: Record of a War Crime*; and David Rohde, *Endgame: The Betrayal and Fall of Srebrenica*.

13   For an account of former chief prosecutor Louise Arbour's energetic efforts to prose-
cute the military and political high command in Bosnia (and later in Kosovo), see
Charles Truehart, "A New Kind of Justice," *Atlantic Monthly*, April 2000, 80–90. For
a critique of the failure of Croatia, Yugoslavia, and the international community to
meet their international legal responsibilities in arresting indictees and transferring
them to the tribunal, see Laura Palmer and Cristina Posa, "The Best-Laid Plans: Implementation of the Dayton Peace Accords in the Courtroom and on the Ground,"
361.

14   The body of Kada's husband was identified in October 2000.

15   On July 11, 1996, the anniversary of the slaughter in Srebrenica, I organized a campaign in which hundreds of international women leaders signed a full page ad in the
International Herald Tribune, demanding that the survivors be allowed to return to
their homes and given word of their missing men and boys. Human rights activist
Bianca Jagger led a pressing campaign to bring the UN face to face with its own complicity in the disaster. A 125-page UN "Srebrenica Report" was published in 1998, wres-
tling with the question "How can this have been allowed to happen?" http://www.
us-israel.org/jsource/un/unga53_55.html (last accessed January 2004).

16   On June 28, 2001, Milosevic was extradited to The Hague, after being imprisoned
in Yugoslavia since April 1 on charges of corruption during his thirteen-year regime.
Milosevic was originally indicted by the UN war tribunal in May 1999 for war crimes
related to Kosovo, including murders, mass deportation, and persecution. After years
of economic mismanagement, sanctions, and NATO bombing, the country was desperate for foreign aid. The United States, World Bank, and EU pledged millions of dollars the day after the extradition. In the wake of Milosevic's extradition, the Bosnian
Serb government indicated readiness to arrest top war criminals.

17   The indictment of Milosevic was announced during the 1999 NATO bombing as the
Yugoslav army moved into Kosovo. The chief prosecutor, Louise Arbour of Canada,
acted despite concerns by U.S. Deputy Secretary of State Strobe Talbott, who was
in delicate negotiations with Boris Yeltsin's special envoy, Victor Chernomyrdin, and
who "feared that an indictment might jeopardize a diplomatic end to the bombing.
Others, like Richard Holbrooke, feared the bombing would fail to break Milosevic,
and the United States would have to do a direct deal with the Serbian leader. "It was
to forestall this possibility — a Houdini-like diplomatic escape by Milosevic — that Arbour brought down her indictment on May 27." Michael Ignatieff, *Virtual War: Kosovo
and Beyond*, 124–25.

18   See Richard Goldstone's foreword in Martha Minow, *Between Vengeance and Forgiveness*, ix–xii.

19   The UN Commission on Refugees asserted as late as October 1992 that "there is no
indication of systematic rapes; it is a matter of wandering gangs." Seifert in Alexandra Stiglmayer, ed., *Mass Rape*, 67–68. See also Dorothy Thomas and Regan Ralph,
"Rape in War: The Case of Bosnia," in Sabrina Petra Ramet, ed., *Gender Politics in
the Western Balkans: Women and Society in Yugoslavia and the Yugoslav Successor States*,
203–18.

20   Infoteka, *To Live With (out) Violence*, 69.

21   The International Criminal Tribunal for the Former Yugoslavia was established under the UN Security Council Resolution 808 on February 23, 1993. "On April 24, 1995, the International Criminal Tribunal for the Former Yugoslavia made headlines by investigating the criminal responsibility of Bosnian Serb leader Radovan Karadzic, Bosnian Serb army commander General Ratko Mladic and a former political head of BS secret police, Mico Stanisic, for crimes ranging from genocide, ethnic cleansing, to the destruction of cultural and historical monuments. The abuses perpetrated as part of 'ethnic cleansing' constitute war crimes, crimes against humanity, and possibly genocide . . . [all] violations of international humanitarian law." Bisera Turkovic, *Bosnia and Herzegovina in the Changing World Order*, 74–75.

22   "The primary threat to security is the continued corrosive political influence of indicted leaders like Karadzic." Payam Akhavan, "Justice in the Hague, Peace in the Former Yugoslavia?," 796. See also Laura Palmer and Cristina Posa, "The Best-Laid Plans," 361–83, for an explanation of the political and security necessity of arresting war crimes indictees still at large in Bosnia.

23   A great strength of international criminal tribunals and truth and reconciliation commissions, such as the Truth and Reconciliation Commission in South Africa, has been the creation of a historical record of the violence convulsing their countries. Galina's comments echo the importance that many thinkers have placed on remembering: "Forgetting the extermination is part of the extermination itself." Jean Baudrillard cited by Martha Minow, *Between Vengeance and Forgiveness*, 118. See also Robert Rotberg and Dennis Thompson, eds., *Truth v. Justice: The Morality of Truth Commissions*.

24   This policy was described to me by the military commanders themselves (including Admiral Snuffy Smith and General Bill Nash) as well as their subordinates on numerous visits to military installations in the two years following Dayton.

25   See Cohen, *Hearts Grown Brutal*, 192.

26   See Leah Curtin, *Sunflowers in the Sand: Stories from Children of War*.

27   The case of Drazen Erdemovic illustrates the dilemma inherent in Alenka's distinction between "ordinary soldiers" and "criminals." In his early twenties, Erdemovic was an ethnic Croat whose pregnant wife was half-Serb; to earn money during the war, he served in armies on all three sides and profited by smuggling people across conflict lines. Erdemovic was serving in the Serb forces at the Srebrenica slaughter, in which he reluctantly (he says) performed "mop-up" operations to eliminate possible witnesses. He became a key witness to the massacre when he agreed to testify before the war crimes tribunal in exchange for his family's safety, which had been threatened by his Serb commander, who doubted Erdemovic's loyalty to the Serb cause. The tribunal sentenced Erdemovic to ten years in prison, following his guilty plea to one count of a crime against humanity. Erdemovic expressed remorse and sobbed while entering his guilty plea, providing this explanation for his actions: "Your Honor, I had to do this. If I'd refused, I would have been killed together with the victims." Quoted in *Prosecutor v. Drazen Erdemovic*, Judgment, in the Appeals Chamber, October 7, 1997,

http://www.un.org/icty/erdemovic/appeal/judgement/erd-aj971007e.htm (last accessed January 2004). See also David Rohde, *Endgame*, 128–29, 307–15, for a detailed account of the dilemmas facing Erdemovic.

Epilogue

1 Daniel Serwer, "The Successor States to Pre-1991 Yugoslavia: Progress and Challenges," U.S. Senate Foreign Relations Committee, Subcommittee on European Affairs hearing, n.d.

2 Warren Zimmermann, private conversation, July 4, 2001.

3 In fact, at U.S. military briefings I witnessed during the war, mothers were described as hysterical agitators and troublemakers for threatening to physically block the road as UN Protection Force soldiers tried to retreat from the "safe havens" they had been sent to protect. Later, talking to the women themselves, I came to see them as heroes, demanding that the international community live up to its word and defend communities where disarmed refugees huddled month after month as the shelling grew louder.

4 Carlotta Gall, in the *International Herald Tribune*, August 2, 2000, describes the return of 15,000 Serbs over an eighteen-month period to Sarajevo. That return could have been managed years earlier, had the international leadership (including military) been willing to put teeth behind the Dayton mandate. Five years later, even with Muslim refugees being evicted to allow Serbs to return to their Sarajevo homes, the nationalist Serbs, emboldened by lack of action by U.S. military, continued to refuse to allow refugees to return in similar numbers to the territory they occupy. And as of this writing, Bosnian Serb Nationalist leader Radovan Karadzic, indicted in July 1995, still roams free in the area of Bosnia patrolled by French troops, even though his general whereabouts are believed to be known.

5 Private conversation with American journalists and funders, in his Sarajevo office, fall 1996.

6 The only ironic exception was Karadzic tapping Biljana Plavsic to be his replacement as President, when he was banned from political office as an alleged war criminal. When she turned toward the West, he became her political enemy.

Profiles

1 I've not tried to write as a historian but rather to stay true to self-descriptions and my own immediate observations. Since our meetings occurred over several years, time-bound details such as ages of children, or the months or years since an event occurred, are only approximately and relatively correct.

2 Sunita Samarah, who staffed our office in Sarajevo, is a talented young lawyer who had

worked during the war for *Zena 21*, a magazine for and about women, and had been an organizer of the conference a few months after the peace was signed, titled "Women Transforming Themselves and Society" (described later). From both experiences, she could identify outstanding women leaders determined to make a difference in their worlds.

3 Alexandra Stiglmayer, ed., *Mass Rape*, 86.

4 "The prevailing attitude is that women in the former Yugoslavia enjoyed a high degree of equality with men. Relative to many western and southern (non-European) countries, this may be true, particularly in terms of education, rates of employment, and healthcare — and particularly in the cities and towns. But . . . a 'glass ceiling' existed — areas that despite the appearance of being open to all persons, in fact were inaccessible or less accessible even to qualified women. For example, in occupations and salaries, political life, and many positions of power and influence, women's rights and interests were subordinate even in the former Yugoslavia. In addition, limits experienced by rural women in particular, and problems of domestic violence, for example, predate the war." From *A National NGO Report on Women's Human Rights in Bosnia and Herzegovina*, 138, compiled by sixteen Bosnian NGOs in cooperation with the International Human Rights Law Group BiH Project. "Even in those industries in which women predominate (e.g., textiles), there are few, if any, women in executive positions. Wherever profits and power are found, the positions are generally reserved for men." Ibid., 157. According to Cynthia Cockburn, under Tito, women were excluded from management or political authority. Even though a quota system ensured 30 percent of the parliamentary positions, few held ministerial positions in the 1970s and 1980s. *The Space between Us*, 158.

Closing Thoughts

1 My sister Helen and I made hundreds of grants through The Hunt Alternatives Fund.
2 See Cynthia Cockburn, *The Space between Us*, 2–3.

Bibliography

Ali, Tariq, ed. *Masters of the Universe? NATO's Balkan Crusade*. London: Verso, 2000.

Akhavan, Payam. "Justice in the Hague, Peace in the Former Yugoslavia?" *Human Rights Quarterly* 20 (November 1998): 737–816.

Allen, Tim, and Jean Seaton. *The Media of Conflict: War Reporting and Representations of Ethnic Violence*. London: Zed Books, 1999.

Anderson, Benedict. *Imagined Communities: Reflections on the Origin and Spread of Nationalism*. London: New Left Books, 1991.

Arendt, Hannah. *The Human Condition*. Chicago: University of Chicago Press, 1958.

Autodafe: International Parliament of Writers. *How Does One Go To War?* New York: Seven Stories Press, 2001.

Baker, James. *The Politics of Diplomacy: Revolution, War and Peace, 1989–1992*. New York: G. P. Putnam's Sons, 1995.

Bec, Janja. *The Shattering of the Soul*. Belgrade: Helsinki Committee for Human Rights in Serbia and Radio B92, 1997.

Bringa, Tone. *Being Muslim the Bosnian Way: Identity and Community in a Central Bosnian Village*. Princeton: Princeton University Press, 1996.

Burg, Steven L., and Paul Shoup. *The War in Bosnia Herzegovina: Ethnic Conflict and International Intervention*. Armonk, N.Y.: M. E. Sharpe, 1999.

Cacace, Rosaria, Arcangelo Menafra, and Agostino Miozzo. *This War Is Not Mine*. Rome: Cooperazione Italiana, 1999.

Christopher, Warren. *Chances of a Lifetime*. New York: Scribner, 2001.

CID (Center for Investigation and Documentation of the Association of Former Prison Camp Inmates of Bosnia-Herzegovina). *I Begged Them to Kill Me: Crime against the Women of Bosnia-Herzegovina*. Sarajevo: BiH, 2000.

Clark, Wesley. *Waging Modern War: Bosnia, Kosovo, and the Future of Combat*. New York: Public Affairs, 2001.

Cockburn, Cynthia. *Gender and Democracy in the Aftermath of War: Women's Organization in Bosnia-Herzegovina*. Utrecht: Universiteit Voor Humanistiek Utrecht, 2000.

———. *The Space between Us: Negotiating Gender and National Identities in Conflict*. London: Zed Books, 1998.

Cohen, Philip J. *Serbia's Secret War: Propaganda and the Deceit of History*. College Station: Texas A&M University Press, 1996.

Cohen, Roger. *Hearts Grown Brutal: Sagas of Sarajevo.* New York: Random House, 1998.

Curtin, Leah. *Sunflowers in the Sand: Stories from Children of War.* New York: Madison Books, 1999.

Damjanovic, Ratomir, Novo Tomic, and Sanja Cosic, eds. *Serbia in the Works of Foreign Authors.* Belgrade: Itaka, 2000.

Domi, Tanya L. "Advancing Women's Political Rights in Bosnia-Herzegovina." *Harriman Review* 14 (November 2002): 36–46.

Donia, Robert J., and John V. A. Fine. *Bosnia and Hercegovina: A Tradition Betrayed.* New York: Columbia University Press, 1995.

Drakulic, Slavenka. *Balkan Express: Fragments from the Other Side of War.* New York: Harper Perennial, 1993.

———. *Café Europa: Life after Communism.* New York: Penguin Books, 1996.

———. *How We Survived Communism and Even Laughed.* New York: Harper Perennial, 1991.

———. *S.: A Novel about the Balkans.* New York: Viking, 2000.

Ensler, Eve. *Necessary Targets: A Story of Women and War.* New York: Villard, 2001.

European Centre for Conflict Prevention. *People Building Peace: Thirty-five Inspiring Stories from around the World.* Utrecht: European Centre for Conflict Prevention, 1999.

FAMA. *Sarajevo Survival Guide.* Sarajevo: FAMA, 1994.

Friedman, Francine. *The Bosnian Muslims: Denial of a Nation.* Boulder: Westview Press, 1996.

Fuss, Diana. *Essentially Speaking: Feminism, Nature and Difference.* New York: Routledge, 1989.

Gilligan, Carol. *In A Different Voice: Psychological Theory and Women's Development.* Cambridge: Harvard University Press, 1993 [1982].

Glenny, Misha. *The Fall of Yugoslavia, The Third Balkan War.* New York: Penguin Books, 1992.

———. *The Rebirth of History: Eastern Europe in the Age of Democracy.* London: Penguin Books, 1990.

Gordy, Eric D. *The Culture of Power in Serbia: Nationalism and the Destruction of Alternatives.* University Park: Pennsylvania State University Press, 1999.

Gow, James. *Legitimacy and the Military: The Yugoslav Crisis.* New York: St. Martin's Press, Inc., 1992.

Griffin, Jennifer. *Surviving Democracy: Where Women Fear Freedom.* New York: Marie Claire, 1997.

Gutman, Roy, and David Rieff. *Crimes of War: What the Public Should Know.* New York: W. W. Norton, 1999.

Hall, Brian. *The Impossible Country: A Journey through the Last Days of Yugoslavia.* New York: Penguin Books, 1994.

Haviv, Ron, Chuck Sudetic, and David Rieff. *Blood and Honey: A Balkan War Journal.* New York: Umbrage Editions, 2000.

Henderson, Michael. *All Her Paths Are Peace: Women Pioneers in Peacemaking.* West Hartford, Conn.: Kumarian Press, 1994.

Herman, Judith. *Trauma and Recovery: The Aftermath of Violence—From Domestic Abuse to Political Terror.* New York: Basic Books, 1997 [1992].

Holbrooke, Richard. *To End a War.* New York: Random House, 1998.

Honig, Jan Willem, and Norbert Both. *Srebrenica: Record of a War Crime.* New York: Penguin Books, 1996.

Hunt, Swanee. "New Faces in the Parliament: Behind the Scenes of the September 1998 Bosnian Election." *Ambassadors Review* (Fall 1998).

———. "Raising their Voices: Women in the New Democracies." *Ambassadors Review* (Fall 1997): 62–67.

———. "Sarajevo Journal." *Rocky Mountain News*, January 1–5, 1996.

———. "Women's Vital Voices." *Journal of Foreign Affairs*, June 1997.

Hunt, Swanee, and Cristina Posa. *Women Waging Peace.* Washington: Foreign Policy, 2001.

Huntington, Samuel P. *The Clash of Civilizations and the Remaking of World Order.* New York: Simon and Schuster, 1996.

ICG (International Crisis Group). *After Milosevic: A Practical Agenda for Lasting Balkans Peace.* Brussels: ICG, 2001.

Ignatieff, Michael. *Virtual War: Kosovo and Beyond.* New York: Picador, 2000.

Infoteka. *To Live With (out) Violence: Final Report [on] Violence against Women [in] Zenica, Bosnia-Herzegovina.* A Second Look, no. 2. Zagreb: Infoteka, 1999.

International Human Rights Law Group in Cooperation with Sixteen Bosnian NGOs. *A National NGO Report on Women's Human Rights in Bosnia and Herzegovina.* Sarajevo: International Human Rights Law Group BiH Project, May 1998.

International Organization on Migration. "Trafficking of Women to the European Union: Characteristics, Trends and Policy Issues." European Conference on Trafficking in Women, June 1996.

Jacobson, Mandy, and Karmen Jelincic, directors. *Calling the Ghosts.* New York: Women Make Movies, 1996.

Kaplan, Robert. *Balkan Ghosts: A Journey through History.* New York: Vintage Books, 1993.

Karahasan, David. *Sarajevo, Exodus of a City.* New York: Kodansha International, 1993.

Kirshenbaum, Gayle. "Women of the Year: Jadranka Cigelj and Nusreta Sivac." *Ms. Magazine*, January–February 1997.

Kurspahic, Kemal. *PrimeTime Crime: Balkan Media in War and Peace.* Washington: United States Institute of Peace, 2003.

Libal, Wolfgang, and Christine von Kohl. *Der Balkan: Stabilität oder Chaos in Europa.* Vienna: Europa Verlag, 2000.

Maas, Peter. *Love Thy Neighbor: A Story of War.* New York: Knopf, 1996.

Magas, Branka. *The Destruction of Yugoslavia: Tracking the Break-Up, 1980–92.* London: Verso, 1993.

Malcolm, Noel. *Bosnia: A Short History*. London: Papermac, 1996 [1994].

Mazower, Mark. *The Balkans: A Short History*. New York: Modern Library Chronicles, 2000.

Mertus, Julie, Jasmina Tesanovic, Habiba Metikos, and Rada Boric, eds. *The Suitcase: Refugee Voices from Bosnia and Croatia*. Berkeley: University of California Press, 1997.

Minow, Martha. *Between Vengeance and Forgiveness: Facing History after Genocide and Mass Violence*. Boston: Beacon Press, 1998.

Mojzes, Paul. *Yugoslavian Inferno*. New York: Continuum, 1994.

————, ed. *Religion and the War in Bosnia*. Atlanta: Scholars Press, 1998.

Neuffer, Elizabeth. *The Key to My Neighbor's House: Seeking Justice in Bosnia and Rwanda*. New York: Picador USA, 2001.

Nikolic-Ristanovic, Vesna, ed. *Women, Violence and War: Wartime Victimization of Refugees in the Balkans*. Budapest: Central European University Press, 1999.

Palmer, Laura, and Cristina Posa. "The Best-Laid Plans: Implementation of the Dayton Peace Accords in the Courtroom and on the Ground." *Harvard Human Rights Journal* 12 (Spring 1999): 361–83.

Pankhurst, Donna. "Issues of Justice and Reconciliation in Complex Political Emergencies: Conceptualising Reconciliation, Justice and Peace." *Third World Quarterly* 20, no. 1 (1999): 239–56.

Pawlikowski, Paul, director and producer. *Serbian Epics*. London: BBC-Bookmark, 1993.

Power, Samantha. *A Problem from Hell: America and the Age of Genocide*. New York: Basic Books, 2002.

Ramet, Pedro, ed. *Yugoslavia in the 1980s*. Boulder: Westview Press, 1985.

Ramet, Sabrina Petra. *Balkan Babel: The Disintegration of Yugoslavia from the Death of Tito to Ethnic War*. Boulder: Westview Press, 1996.

————, ed. *Gender Politics in the Western Balkans: Women and Society in Yugoslavia and the Yugoslav Successor States*. State College: Pennsylvania State University Press, 1999.

Rattner, Steven, and Michael Froman. *Promoting Sustainable Economies in the Balkans*. Report of an Independent Task Force Sponsored by the Council on Foreign Relations, 2000.

Rieff, David. *Slaughterhouse: Bosnia and the Failure of the West*. New York: Touchstone, 1996.

Rohde, David. *Endgame: The Betrayal and Fall of Srebrenica: Europe's Worst Massacre since World War II*. New York: Farrar, Straus and Giroux, 1997.

Rosenberg, Tina. *The Haunted Land: Facing Europe's Ghosts after Communism*. New York: Vintage Books, 1995.

Rotberg, Robert, and Dennis Thompson. *Truth v. Justice: The Morality of Truth Commissions*. Princeton: Princeton University Press, 2000.

Scharf, Michael P. *Balkan Justice: The Story behind the First International War Crimes Trial since Nuremberg*. Durham: Carolina Academic Press, 1997.

Schlegel, Alice, ed. *Sexual Stratification: A Cross-Cultural View*. New York: Columbia University Press, 1977.

Sell, Louis. *Slobodan Milosevic and the Destruction of Yugoslavia*. Durham: Duke University Press, 2002.

Sells, Michael A. *The Bridge Betrayed: Religion and Genocide in Bosnia*. Vol. 2. Berkeley: University of California Press, 1998.

Silber, Laura, and Allan Little. *Yugoslavia: Death of a Nation*. New York: Penguin Books/BBC Books, 1996.

Spelman, Elizabeth. *Inessential Woman: Problems of Exclusion in Feminist Thought*. Boston: Beacon Press, 1988.

Stiglmayer, Alexandra, ed. *Mass Rape: The War against Women in Bosnia-Herzegovina*. Lincoln: University of Nebraska Press, 1994.

Südosteuropäischer Dialog. *Balkan*. Heft 1–5. Vienna: Agens-Werk, 2000.

Tanner, Marcus. *Croatia: A Nation Forged in War*. New Haven: Yale University Press, 1997.

Thomas, Robert. *The Politics of Serbia in the 1990s*. New York: Columbia University Press, 1999.

Turkovic, Bisera. *Bosnia and Herzegovina in the Changing World Order*. Sarajevo: Saraj-Invest, 1996.

van Tongeren, Paul, ed. *People Building Peace: Thirty-five Inspiring Stories from Around the World*. Utrecht: European Centre for Conflict Prevention, 1999.

Waller, Todd W., and Lorenza Fabretti, producers. *Killing Time: Women Activists Awaiting Justice*. Italy-USA: Brave Dog Dead Dog Productions, 2001.

Weber, Renate, and Nicole Watson, eds. *Women 2000: An Investigation into the Status of Women's Rights in Central and South-Eastern Europe and the Newly Independent States*. Vienna: Agens-Werk and Geyer + Reisser with the International Helsinki Federation for Human Rights, 2000.

Wiesenthal, Simon. *The Sunflower: On the Possibilities and Limits of Forgiveness*. New York: Schocken Books, 1998 [1976].

Woodward, Susan L. *Balkan Tragedy: Chaos and Dissolution after the Cold War*. Washington: Brookings Institution Press, 1993.

Ziga, Jusuf. *The Tradition of Bosnia Which Has Been Betrayed*. Sarajevo, 2001.

Zimmermann, Warren. *Origins of a Catastrophe*. New York: Times Books, 1996.

Inside the National Library in Sarajevo. December 1995.

Index

Names of interviewees are cited in direct order (e.g., Alenka Savic).
Locators in italics indicate portraits and profiles of interviewees.

SWANEE HUNT

is Director of the Women and Public Policy Program at

the John F. Kennedy School of Government, Harvard University,

and President of the Hunt Alternatives Fund. She was

previously the U.S. Ambassador to Austria.

Library of Congress Cataloging-in-Publication Data
Hunt, Swanee.
This was not our war :
Bosnian women reclaiming the peace / Swanee Hunt ;
foreword by William Jefferson Clinton.
p. cm.
Includes bibliographical references and index.
ISBN 0-8223-3355-4 (cloth : alk. paper)
1. Yugoslav War, 1991–1995 — Bosnia and Hercegovina —
Women.   2. Yugoslav War, 1991–1995 — Protest movements.
3. Bosnia and Hercegovina — Politics and government — 1992–
4. Hunt, Swanee — Travel — Bosnia and Hercegovina.
I. Title.
DR1313.7.W65H86   2004
949.703'082 — dc22
2004006832